THE GREATEST AIR COMBAT
STORIES EVER TOLD

THE GREATEST AIR COMBAT STORIES EVER TOLD

EDITED BY TOM McCARTHY

Guilford, Connecticut

An imprint of Globe Pequot
Distributed by NATIONAL BOOK NETWORK

British Library Cataloguing in Publication Information Available

Library of Congress Cataloging-in-Publication Data

Names: McCarthy, Tom, 1953–, editor.
Title: The greatest air combat stories ever told / edited by Tom McCarthy.
Description: Guilford, Connecticut : Lyons Press, [2017] | Includes bibliographical references.
  | Description based on print version record and CIP data provided by publisher; resource not
  viewed.
Identifiers: LCCN 2017009075 (print) | LCCN 2017012713 (ebook) | ISBN 9781493027019
  (electronic) | ISBN 9781493027002 (pbk. : alk. paper)
Subjects: LCSH: Air warfare—Anecdotes. | Air pilots, Military—Biography—Anecdotes. |
  Combat.
Classification: LCC UG630 (ebook) | LCC UG630 .G785 2017 (print) | DDC 358.40092/2—
  dc23
LC record available at https://lccn.loc.gov/2017009075

♾™ The paper used in this publication meets the minimum requirements of American National
Standard for Information Sciences—Permanence of Paper for Printed Library Materials, ANSI/
NISO Z39.48-1992.

Contents

Introduction

Courage is not the absence of fear but rather the control of it. The pilots in this stirring collection had every reason to be afraid. A mistake, even the smallest lapse of concentration, meant trouble. The most fleeting loss of focus—the sort that most of us anchored firmly on the ground make every day—meant death. It was usually not a pretty death, either. It was not floating effervescently to the ground and daintily meeting their maker. Pilots went in headfirst at 150 miles an hour or were atomized in explosive collisions or torn apart by machine-gun blasts. They were shot as they parachuted to the ground or were captured and tortured. It was never an easy ending for combat pilots caught on the wrong side of fate. One is compelled to wonder, "What were they thinking about in their final seconds?"

But let's not hover over the grimness of their heroic occupation. These pilots wanted to do what they did, death and untimely demises be damned. They knew the one simple fact that every wartime pilot knows: Make a mistake in combat, and it will be your last. These guys were ultimately defiant and skilled and properly—shall we say—grounded. They knew what they were doing. They volunteered for the work, and then they honed their skills and tested them to the limit every day.

Pilots in flimsy and fragile biplanes did it. So did the pilots of the clunky, totally inapt planes thrown into service in the early days of the Battle of Britain. So did the pilots of the magnificent, state-of-the-art F-16s. The stories here, from the first days of World War I, when the more astute war planners saw the powerful and ominous potential of air power, through Word War II and Korea and Vietnam to the sand-blown chaos of the Iraqi desert, are all about courage, unshakable and resolute. These pilots might have lived more than one hundred years apart, but there is no doubt that they had much in common. One can see them sitting together after a long day of combat and toasting each other and talking warmly—planning the next day's efforts and looking forward to facing the odds again. No doubt they'd be scoffing at the enemy and others who might have second thoughts about going up again.

All the pilots here shared this trait—this calm, almost casual acceptance that, if their careers were to end, they would end rather abruptly and certainly violently. Yet they all started the engine and taxied down the runway to uncertain results. The shocked and unprepared Americans who shot into the air over the Philippines and into swarms of attacked Japanese Zeros did not have second thoughts about doing so. For many, those were their final thoughts. The odds were simply overwhelming and, at first, favored the attacking Japanese.

What about the RAF pilots who took off after the invading Germans over the English Channel at the beginning of the Second World War? Some were assigned to fly an ill-conceived old plane, whose mounted machine guns—their only offense—could only fire backward. That, of course, meant that any Luftwaffe pilot worth his salt knew he had only get ahead of the doomed RAF pilot and blow him to kingdom come. Many did. Yet the RAF kept coming—even as their numbers shrank alarmingly every day.

That's another common trait of the pilots on these pages—an almost insouciant view of their lethal occupation. Maybe that's the main ingredient. Having an unshakable nonchalance about their work seems to have been one of the required traits to get the job. Death was almost certain, and if you thought about it too much—dwelled on it—you would never leave the solidness of the ground again. One has only to take a quick glance at the list of the RAF 60 Squadron members here to see their chance of survival. It is a chilling list, to say the least. It says far more than what the numbered names might indicate.

One has only to view that list with a commander's calm and unemotional recounting of the death of one of their own: "It is thought that the pilot was Freiherr von Richthofen, the elder. This machine was venturing well over our side of the line on March 6, 1917, and went on and engaged and shot down Evelyn Graves, whose machine caught fire. When picked up, he was found to have been shot through the head, so that he was spared the pain of death by burning."

The Red Baron looked at his deadly vocation this way:

> *My father discriminates between a sportsman and a butcher. The former shoots for fun. When I have shot down an Englishman, my hunting passion is satisfied for a quarter of an hour. Therefore, I do not succeed in shooting two Englishmen in succession. If one of them comes down, I have the feeling of complete satisfaction. Only much, much later, I have overcome my instinct and have become a butcher.*

The only things that changed between 60 Squadron and the Red Baron and the pilots of today were the machines with which they plied their destructive and fatal crafts. The pilots on these pages are all modest, all calm and understated, and all superbly skilled. More than anything, they were all courageous.

Are the recollections of an F-16 pilot in training that much different from those of the Red Baron's nearly one hundred years before?

> *You get so you can do something most people would say is insanely dangerous and enjoy it. It's way crazy cool. Your mind is operating so fast you can count fence posts at 5,000 feet and 500 knots. You fly over I-10 and you can just in a flash see the blue car with a semi behind it—and twelve or fourteen cactus on top of that mountain—and a bird went by just above to the left while I was doing my radar fix. Your cross-check is so reactive and automated that you don't miss anything. The danger adds to the thrill. That includes the possibility that someone out there wants to kill you.*

Pilots know that. They just never seemed to let that bother them.

CHAPTER ONE

Tallyho! Bandits over Clark

John Toland

As the last raider wheeled and left the wreckage of Pearl Harbor, other Japanese planes were hitting Singapore. An hour and a half later, the Philippines and Guam were lightly bombed. Then Hong Kong's airfield was attacked, its tiny air force wiped out.

Two hours after this air raid, the strategic atoll of Wake, surprisingly, was still untouched. At a few minutes before noon, in the radio trailer of the small Army communications detail, Sergeant James Rex was busy relaying messages from the Philippines to the States, since direct contact had been lost. All morning, he had been trying to pass on news of Pearl Harbor to operators in Australia and New Guinea, but they kept telling him to stop kidding, and he'd finally given up.

At the Pan-American base on Peale, the tiny island just off the northwest tip of the main island, the *Clipper* had just been emptied of passengers and mail. At dawn it had taken off for Guam but returned when the skipper, John H. Hamilton, learned of war. Hamilton was almost ready to take his ship on a voluntary patrol. He was talking by phone to Major Paul Putnam, the commander of Marine Fighting Squadron 211, who was five miles away in a tent at the edge of the airstrip on the main island.

Putnam hung up the phone, stepped out of the tent, and looked across the bald, narrow 3,000-foot long strip. Eight planes were scattered at 50-yard intervals. Six other planes were being warmed up, two to escort the *Clipper* and four to relieve the patrol then in the air. Even

3

though there had been a constant air watch since dawn, Putnam was worried. Other equipment had arrived recently, such as a garbage truck, but they still had no listening device, no radar.

At 11:58 a.m. Putnam happened to look to the south, where a low-lying rain squall was sweeping in. He saw planes only 1,500 feet up, gliding noiselessly, eerily out of the squall.

"Take cover—bomber," he shouted. Most of the men were paralyzed a few seconds as they stared at the 34 medium bombers. Others reacted instantly and ran toward their foxhole. There was no foxhole near Putnam, but 100 yards away was the head. Before the first fragmentation bomb fell, he was running. In high school he had once raced 100 yards in 10.2 seconds. Today he knew he would break 10 seconds. Out of the corner of his eye, he saw bombs falling, about 12 from each plane. Still short of the head, he dove when he heard machine guns' sputter. He slid on his belly into the open latrine, headfirst, his legs dangling in the air. His hand and nose were covered with filth, but he was glad to be there.

In five minutes it was all over. Most of the raiders disappeared, but ten turned and raked the Pan-American station. The hotel was blasted, several buildings completely destroyed, fuel tanks set afire. Ten employees, all Guamanians, were killed.

The airfield on Wake was an inferno. Seven of the parked planes and the two 12,500-gallon aviation gasoline tanks were blazing. Parts of bodies were scattered; the wounded moaned. Putnam, himself grazed by a bullet in the back and dazed by a concussion, refused first-aid treatment as he tried to bring organization from chaos. His air force was crippled. Half of his men were killed or wounded, and there were only four undamaged planes left to protect the island.

At Peale, workers feverishly patched the many bullet holes in the *Clipper*. The passengers, all unwounded, were loaded. Then, after throwing off two Guamanian stowaways, as many employees as possible boarded. At 1:00 p.m. the big plane took off, heading for Midway.

On the island of Kwajalein, about 650 miles south, the main body of the Wake Invasion Force was almost ready to leave. Tokyo hadn't given Rear Admiral Samichi Kajioka, the overall commander, a definite deadline for conquest. It was too simple a job. As the last of the Japanese invaders were climbing aboard, word came from returning bombers that all but four planes on Wake had been destroyed. Kajioka's mission now seemed ridiculously easy. Wake should be taken in two days.

Earlier that morning, Major General Lewis Brereton, commander of MacArthur's Far East Force, reported to No. 1 Victoria Street in the Walled City section of Manila. It was almost 5:00 a.m., December 8, 2.5 hours after the first bomb had fallen on Hawaii. Unable to see MacArthur, then in conference with Admiral Hart, he was talking with General Sutherland, so often the buffer between the commanding general and his subordinates.

"I'd like to mount all the B-17s at Clark Field for missions to Formosa," said Brereton. He wanted his Flying Fortresses to leave immediately after daylight and bomb Takao Harbor in southern Formosa, about 600 miles to the north.

Sutherland told him to go ahead and make preparations but warned him to make no final commitment until approval by MacArthur was granted. Brereton left. There was nothing now for him to do but wait, since he had already alerted his headquarters at Nielson Field to prepare the Flying Fortresses for the mission to Formosa. For Brereton, eager to hit the Japanese before they hit him, the next hour crawled with painful slowness.

A few minutes later, dawn and the Japanese reached the Philippines simultaneously. On Mindanao, the southernmost of the major islands, Japanese Navy dive bombers swept in from an island to the east, Palau, and attacked the seaplane tender, William Preston, and two PBYs in Davo Harbor. The ship evaded the bombs, but the two planes were sunk, and the first American in the Philippines, Ensign Robert Tills, was killed. At about the same moment, Army Zeros from Formosa hit the radio station in Aparri, a good-sized town on the north coast of Brereton's own island, Luzon, the northernmost of the major islands.

But the Far East Air Force chief knew nothing about these attacks so close to his own two main bomber bases—Clark Field in central Luzon and Del Monte Field in northern Mindanao—as he impatiently returned to No. 1 Victoria Street at 7:15 a.m. Brereton hurried into Sutherland's office. Across the hall, Colonel William Morse, one of MacArthur's staff officers, could hear the two men talking through the open doors.

"I want to go up and bomb Takao," said Brereton said insistently.

"I'll ask the general," said Sutherland. Morse saw the chief of staff walk into MacArthur's office and return a moment later. "The general says no. Don't make the first overt act."

Morse then heard Brereton protest that bombing Pearl Harbor was certainly an overt act. Sutherland was unmoved. Besides, he felt that Brereton knew very little about the targets on Formosa, since there had been almost no reconnaissance. Such a raid on Formosa would just be a wild stab. Brereton's role for the present, he said, was defense.

Half an hour later, Brereton reached his headquarters, Nielson Field. On the southern outskirts of Manila, it was on a barren plain, protected by no natural cover. The hangar roof, painted in bold black and yellow squares, was an inviting target.

His staff was waiting eagerly. Captain Allison Ind, the intelligence officer, had assembled target folders on Formosa, and although he had no maps indicating the best approaches and bomb release lines, the information was as good as it would be for a long time to come.

Brereton, face pale, entered his office. "What's your decision about bombing Formosa?" he asked the staff.

They had been arguing about the bombing ever since dawn but had now agreed the B-17 Flying Fortress at Clark Field should set out immediately for Formosa.

"No," said Brereton, his jaw hardening. "We can't attack till we're fired on." He explained that Sutherland had ordered him to prepare the B-17s but to take no offensive action. The staff officers were incredulous. If they didn't strike now, they probably wouldn't get a second chance.

The problem was much more complex than the airmen realized. Although the Philippines would soon be attacked, many Filipino authorities had high hopes the Japanese would consider them an independent nation. If he made a wrong move now, MacArthur knew his whole delicately constructed plan of local self-defense might collapse. He also remembered Marshall's recent orders: "If hostilities cannot be avoided, the United States desires that Japan commit the first overt act."

As Brereton was ordering several planes to Formosa on photo-recon-naissance in case approval from MacArthur came through, he was called to the phone. It was Major General Henry "Hap" Arnold, commanding general of the Army Air Forces in Washington. Arnold warned him how everyone had been "caught napping" at Pearl Harbor. Every precaution should be taken in the Philippines. He didn't want Brereton's air force destroyed the same way.

In western Formosa, Japanese Navy officers of the 11th Air Fleet were just as disgusted and disappointed as the American fliers. Heavy fog surrounded their fields. They were to have taken off before dawn for strikes at the American fighter bases—Nielson, Nichols, and Iba—and the main target, Clark Field. As the hours passed, worry grew that the Clark-based Flying Fortresses would suddenly appear and wipe out their own planes, gassed and lined neatly up on the runways.

East of the Navy fields, the fog over the Japanese Army bases had lifted at dawn. One flight had already bombed Aparri. Other flights were nearing their targets: Baguio, the former summer capital, about 85 air miles north of Clark, and Tuguegarao, 50 miles south of Aparri. But the 11th Air Fleet men were not at all cheered by the better weather of their Army brothers. They knew the Army was bombing merely tactical targets. The fate of the entire Philippines campaign depended on the success of their own mission: quick destruction of the main body of MacArthur's fighters and bombers. If the weather didn't clear soon, all might be lost.

Even at 9:00 that morning, most Filipino villages were still completely unaware that war had come to their country. Hundreds of barrio fiestas were starting all over the islands—except for the Moslem-worshiping Moros of Mindanao, the Igorots and Negritos of Luzon, and other tribes untouched by civilization—most Filipinos had adopted the religion of their first conquerors, the Spaniards.

But in Manila, almost every one of its 600,000 people had heard the news by breakfast because of the newspaper extras and Don Bell's frequent news broadcasts over KMZH. Even these reports didn't completely convince many Americans. Although everyone had been sure war was coming, very few were mentally prepared to accept it. Many remembered the panic caused by Orson Welles's broadcast on the invasion from Mars.

In the city's suburbs at Nielson Field, the Air Warning Room was receiving reports of bombers heading for Lingayen Gulf. These were the Japanese Army bombers bound for Baguio, but everyone at Nielson thought their target was Clark Field. The B-17 base was warned, and soon all but one of the Flying Fortresses took the air bombless, in fear of being caught on the ground. At the same time, 18 P-40s from Clark and 18 from Nichols Field, on the outskirts of Manila, headed for Lingayen Gulf to intercept the invaders.

Back at Nielson scores of reports were pouring in: enemy battleships sighted off the northern coast of Luzon; three Japanese flying boats seen over the tiny islands north of Luzon. As messages piled up, all civilian secretaries were abruptly evacuated in case of a raid.

At the height of the ensuing confusion, at 9:25 a.m., two even more startling reports came in. Luzon itself had been bombed at Baguio and Tuguegarao. Now there could be no argument about an "overt act." Brereton picked up the phone and told Sutherland about the attacks. "If Clark Field is attacked, we won't be able to operate on it." He again begged for permission to bomb Formosa. His face fell, and he hung up. Turning to Lieutenant Colonel Eugene Eubank, commander of the B-17s, he shook his head. Permission not granted. Eubank started back for Clark Field at 10:10 a.m.

Four minutes later a call came from No. 1 Victoria Street. Offensive air action against Formosa was authorized. But it seemed too late to hit Takao Harbor as planned. Brereton's staff hastily plotted new missions.

In Formosa activity was just as frenzied at 10:10 a.m. The fog had cleared. On the Japanese Navy fields, 196 planes were warming up for takeoff. Suddenly sirens all over the island screamed. American planes were reported approaching Formosa. Gas masks were hurriedly passed out. The horde of medium bombers and Zero fighters hastily took to the air on two separate missions. Fifty-three bombers and 63 fighters were to wipe out the fighter field at Iba; 54 bombers and 36 fighters were to hit the main target, Clark Field.

Just as the great armada was leaving Formosa, the approaching planes which had alerted the entire island were spotted. Fighters left the Navy formation and sped to the attack. Just in time red suns were seen on the "Americans'" wing tips. They were Japanese Army bombers returning from the Baguio and Tuguegarao missions.

In the Philippines the big Flying Fortresses milling aimlessly around Mt. Arayat in fear of being caught on the ground by these same enemy Army bombers were now getting permission to return to Clark Field. The alert was over; false alarm. As soon as they landed and lined up neatly, P-40s flying their cover came in for gas and lunch. By 11:00 a.m. the terrific tension of the morning slackened. Calm had returned to Clark Field.

Forty miles west of the Clark Field, across the rugged Zambales Mountains and on the South China Sea, was Iba, a village consisting of little but nipa huts. Next to it was a single grass landing strip, bordered on its west side by a sandy beach. After Nichols it was the most important fighter field in the Philippines. In addition to its 18 combat-ready P-40s, it had the only working radar in MacArthur's command.

The Iba pilots were dog-tired. Since 2:00 a.m. they'd been chasing phantoms seen on the screen in the half-buried radar shack. Now they were sitting in their planes, smoking cigars, waiting for the next alert. Some were kidding the squadron commander, Lieutenant Henry Thorne. They felt he should think up a memorable fighting phrase for that first day of war. Someone suggested, "Damn the torpedoes, and take the hills."

At 11:27 a.m. the radar screen was again alive. A big formation was coming in across the China Sea. Thorne ordered his men to start their motors. The chase was on once more. Three minutes later Iba was telling Air Warning at Nielson Field that a large formation was presumably heading for Manila. Immediately 18 fighters from nearby Nichols were sent to patrol Bataan and Manila Bay.

In Manila air raid sirens wailed, but there was still no panic on the streets. Alarms, by now, were coming by telephone and telegraph from towns all along the northwest coast of Luzon. Some spoke of 27 planes, apparently fighters, others of 54 heavy bombers. The plotters tried to make sense of the tangled information. Apparently one big group was heading for Manila and several for Clark Field.

At Fort Stotsenberg, the base of the Flying Fortresses a mile away, it was still calm. No sirens screeched. Cavalrymen were eating lunch. So were mechanics and air crew.

At 11:45 a.m. Colonel Alexander Campbell, the aircraft warning officer at Nielson, sent a teletype to Clark. But the message was not getting through. Radio was then tried. Still Clark could not be reached. Evidently the operator was having lunch. Colonel Campbell finally got a faint telephone connection with Clark. A junior officer assured Campbell he would pass on the news to the base commander or operations officer immediately.

It was 11:56 a.m. While sirens shrieked and all except key personnel were trying to find cover on the barren Nielson Field, Brereton was telephoning Sutherland. The new bombing missions had been drawn up. The Flying Fortresses at Clark would hit known fields in southern Formosa at dusk; the other 14 B-17s, now 550 miles to the south at the Del Monte pineapple plantation in Mindanao, would fly up to Clark, arriving after dark, and prepare for raid on Formosa the next dawn. Sutherland approved.

By 12:10 p.m. all fighter pilots on Luzon were either in the air or waiting for orders to intercept the oncoming attackers. All, that is, but the fighters in the Clark Field area. Forty minutes earlier, the 18 P-35s at Del Carmen, 14 miles south of the member base, had been ordered to fly cover over Clark, but the message never arrived. At Clark itself, the junior officer who had talked with Colonel Campbell had not yet passed on the warning.

Even the alerted pursuit planes were becoming hopelessly tangled because of poor communications and confused orders. Twelve of Iba's 18 planes were still circling above their own field. But 6 planes of B Flight, losing radio communication, had sped to Manila, looking for the Japanese. Suddenly their radios cleared up. They heard, "Tallyho!" Then a voice shouted, "Bandits over Clark!" The 6 P-40s streaked, full throttle, to the north.

The 12 fighters hovering over Nichols heard the same call. As they headed for Clark, the squadron commander, Lieutenant William Dyess, radioed Nielson. Brereton's headquarters told Dyess to come back and patrol Manila Bay.

By now the six planes of Iba's errant B Flight were in sight of Clark. All was peaceful. Another false alarm. They turned west, heading for home.

It was now 12:25 p.m., and not a pursuit plane was flying cover over the parked Flying Fortresses at Clark. At that moment 27 new-type "Betty" bombers, with flaming-red suns on their wings, roared over Tarlac, only 20 miles to the north. They were heading directly for Clark. An excited Filipino plane observer ran to the telegraph office to make his report.

At Clark Field many of the ground crew were walking unconcernedly from the mess halls to the flight line. Ordnance men were loading bombs on the big, unpainted Flying Fortresses. Pilots of the 18 P-40Bs, under Lieutenant Joe Moore, were sitting in their planes at the edge of the field near their empty fuel drum revetments. Many of the men were still eating. At the 30th Squadron mess hall, mechanics and Flying Fortress crewmen were listening to Don Bell broadcasting the news.

"There is an unconfirmed report," said Bell, "that they're bombing Clark Field."

Since the only noise was the usual clatter of talk, dishes, knives, and forks, Bell's words were greeted with derision and laughter. Many of the men still refused to believe the Pearl Harbor reports, thinking it was probably just some harebrained general's idea of putting everyone on the alert.

———

The first of the two flights of Japanese bombers were within sight of Clark. In fact, their crews had spotted the mass of B-17s, shining in the bright sun, from Tarlac. Their prey was ridiculously obvious, sitting out in the great, unprotected central Luzon plain. As an extra guidepost, Mt. Arayat, 15 miles east of the field, stuck up like a huge traffic marker. No one could miss this 3,867-foot lonely peak standing in the idle miles of plain, its cone dented, according to native lore, when Noah's ark landed.

Now, the neat outlines of Fort Stotsenberg became distinct to the bomber pilots, with its white buildings, lines of acacia and mango trees, and the big polo field. A mile east stretched Clark Field. Not a single protecting pursuit plane was above it. At first the Japanese pilots couldn't believe what they saw: rows and rows of parked P-40s and Flying Fortresses. It was incredible luck. Almost ten hours after Pearl Harbor, every plane based at Clark was a helpless, sitting target.

The second flight of 27 old-type "Nell" bombers swung in behind the leading Betties. Suddenly 36 Zero fighters were hovering above the bombers like shepherds. Everything was working with precision. It was 12:35 p.m.

George Setzer, who had the taxi concession at Fort Stotsenberg, was just driving out the gate. Hearing a growing roar, he stopped the car. He and his daughter, Stella, got out. They saw a mass of silver planes coming from the northwest.

"It's about time they came to help us," he said joyfully. On the perimeter of the airfield, New Mexican National Guardsmen of the 200th Coast Artillery were having lunch or loafing around their 37-mm. and 3-inch anti-aircraft guns. They, too, thought the approaching bombers were friendly. At the cry, "Here comes the Navy," Sergeant Dwaine Davis of Carlsbad grabbed the movie camera bought from company funds and began taking pictures.

"Why are they dropping tin foil?" asked someone.

"That's not tinfoil, and those are goddamn Japs!"

At the west end was a sound as of rushing freight trains.

At the west end of the field, a crew chief of the 20th Pursuit Squadron was standing in front of the operations tent. He looked up. "Good God Almighty," he shouted. "Yonder they come!"

Hearing this, Lieutenant Joe Moore, the squadron commander, raced for his P-40. Followed by six others, he quickly taxied into position. He shot into the air, swung wide, and started a maximum power climb. Two others got into the air, but the last four planes were hit by bombs.

Corporal Douglas Logan, a B-17 gunner and cameraman, was at Headquarters Building, watching Major Birrell Walsh conduct the briefing for the photographic mission over Formosa at a blackboard. Just left of Logan stood Colonel Eubank, the bomber commander. Logan saw him look absently out the window at the sky and turn away. The corporal looked out and saw men running frantically on the field.

Eubank, realizing what he had seen, jumped back to the window, then yelled, "Take cover, men! Here they come!"

As everyone headed for the rear door, a stick of bombs exploded. The last to reach the door was Logan. Suddenly the floor pitched. Logan flopped; as he rolled toward a corner, he instinctively put his hands over his face.

The air raid siren was now wailing. Someone shouted to get out of the hangars. Men began to saunter out. Above, they saw planes in a great *V*. It was such a beautiful formation, they were thrilled—until they realized bombs were falling on the P-40s and B-17s at the far end of the field. They dove for the trenches, recently built by the base commander, Lieutenant Colonel Lester Maitland, and till now chidingly referred to as "Maitland's folly."

At the west end of the runway, Corporal Durwood Brooks, a combat radio operator, was sprawled on his bunk when he heard the first bombs fall. He sprang up and ran into the latrine; then he wheeled and ran outside toward a row of slit trenches. They were filled with white-clad cooks. He looked and saw three *V*s forming one great *V*. It was so perfect it was beautiful. He watched in fascination until a bomb hit 100 yards away. He was shocked. Someone was trying to kill him. He ran to the library and hid behind a heavy wooden piling. Every time a bomb hit, he seemed to rise a foot in the air.

Except for the bombs dropped on the pursuit planes about to take off, the raiders were concentrating on hangars, shops, and buildings. Anti-aircraftmen of the New Mexico National Guard were shooting 37-mm. and 3-inch guns at the passing formations. It was the first time most of the men had fired live ammunition. Much of their training in the United States had been with broomsticks and boxes or wooden models. Even if their bursts were exploding far below the targets, it was satisfying and somehow exhilarating to shoot finally in earnest.

At Fort Stotsenberg, cavalrymen were standing under mango trees with their horses. They were proud of their mounts. Not one had panicked, even though the ground shook from reverberations and flak from Clark Field clattered down on all sides.

Major General Jonathan "Skinny" Wainwright was watching the bombing from outside his headquarters. His houseboy ran to him, eyes bugged with terror. He was wearing the general's steel helmet. "Mother of God, General, what shall I do?"

"Go get me a bottle of beer," yelled the general above the din. A moment later his aide, Captain Tom Dooley, drove up.

"Tom, you damn fool," shouted Wainwright angrily. "You didn't drive past Clark during this bombing, did you?"

"You sent me an order to report as fast as I could."

Wainwright walked into his headquarters and wrote Dooley an order for a Silver Star.

Abruptly the bombing of Clark stopped. Corporal Brooks dazedly walked toward the flight line. The idea of war was new and terrifying. Bodies and parts of bodies were lying all over. In a slit trench, he saw two Filipino pin boys. They were good friends, killed by someone who hadn't even seen them. Brooks couldn't figure it out. Then he saw another friend, a Polish boy of 19. By some freak he was blown up like a balloon by an explosive bullet and to Brooks looked almost transparent.

Others staggered from the trenches. In the sudden silence, the groans of the wounded could be heard. Many of the buildings were burning. The big oil dump blazed, sending dark rolls of smoke across the field.

As Colonel Eubank started a hurried inspection of the group, the two B-17s being painted were taxied unharmed out of their burning hangar. Eubank learned only a few of the Flying Fortresses parked on the field were damaged. His bombers had been saved by a miracle.

Lieutenant Joe Moore was now about 20,000 feet above Clark in his P-40, with Lieutenant Randall Keator on his tail. Trailing half a mile behind and 3,000 feet below was Lieutenant Edwin Gilmore, the third of the pursuit pilots to take off successfully from Clark. Nine Zeros suddenly swooped down on Gilmore. Moore and Keator jumped the Japanese. Almost instantly, Keator shot down a Zero. It was the first American kill over the Philippines. A moment later, Moore found a Japanese in his sights. As Moore pulled the trigger, he wondered how it would feel to shoot live ammunition. Up until now it had been forbidden because of its scarcity. A Zero blew up in his face. He dove on another target. There was a second explosion.

Pilots of the 34th Pursuit Squadron in Del Carmen, 14 miles to the south, saw smoke rising from Clark Field. Without orders they took off in their worn P-35s. Before they reached Clark, several Zeros confidently attacked the much larger American group. Easily out-maneuvering the outdated 35s, the Japanese drove them off.

At 12:40 p.m. the 12 P-40s of the Flights A and C were still circling over their field at Iba, looking anxiously for raiders. Suddenly, over their radios they heard a hysterical voice shouting, "All pursuits to Clark Field! All pursuits to Clark! Enemy bombers overhead!" Then they heard the crash of bombs in their headsets. They raced to the east.

Standing near the strip at Iba, Second Lieutenant Glenn Cave watched the P-40s disappear. A moment later, at 12:44 p.m., another pilot said, "Look at that pretty formation of B-17s."

Cave looked to the west. He counted 52 planes in perfect formation at 13,000 feet. "You're crazy," he said, "there aren't that many B-17s in the Philippines." Black objects started wobbling from the planes. The two pilots dove into one of the few foxholes on the beach. Cave landed first, the other man on top of him. As bombs exploded and the earth shook, he was glad he was the man on the bottom.

At that moment the six Iba planes of B Flight which had flown to Manila and returned when they heard the mysterious false alarm from Clark were innocently approaching their home field for landing. The control tower frantically called incoming planes, warning of the bombers high overhead, but the radios of the P-40s were jammed.

As the first plane touched down, Second Lieutenant Andy Kreiger, pilot of the plane flying cover for the other five, saw the field explode in a great blinding flash. Kreiger climbed away so fast he had to level off at 10,000 feet to let his engine cool. Looking down, he saw what looked like a squadron of P-35s circling the field. They were crazy to try and land on that bombed-out strip. Then he saw they had big red spots on the wings—Japanese! He dove into their circle and shot at the plane ahead. When tracers suddenly zipped past him, he turned and saw three Zeros on his tail.

On the field below, Cave also thought the planes swooping down were P-35s. Red lights on the wings were blinking. Cave was puzzled. Suddenly bullets spattered in the sand. He realized he was being strafed. He heard a deep rumble. Another flight of bombers was making its run. This time the other man got to the bottom of the foxhole first. Cave looked at his legs sticking up and wondered if they'd be hit.

Halfway to Clark, the other Iba pursuit planes heard Lieutenant Krieger call, "All 3rd Pursuit to Iba." Half of the 12 planes turned back. But Lieutenant Fred Roberts and five other Iba Pursuit pilots flew headlong into the Zero fighters preparing to dive onto Clark Field. Almost out of gas, three Americans were quickly shot down. To Roberts's amazement the Japanese planes were faster, more maneuverable, and climbed at a terrifying rate. How could these possibly be Japanese? He and other pilots had been told there was no such thing as a good Japanese fighter plane.

He didn't know, of course, that exact data on these Zeros had been sent to the War Department by the brilliant, unorthodox Clair Chennault in the fall of 1940. The chief of the Flying Tigers had also revealed how the heavier P-40 could master the faster Zero, but this information, which could have saved the lives of bewildered American pilots dying at that moment, had been filed and forgotten. Chennault was not at all popular with Air Corps commanders.

Holes appeared in Roberts's wings. Suddenly a cable at his feet was shot out. He felt a sting in his leg, then numbness. The needle of his gas gauge wobbled near empty. He pulled sharply to the west, heading for Iba.

As he crossed the Zambales Mountains, smoke was rising from his home field. Tiny objects, obviously Japanese strafers, were diving and circling, but he had to come in. As he approached the field, he tried to lower his wheels. Something was wrong. As he swung in behind a two-place Japanese fighter, the man in its rear began blinking a red light at him. Roberts loosed a burst and turned out to sea. With only ten gallons of fuel, he decided to beach his plane. He headed toward the water at 120 miles an hour, then realized he'd misjudged the distance. He was too high. He quickly nosed down, crashing into the surf 50 yards from the shore.

He swam to the beach. The barracks was burning. So were other buildings and a gas truck. He heard a pig squeal and looked toward what had been the village of Iba. All the nipa shacks were blazing; palm trees were mowed down; carts were tipped over; horses lay dead, feet in the air. Children screamed in terror. Filipinos were moaning, "Help me, Joe."

The strip was a mass of craters. Several P-40s were crackling. The radar shack was a shambles, its operator killed. The control tower was riddled with bullets, its crew of four dead.

Disaster had struck suddenly. Iba was completely destroyed, and most of the survivors were in a state of shock. The coolest man was not a combat pilot but the young flight surgeon, Lieutenant Frank Richardson. Taking charge, he commandeered a bus, quickly loaded the wounded, and headed for Manila.

Back at Clark, as the survivors stared unbelieving at the wreckage, there was a cry, "Here come the strafers!"

The Zeros which had been circling far above the bombers were diving. Their main targets were the big Flying Fortresses and P-40s parked on the field. Soon they were joined by 44 of the 53 Zeros from Iba, now looking for new targets. One by one the parked Fortresses exploded with great roars as tracers ignited their gas tanks.

"Get in the woods," shouted an officer to men in the big ditch near the main hangar. Several dozen men scrambled out of the deep straight ditch and headed for the nearby woods as three Zeros swept over, riddling the area.

A score of white-coated Chinese dashed out of Charlie Corn's PX restaurant. A Zero swooped, and the ground was instantly white with their bodies. Nearby, Corporal Brooks was looking helplessly for quick shelter. He threw himself at a shallow ditch, digging frantically with hands and feet as two Zeros dove at him, their bullets squealing past. He ran to a deeper ditch and jumped onto a master sergeant.

"Excuse me," he said.

"Never mind," said the sergeant. "That's just one more it has to go through to get at me."

In a nearby trench, an antique water-cooled .30-caliber machine gun was spitting bullets at the strafers. A youthful mechanic was pumping it to keep it cool. After the first wave passed, the young man still kept pumping frantically as if in a trance.

A truck swung by, blood dripping out the sides. It was filled with wounded heading for the Fort Stotsenberg Hospital. Other wounded were walking dazedly, eyes blank.

The Zeros now had little opposition, except for the machine guns of the 200th Field Artillery and the 192nd and 184th Tank Battalions. When the water-cooled barrels of the artillerymen's old Browning burned out, the gunner grabbed rifles and shot at the swooping Zeros.

As suddenly as it started, the attack was over. Great black clouds of smoke covered the field. All the parked P-40s and 30 medium bomber and observation planes were burning. All but three of the Flying Fortresses were completely destroyed. In one raid the Japanese Navy airmen had knocked out half of MacArthur's Far East Air Force. Too late, America had learned what the lessons of war in Europe should have taught; a heavy bomber force without adequate fighter protection, air warning, and anti-aircraft guns is helpless, useless.

The returning Japanese planes were checking in. Not a bomber had been lost, and only seven fighters were missing. The claimed results were so fantastic—25 planes shot down and 71 destroyed or so severely damaged on the ground—that conservative officers at Formosa were dubious. Yet as claim piled on claim, it was obvious that, even allowing for the natural optimism of all fliers, complete surprise had been achieved. It was a second Pearl Harbor.

At Imperial Navy Headquarters in Tokyo, the news was received with another enthusiastic demonstration. In half a day, two of the three most powerful deterrents to complete success in Southeast Asia had been cancelled: the Pacific Fleet and MacArthur's Air Force. The third was

British Admiral "Tom Thumb" Phillips's powerful striking force. According to the last reconnaissance report, the battleship *Prince of Wales* and the battle cruiser *Repulse* were still in Singapore Harbor—too shallow for their conventional aerial torpedoes and well protected by anti-aircraft batteries.

If only the two big ships could be lured into the open sea.

CHAPTER TWO

Home Town Hero

Colonel Robert Barr Smith (Ret.)
and Laurence J. Yadon

SHORTLY AFTER THE WAR ENDED IN NOVEMBER 1918, ALMOST EVERY-
one in Columbus, Ohio, stood in awe at the train station to greet native
son Edward Vernon Rickenbacker, the greatest American ace of the
conflict. Within a few weeks, he was feted by some 300,000 people in
Los Angeles, toasted as the greatest aviator of the war by the New York
elite, and praised in a lengthy telegram prepared for the occasion by the
president of the United States.

Yet within eight years, Eddie was flat broke, indebted to the tune
of $3.4 million in modern money by the failure of Rickenbacker Motor
Company. The next year he was nearly killed by a pencil pushed into his
chest during a bizarre automobile accident. "You crawl out alone, or you
stay there," Eddie later remembered. When he did, Carl Fisher, a near-
sighted automotive visionary, manufacturer, and investor offered him a
hand up.

Fisher owned a fledgling operation known then and now as the Indianapolis Motor Speedway. Fisher opened "the Indy" in February 1909 as
a proving ground. By late 1927, "the brickyard," so named for its early
racing surface, was so badly in need of repairs that Fisher considered
giving up and handing Indy over to real estate developers.

Eddie bought the track and developed a golf course nearby, all with
borrowed money, all at a good profit.

Soon, he brokered a sale of Bendix Aviation to General Motors, using his finder's fee to pay off the debts from his Rickenbacker Motor Company bankruptcy. In November 1934, while serving as public relations manager for Eastern Airlines, he flew a DC-2 from New York to Miami and back again to great fanfare, setting the stage to become general manager and, four years later, the majority stockholder.

In May 1935, he offered the first shuttle flights ever between New York (Newark, New Jersey) and Washington, DC. Although he quarreled with the newly created Civil Aeronautics Board, he jealously promoted airport development nationwide.

Between September 1939 and December 1940, he transitioned from America First isolationist to full-blown interventionist and told reporters he expected the country to be at war by the following summer.

Eddie was expecting an uneventful business trip to Atlanta on Wednesday, February 26, 1941. He boarded the Eastern Airline "Mexico Flyer" at the airport named for his friend Fiorello La Guardia, who had been commissioned to fly the very same day in 1917 as had Eddie.

But that evening near Atlanta, when Eddie felt the left wing brush a tree during the landing, he jumped up and ran for his life toward the rear of the plane, even as the pilot overcorrected, striking a large pine tree with the right wing.

Seconds later, Eddie was wedged between the bulkhead and the gas tank in the darkness with a shard of metal which he could not see pointing directly at his left eye. "Does anyone have a match?" another injured passenger yelled. Eddie warned him that the entire plane was now soaked in gasoline. Moments later, he tried to free himself. The next morning rescuers found Eddie nearly dead, the injured eye hanging on his cheek nearly severed.

Yet six months later, when he arrived back at La Guardia, he told reporters he then suffered from only a few aches and pains. When they asked him whether the United States should get into World War II, Eddie simply replied, "We are in it and have been for a year."

During those first few months after Pearl Harbor, he toured forty-one stateside airbases in thirty-two days, bolstering morale among airmen who would soon be on their way to dangerous assignments overseas.

The press described him as grim, powerful, and determined, prompting Secretary of War Henry L. Stimson to send Eddie on a secret, highly sensitive assignment to confront an American god of war.

Although now headquartered in remote New Guinea, Douglas MacArthur was making trouble for the president. This wasn't the first time, but most recently his target was George C. Marshall, chairman of the Joint Chiefs of Staff. No one was better suited than Eddie to quiet down MacArthur.

The battleship *Oklahoma* was still listing with its bottom up, fully visible from the airfield at Pearl Harbor on the evening of October 20, 1942, when Eddie and his assigned assistant Colonel Hans Adamson boarded a B-17 bomber specially fitted for the trip. Adamson had popularized dinosaurs to the American public while working at the Museum of Natural History in New York.

"I wonder why they are bringing this cripple on board the plane?" wondered flight engineer Johnny Barteck, the youngest man there: Eddie was stooped over, walking with a cane, looking much older than his fifty-two years. Barteck thought Eddie should be in a hospital, not traveling across the Pacific.

Their first flight, at about 10:30, was very short, indeed. The landing gear locked in place during takeoff, putting everyone on board in danger. After an emergency landing, the crew carried their equipment to another plane in the darkness, followed by the passengers. They left Pearl Harbor at 1:30 in the morning.

Once aloft, Eddie spent some time in the cockpit drinking orange juice and coffee with the pilots as the sun rose over the Central Pacific. They began a routine descent to Canton Island at 9:30, only to discover that their intermediate destination had disappeared. Or so it seemed.

Captain Bill Cherry, a drawling Texan wearing cowboy boots, now realized that tailwinds had been stronger than expected, pushing them beyond Canton. Worse yet, nobody noticed that the internal works of the delicate octant used to fix longitude and latitude had been severely damaged during the crash landing. The airbase at Canton Island couldn't give them a radio bearing because the equipment for doing so had just arrived but hadn't been unpacked. Palmyra Island to their north couldn't help either. Even as the radio operator sent SOS messages across the airwaves, the pilots began preparing for the first B-17 water landing in history. The copilot was almost cut in two as the plane plunged into eight-foot waves at ninety miles per hour.

Crippled though he was, Eddie helped a crew member push three emergency rafts out of the plane into the rolling waves before leading everyone onto the wing. Within six minutes, eight men watched the B-17 sink, knowing they hadn't had time to retrieve food or water. All they had were four oranges, two fish hooks, and some string.

They would have been quite a sight if they hadn't been alone in the middle of the Central Pacific. Most had ditched their shoes and pants, anticipating a swim to the rafts, which most had avoided. Eddie was the best dressed, sporting an expensive blue summer suit and gray fedora. Whatever the reason, Eddie took over informal command of the survivors.

During the first week, he split and portioned out the oranges. As the second week began, they began daydreaming out loud about a banquet at the Mark Hopkins Hotel, high on a San Francisco hill, just before blindness afflicted most of them.

Eddie saved them from starvation on day eight by snagging a sea swallow which landed on his fedora. Nothing went to waste; the intestines soon attracted a small mackerel and a sea bass. Better still, a rainstorm that evening brought fresh water.

Eddie saved them all again by becoming a taskmaster, offering kindness and verbal abuse in equal measure, whatever it took to keep the men's chins from sagging onto their chests. The single exception was young Alex Kaczmarczyk, who couldn't resist slurping some seawater in the darkness and later died in Eddie's arms.

A flying fish which soared into one of the rafts ended any thoughts of cannibalizing young Alex anyone might have had. Captain Cherry overruled Eddie and insisted that the three rafts split up to increase their chances of being seen, a decision that may have saved their lives.

Planes began to appear, oblivious to the men shouting at them far below. Finally, on November 13, 1942, they were spotted by a pair of seaplanes and ferried aboard PT boats.

"God, Eddie, I'm glad to see you," MacArthur said when they met twenty-four days later at the Port Moresby airfield. Eddie later learned that the search had been abandoned until his wife Adelaide persuaded General Henry H. "Hap" Arnold to resume it. MacArthur didn't blame Eddie for the warning from F. D. R. which he carried and arranged for him to visit Guadalcanal before returning stateside.

The next year Eddie and copilot James C. Whittaker published separate accounts of the ordeal. In 1945, Eddie published a memoir about his dangerous life and speculations about the hereafter, a book thousands of people found inspiring. Throughout the war years, he promoted industrial defense, appeared before Congress, and flew to the U.S.S.R. on behalf of the president.

Eddie stepped down as Eastern CEO in October 1959, resigning his chairmanship four years later. He spent the rest of his life speaking on causes he believed in. His memoir was published in 1967, six years before his death in Zurich, Switzerland, far from the floor of the glass factory in Columbus.

Eddie was born there October 8, 1890, the third child of former starch-factory worker Elizabeth Basler Rickenbacker and her husband, William, an often-unemployed brewer. When Eddie was fourteen, his father was mortally wounded in a fight during his lunch hour while helping pour a cement sidewalk. The day after the funeral, Eddie quit school and began working at the Federal Glass Factory, but he soon talked his way into a job as an apprentice auto mechanic.

In the spring of 1906, he began working for the Oscar Lear Automobile Company, which soon thereafter began racing cars. Company partner Lee Frayer was responsible for monitoring gauges, tire pressure, and opponents approaching from behind. In those days, riding mechanics were not as well protected as race drivers and died three times as often in accidents.

Although the Frayer-Rickenbacker team didn't finish the race, Frayer soon became a father figure for Eddie.

He soon began driving in races himself, changed his name to Rickenbacker, and gave himself the middle name Vernon in July 1915 to affirm his American origins in an era when German-Americans were not always welcomed. Yet, one sponsor promoted him as "Barron Rickenbacker," a young Prussian nobleman who absconded from the Vienna Military Institute in a stolen Mercedes. Along the way, he worked for or with William K. Vanderbilt, Fred and Augie Duesenberg, Barney Oldfield, pioneer filmmaker Max Sennett, and other luminaries of the early auto-racing world. He never set a land speed record, as some biographers have claimed, but he did drive five races at the Indianapolis Motor Speedway.

Eddie became nationally famous by winning seven major races, finishing second twice and third five times, before ending his racing career in Los Angeles, November 30, 1916; that month aviation stole his heart in Riverside.

He saw a plane on the ground in a field and introduced himself to pioneer flyer and designer Glenn Martin. His first flight that day with Martin made Eddie dizzy, but his mind was made up.

About a month after that first plane ride, Eddie was on a ship bound for Liverpool, England. He'd been invited to visit the Sunbeam Motor Works in Wolverhampton, but there was a problem. Britain went to war in August 1914, and "Baron Rickenbacker" had captured the attention of British intelligence agents. He was detained, searched, and mortified by having lemon juice rubbed into his body to detect invisible ink messages. Ten days later, the agents released him.

On the return cruise to New York, he had an idea. Eddie told reporters that if the United States ever became involved in the war, he would recruit fifty drivers and mechanics to join an American flying corps. Five of America's top drivers volunteered immediately.

When Congress declared war on Germany April 6, 1917, Eddie raced to Washington, but the Army turned him down. Two months later he joined the American Expeditionary Force sailing from New York to Europe—but as a driver.

There is no official documentation establishing that Eddie chauffeured General John J. Pershing on tours of the front in France, although American newspapers reported that he did. He definitely drove Major T. F. Dodd, second-in-command to Colonel Billy Mitchell, founder of the American Air Service.

While so serving, Eddie witnessed German bombardments of Nancy from Point-Saint-Vincent nearby. On the return trip, Eddie fixed an engine problem on Mitchell's personal vehicle and soon became his driver. By August, Eddie persuaded Mitchell that he should be sent to flight school.

Shortly thereafter, someone, maybe even Mitchell, changed the age in Eddie's military records from twenty-seven to twenty-five, just young enough to qualify for preliminary flight training at Tours. From there he was off to Issoudon, some one hundred miles south of Paris, there to become chief engineer, a ground job. The air base there was sheer chaos, a rock-filled mud hole lined by crates, gasoline barrels, and even bathtubs awaiting construction of living quarters. Quentin Roosevelt, son of a past president, and Hamilton Coolidge, son of future president Calvin Coolidge, were among the pilots stationed there.

The French Nieuport 23 planes then flown out of Issoudon reminded Hamilton Coolidge of toys. Although not officially assigned, Eddie took a Nieuport out for practice, demonstrated a controlled tail-spin in late December, and graduated from advanced flight school the next month.

On March 6, 1918, he joined fourteen other pilots ferrying unarmed planes from Paris to Villeneuve-les-Vertus (Villeneuve); plagued by mechanical problems, only six reached their destination. Yet the Americans had no alternative to the Nieuports, which the French had abandoned for the sturdier SPAD XIII. Worse still, the Nieuports had dangerous wing and engine design problems which sometimes cost pilots their lives.

Eddie and the other pilots stationed at Villeneuve became part of the 94th Aero Pursuit Squadron of the 1st Pursuit Group, just in time for a German offensive which was nearly successful. The 94th flew its first hostile mission on March 28 without incident, but Major Raoul Lufberry embarrassed Rickenbacker and Eddie's fellow rookie, Douglas Campbell, by pointing out that they failed to notice several other airplanes, including a pair of enemy biplanes which flew beneath them.

April 12 found Eddie painting the new and eventually emblematic hat-in-the-ring insignia of the 94th on the fuselage of his plane.

Next day, two of his comrades scored the first American kills of the war. Eddie's turn came two weeks later on April 27, when he helped his flight leader force a German Pfalz D-III into the ground. Ten days later Eddie and another flier engaged four German fighters. Eddie attacked from above, knocking down his prey, as had James N. Hall, who didn't return. Soon, the Germans sent word that Hall was injured and captured. Eddie replaced Hall as flight leader.

During a May 17 patrol, Eddie shot down a German Albatros, just before noticing two others closing in behind him. He ripped the leading edge of his upper right wing trying to gain altitude, then went into a 10,000-foot free fall; according to his own account, he only regained control 200 feet above certain death.

Eddie scored a third kill five days later and a fourth on May 28, bringing him into competition with Douglas Campbell to become the first American "ace." This expression for five kills is of uncertain origin but was adopted by the Allies as early as 1915.

Two mornings later he was in the air again, even though he had not been assigned to fly that day. He rose to 15,000 feet just in time to see some German fighters begin an attack on British and American fighters returning from a mission. One of the Germans would not fly again, and "Baron Rickenbacker" nearly ran out of fuel returning from a June 5 mission. He spent ten days in Paris recovering from exhaustion, only to be hospitalized for the same problem twenty-one days later, even as his unit was relocated to Touquin in the Chateau Thierry sector, the very center of the battlefront.

Eddie was back in the air on July 10, now flying a SPAD XVIII he commandeered at Orly. His first SPAD flight caused him such ear pain that he was sent to a Paris hospital. Three days later his friend Quentin Roosevelt was killed in air combat. While grounded yet again, Eddie dreamed that his friend Walter Smythe was killed in a midair collision. So it was no surprise when an orderly appeared to announce that it was so.

The Allied leadership refused to permit pilots to wear parachutes, the "chair-borne rangers" in leadership positions opining that the easy availability of 'chutes would encourage pilots to abandon their planes at the slightest hint of trouble. Eddie considered this to be criminal negligence.

Eddie was back at the front on September 6, waiting for the stormy weather to break, even as the Allies planned the great assault which would begin six days later. He was in the air that day, strafing German troops retreating on the highway to Vignuelles, a major Allied objective. Eight days later, in the air above Metz, Eddie spotted and shadowed four Fokker fighters closing in on some American bombers. He picked one off only to realize that he was tangling with Baron Richthofen's fabled squadron. Within seconds, he was fighting for his life with the group leader on his tail but escaped. His seventh kill came the next day, succeeding Endicott Putnam as the greatest "ace of aces" then living, Putnam being mortally wounded several days before near Toul.

Even then, Frank Luke of the 27th Aero Squadron began to emerge as the new competition within the 1st Pursuit Group, shooting down two balloons at dusk on September 18, prompting a bacchanalia the next evening.

Five days later, Eddie was picked to command the 94th Aero Squadron, despite his lack of stateside flight training, because his colleagues trusted his strategic decisions as much as his skills in the air. Billy Mitchell himself complimented his judgment, fighting élan, and dexterity fifty-years later. He went aloft that very day, promptly found a quintet of Fokkers, and attacked "with the sun on his shoulder," downing two Germans with hundred-round bursts.

Two days later, on September 26, the 1st Pursuit Group was ordered into the air several hours before dawn to support American and French troops attacking around Montfaucon; it was their first night mission. Eddie destroyed at least three enemy balloons that morning before playing chicken head to head with a Fokker. He ended that duel by doing a half roll followed by a half loop, positioning his fighter for his tenth kill before limping into a small Allied airfield.

As the Allied armies struggled to break through the Hindenburg line, Billy Mitchell gave them a special mission in early October, sending thirty planes to destroy three strategically located observation balloons. Eddie picked Ham Coolidge, son of future president Calvin Coolidge, as the lead balloon-strafer. He deftly dodged one of the manned balloons. Then, after destroying the first, he shot down an attacking Fokker, before escaping to Allied lines. Several days later they were in the air again with refined tactics, twenty-four planes spread across a three-mile front, hunting observation balloons, with Eddie commanding. He downed one Fokker in a dogfight, then one more, in the process rescuing Jimmy Meissner but at a cost.

Eddie's friend Wilbert White saved another pilot by intentionally colliding with an attacking Fokker. Badly shaken by the loss, Eddie sojourned in Paris for three days. By October 23, he was back behind the German lines, fighting four Fokkers, two of which he shot down before he returned home. Four days after that, Eddie took out another, just before Ham Coolidge was killed by anti-aircraft fire. Victories twenty-five and twenty-six (by most accounts) came on October 30. Word came on the evening of November 10 that the war would end the next day. In a last act of defiance, Eddie flew over the lines, firing the last of his ammunition toward the enemy, minutes before the armistice.

CHAPTER THREE

Fallen Angel

The Final Seconds of Extortion 17

Don Brown

*EDITOR'S NOTE: ON AUGUST 6, 2011, TALIBAN FORCES SHOT DOWN A HELICOP-
ter, call sign "Extortion 17." The attack killed the Air National Guard crew,
seven unidentified members of the Afghan military, and seventeen members
of Navy SEAL Team Six—the same team that had killed Osama Bin Laden
just ninety days before. The investigations that followed pointed to a cover-up.*

In reading the transmission describing the shoot-down in real time,
keep two things in mind. First, Extortion 17, per the testimony of the
Apache pilots at exhibit 53, page 37, was between 100 and 150 feet off the
ground when hit by an RPG. At page 52 of that same exhibit, the transcript noted that the chopper had slowed her airspeed to "80 knots or less."

Eighty knots is 92 miles per hour. We don't really know what "or less"
means, except that it's less than 92 miles per hour. But it seems doubtful
that the chopper would be flying 92 miles per hour as it entered the
landing zone. Helicopters slow and feather as they are about to set down.
So that part (92 miles per hour) is not believable. The "or less" part is
believable. The question is, "How much less?" Probably considerably less.

Also keep in mind reports from flight control that the chopper was
not moving at all. So the chopper was very low at this point, was truly
about to land, and was so close to the ground that the RPG shot had to
have been a point-blank shot.

Remember that on the tape at 34 seconds past 2:38 a.m. local time,
Bryan Nichols (or someone impersonating him) said, "One minute. One
minute."

Sixty-eight seconds later, at 22:09:46 (2:39:46 local time), the aircraft had already been delayed, eight seconds behind the pilot's latest estimate. But strangely, it's still apparently hovering in the sky, just hanging there as a target, for reasons that remain a mystery.

In this portion of the transcript, "BS" is the backseat pilot in the Apache helicopter, or the lead pilot of gun 1. "FS" is the front-seat pilot, or copilot, of gun 1.

The sequence begins with the lead pilot of gun 1 (BS) announcing, "I just saw a flash."

Note the tragic announcement of "fallen angel," the military distress code announcing that a U.S. military aircraft has gone down.

FINAL SEGMENT 3

22:09:46	BS:	I just saw a flash. Did you see a flash?
22:09:48	FS:	Yeah, they're being shot at.
22:09:52		H17 traffic. CH-47 transitioning south. [INAUDIBLE].
22:09:55	BS:	What is that?
22:09:58	FS:	Dude, I think they just got shot.
22:10:01	BS:	Are you shot?
22:10:03	FS:	Are you on that?
22:10:05	FS:	I'm on it, sir! [Extortion 17] is down.
22:10:12		Roger.
22:10:13	BS:	Coalition traffic; we have a fallen angel. Fallen angel. It's [Extortion 17].
22:10:26	BS:	[EXPLETIVE].
22:10:33	FS:	. . .
22:10:39	BS:	We pushed.
22:10:41	BS:	Go ahead.
22:10:42	FS:	Roger. We have a fallen angel. [Extortion 17] was shot down in the Tangi Valley. [INAUDIBLE].
22:10:45	BS:	Coalition traffic, anybody out there? We have a fallen angel CTAF.
22:10:50		[Gun 1], H-17. Say location.

22:10:53	BS:	Location Tangi Valley. Tangi Valley, and we're up on 338.45 on in the green plain text.
22:10:58		[INAUDIBLE].
22:11:01	FS:	Roger, what we're remaining [INAUDIBLE] 33/45.
22:11:04	BS:	Roger. Roger. Right now, currently it's one Chinook down. How copy?
22:11:08		Roger. [Extortion 17] is down.
22:11:11		That's a good copy. We're already made on SATCOM [INAUDIBLE].
22:11:21	BS:	1 this is 2. Do you have anything?
22:11:24	BS:	We got nothing at this time. We got a wreckage on fire.
22:11:28	FS:	Alright, the calls been made to X.
22:11:31	BS:	I have [Extortion 17] right now down in the Airborne Valley by Hotel coming in on CTAF.
22:11:38	FS:	Right, I'm going stay up here and develop things. Where are you at?
22:11:43	FS:	Roger, we are circling overhead. I saw where the [EXPLETIVE] explosion came from, man. I'm searching the buildings. If I see [EXPLETIVE] anybody with a weapon, I'm firing.
22:11:52		Helo common.
22:11:58	FS:	
22:11:59	BS:	[Call sign deleted] Go.
22:12:11	BS:	[Call sign deleted], this is [Call sign deleted] on Helo common. Go.
22:12:17	FS:	Did you see any survivors down there?
22:12:19	BS:	I'm not seeing any.
22:12:20	BS:	No, I'm not seeing anything right now. It is a ball of fire. It looks bad.
22:12:24	FS:	Okay.
22:12:26	BS:	Another explosion.
22:12:28	FS:	I got secondaries. Are they shooting them still?
22:12:34	BS:	No. I got secondary. I think that's fuel.

The sudden, almost panic-like reaction in the voices of the Apache pilots marked a very sad and dramatic moment for the Americans aboard Extortion 17. Their deaths, here, are recorded in real time. Indeed, this was a difficult passage to read. It's at this point, as precisely reflected on the gun tape, in a horrible flash at a moment frozen in time, that lives, American lives, were changed forever.

Braydon Nichols lost his father, and Kimberly Vaughn lost her husband. Billy and Karen Vaughn lost their son. The two Vaughn children, Reagan and Chamberlain, in the horrible instant of a blinding moment, were forever fatherless.

Charles Strange, a blue-collar worker from Philadelphia, lost his son Michael, who was a Navy cryptologist supporting the SEAL team, and Candie Reagan lost her longtime fiancé, Patrick Hamburger.

Young Payton Hamburger, just two years old, would never see her father again.

Before dissecting specific timeframes, it's important to note that this shoot-down was not just witnessed by the Apache pilots, who were discussing it here in real time. It was also witnessed by the AC-130 pilot, along with several of his crewmembers. The pilot testified that three shots were fired and that either the first or the second shot appeared to strike the chopper.

Meanwhile, another member of the AC-130 crew, the left scanner, testified that the second RPG hit the chopper.

The first excerpt, taken from exhibit 40, page 25, was the aircraft commander's testimony describing that he saw three shots fired at Extortion 17. Remember that the AC-130 was circling 7,000 to 8,000 feet overhead.

AC-130 Commander: Shortly after the burn came on, we saw—I saw three RPG shots, kind of just ripple—one, two, three—coming from the south to the north. I was in the southern part of the orbit, and I saw, what I saw was either the first or second one make an initial hit and just a massive explosion, and it just seemed to be stationary, and it just dropped.

Now here is the left scanner's testimony, at page 27 of exhibit 40:

> **Left Scanner:** I was sitting left scanner. I have a single monocle that I look out of—NVGs, so I had like one eye that's just looking normal and one eye looking through the NVG. From my perspective the second RPG did hit directly. It made direct contact with the helicopter.
>
> **IO-DEP:** The first RPG?
>
> **Left scanner:** The second RPG.
>
> **IO-DEP:** The second RPG; I'm sorry.
>
> **Left Scanner:** I think the first RPG went underneath the helicopter, from my perspective. The second one did make a direct hit with the helicopter, and there was a fairly large explosion in the air, but it was split seconds between the time the helicopter was hit. There was that explosion, and then it hit the ground, and then there was an explosion.

This testimony was highly relevant for two reasons. First, the aircraft commander revealed that three shots were fired at Extortion 17. But the second revelation, as alluded to earlier, is significant. The commander said, "Shortly after the burn came on, we saw—I saw three RPG shots, kind of just ripple—one, two, three—coming from the south to the north."

Note the testimony here was not "shortly after the burn went out" but rather "shortly after the burn came on, we saw three RPG [rocket-propelled grenade] shots." So the pilot of the AC-130 testified that the burn was on at the time of shoot-down. This is inconsistent with the Apache gun tape recording of "burn's out" at the 22:08:37 mark.

Now, remaining for the moment in exhibit 40 of the Colt Report (interviews of AC-130 crew), take a look at a series of questions asked by the deputy investigating officer, beginning at page 27. These questions were directed at two AC-130 crewmembers, namely the television sensor operator and the left scanner.

On the question of how long the burn lasted, the television sensor operator's testimony was most crucial because he was the airman who actually operated the burn.

> **Television Sensor Operator:** When he called that he saw RPGs come up, I turned off the burn, slid over to him, and that's when I saw the third RPG. And, the third RPG had already started coming out of the tube when the Helo was already on the deck—it was already on the ground—impacted with the ground. And, at that point, I mean, the first or second one had to have hit it, and it was a massive fireball. I mean, it just lit up.

On the question of when the burn ended, the television sensor operator's testimony is compelling. "When he called that he saw RPGs come up, I turned off the burn, slid over to him, and that's when I saw the third RPG." He turned the burn off after the RPGs were launched. This means that the landing zone, and perhaps even the chopper, were being spotlighted by the bright, wide burn at the moment of shoot-down. This also means that the enemy on the ground, with a relatively inexpensive set of night-vision goggles (NVGs) had plenty of time to focus on the spot-lit landing zone, to ready his RPG, and to fire as the helicopter descended through the ultraviolet light.

It's clear that the possibility of the "burn" illuminating the chopper and making it a more visible target became a concern, at least to members of the AC-130 gun crew.

The navigator of the AC-130, at page 48, testified and verified other testimony that the burn size was roughly the size of a football field but also noted that he didn't believe the burn could have highlighted the aircraft.

> **Navigator:** Our burn is probably roughly the equivalent to the size of a football field, and we're down here to the south of HLZ. I don't believe there's any way that our burn could have highlighted the aircraft.

A couple of points about the navigator's comments. First, it's clear, at least at this point, that there was a concern about the burn lighting the helicopter. That's why the navigator says, "I don't believe there's any way that our burn could have highlighted the aircraft."

Of course, it really doesn't matter whether the burn highlighted the aircraft because the burn put a big bright spot, the size of a football field, on the ground at the exact spot that the helicopter (Extortion 17) was flying to. All the Taliban had to do was get their RPGs, run to the edge of the big bright spot on the ground, stay back just behind the bright lights, wait until the helicopter flew in toward them, then point in the air, and aim toward the noise.

Pay close attention to the navigator's testimony regarding directions. He said because "we're down here south of the HLZ"; in other words the AC-130 was spotting the HLZ (acronym for helicopter landing zone) from an aerial position almost over the landing zone but just south of it.

Compare that with the AC-130 commander's testimony on directions, found at page 40 of exhibit 5:

AC-130 Commander: And they're changing their run—in heading it sounded like they are coming from the northwest now, and so there was that delay, and then we heard the one-minute-out call, put the burn on. Shortly after the burn came on, we saw—I saw three RPG shots, kind of just ripple—one, two, three—coming from the south to the north. I was in the southern part of the orbit, and I saw, what I saw was either the first or second one make an initial hit and just a massive explosion, and it just seemed to be stationary, and it just dropped.

A couple of relevant points from this portion of the AC-130 pilot's testimony. First, Extortion 17 was coming, that is converging on the landing zone, from the northwest. Because the gunship was converging from the south, the gunship was firing down its light beam at a slightly different angle from the helicopter's approach.

Because the chopper and gunship were approaching the landing zone from slightly different angles, the plane from the south, the chopper from the northwest, the gunship's navigator assumed that the light did not clip the helicopter.

Maybe the light did not clip the chopper. Maybe it did.

Again, it doesn't matter because the target stage was painted with the AC-130's powerful light. This long illumination gave the Taliban time to know where to stand and shoot.

To better understand where the AC-130 was flying in relation to the landing zone, turn to exhibit 83 of the Colt Report, the transcript of the second day of testimony from the AC-130 gunship. Exhibit 40 included the first day of testimony of the AC-130 crew, conducted August 18, 2011, and exhibit 83 was the continuation of that testimony, taken on August 19, 2011.

In his opening statement on August 19, at page 3 of exhibit 83, the AC-130 aircraft commander explained that the gunship was actually flying in a tight, circling pattern over the landing zone.

> **AC-130 Commander:** [I was] the aircraft commander on that night. We were on [the] southern part of the orbit, and we were essentially [performing a] 1.5-nautical-mile radius wheel, counterclockwise around the helicopter landing zone [HLZ] at the point when I saw the rocket-propelled grenade [RPG]. Now the helo was calling one minute out, and we set up a contract to put down our burn, which is actually just a football [field]–size flashlight, infrared flashlight that you can see on NVGs.

So the AC-130 was basically flying a tight, counterclockwise orbit around the landing zone, with a radius of only 1.5 nautical miles, shining down its burn on the landing zone. The aircraft commander noted that the burn could be seen with NVGs, or night-vision goggles.

Remember, the Taliban would need NVGs (night-vision goggles) for the ultraviolet burn from the AC-130 to have been a fatally defective mistake. Without NVGs, the ultraviolet burn would have been invisible to the naked eye.

Chapter Four

The Skies over Midway

John Lundstrom

WHILE THE EXHAUSTED PILOTS SLEPT OR TRIED TO, AN EQUALLY TIRED Admiral Raymond Ames Spruance thought hard in the early hours of 5 June about how to avoid a possible night counterattack by the enemy and yet position his battered and bruised carrier air groups where they could do some good after daybreak. He withdrew Task Force 16 eastward until 0200, then reversed course westward to approach the Japanese once again. From submarine alerts, he learned of an enemy force bearing down on Midway and at 0420 came around to the southwest to move into direct support range of the island. The ships glided into a band of bad weather; fog and rain greatly reduced visibility and threatened air operations if those conditions persisted after sunrise. As on the previous day, Spruance relied on Midway-based planes to conduct searches and follow up air strikes. Carefully he husbanded what dive bombers he had (his torpedo squadrons had virtually been destroyed) to unleash them should Japanese carriers turn up. The American carrier planes had sunk or maimed four enemy flattops, Spruance knew, but it was within the realm of possibility the Japanese might have a tough old bird like the *Yorktown* out there and back in action. Perhaps a fifth enemy carrier also lurked nearby, something that earlier intelligence estimates had warned about.

Dawn found Task Force 16 socked in, so Spruance depended more than ever on Midway's faithful patrol squadrons. At 0630, a PBY radioed a position report for two Japanese "battleships bearing 264

45

degrees, distance 125 miles from Midway." They lay within range of his SBDs, but Spruance had to know where enemy flattops were before he committed his strike planes. Ninety minutes later, another flying boat located one burning carrier, two battleships, three cruisers, and several destroyers, bearing 324 degrees, distance 240 miles from Midway. Twenty minutes later, another report reached the *Enterprise*—this one placing an enemy carrier bearing 335 degrees, distance 250 miles from Midway, out in the same area as the burning flattop. Conditions still did not permit immediate flight operations by the American flattops, and Spruance decided to wait a bit longer to see what the far-reaching search planes might turn up.

First scheduled flight operations on board the *Enterprise* that morning involved fighters for the combat air patrol, and "the Big E" readied a dozen F4Fs to go. Among them were six from Fighting Three: Thach's contingent was warned by the air department to "pack their toothbrushes" and be prepared to land on board the Hornet. The evening before, Spruance's staff had assessed the situation and found an excess of F4Fs on board the *Enterprise* and a lack of them on board the *Hornet*. Consequently they decided to shift Thach and most of his *Yorktown* refugees over to the Hornet, where he would take command of the composite fighting squadron. Left on board the *Enterprise* were Scott McCuskey and Dick Wright with two VF-3 F4Fs (F-3 and the wrecked F-17).

The twelve CAP fighters started taking off at 0825 from the *Enterprise*, while the *Hornet* remained quiet. For a change, 5 June proved a very quiet day for the fighters. They encountered no enemy aircraft (there were not many left to encounter!), and what snoopers were out (cruiser floatplanes) did not locate Task Force 16. About the most exciting contact came early, at 0900, when the CAO spotted an object floating on the sea. That turned out to be a disabled PBY flying boat from Midway. The fighters alerted Spruance, who sent the destroyer *Monaghan* to the *Catalina*'s assistance.

Later that morning, when Thach's patrol was over, he took the six VF-3 Wildcats over to the *Hornet* and landed on board, where they increased the *Hornet*'s complement of fighters to twenty-nine (fifteen from Fighting Eight and fourteen from Fighting Three). The Yorktowners were made to feel most welcome. Thach assumed command of something designated "VF-3/42/8." Since December he had personally operated all five of the Pacific Fleet's big carriers: the *Saratoga*, *Lexington*, *Yorktown*, and *Enterprise*, and now the *Hornet*. Quite likely he was the only pilot to do so. Eddie O'Neill, VF-8's own executive officer, went on the sick list. Replacing him as temporary XO was Bruce Harwood, while Warren Ford became flight officer.

In the reader room, Thach conferred with his pilots to get acquainted and work out a squadron flight organization. He took the opportunity finally to abolish even an administrative organization in six-plane divisions, as that had ruined his escort plans on the fourth. The composite squadron would have four-plane divisions, composed of pairs whose pilots had flown with each other. Thach did not try to integrate the sections but kept the different squadron pilots and F4Fs with one another.

By 1100, Spruance had determined to his own satisfaction that the Japanese no longer posed a direct threat to Midway. He changed course to the northwest and bent on twenty-five knots to pursue the carrier or carriers located that morning by the PBYs. Task Force 16 would not be within range to launch SBDs until well into the afternoon. Meanwhile, Browning, the chief of staff, worked up planes that were to see the SBDs, armed with 1,000-lb. bombs, launched at a range of 275 miles. The orders shocked Wade McClusky and his squadron commanders out of their socks. In the presence of the admiral, they protested most vocally to Browning. Spruance overruled the chief of staff, delayed the launch for an hour, and told the air officers to arm the Dauntlesses with 500-lb. bombs. There was no thought of sending the fighters, given the long flight, to the targets. For the F4F-4 Wildcats, it was simply out of reach.

The *Hornet* was the first to launch, once Spruance gave the go-ahead. At 1512 she sent aloft a deckload of twelve SBDs from Bombing Eight led personally by Ring, the group commander. Ring set off immediately for the target, said to bear 324 degrees, distance 240 miles. The *Hornet*'s second deckload, fourteen SBDs under VS-8's skipper, Walter Rodee, left at 1542. En route, Ring spotted what he believed was a light cruiser but pressed on to the target, thought to contain one carrier, two battleships, two cruisers, and five destroyers—the remnants of *Kidō Butai*. Ring took his aircraft out 315 miles but saw no other enemy vessels. On the flight back, he again encountered the "light cruiser," and this time he attacked. The quarry was actually the destroyer *Tanikaze*, detached by Nagumo to ensure that the carrier *Hiryu* had really sunk. The *Tanikaze* skillfully evaded all bombs. Rodee had worse luck. He flew out to the end of the navigation leg without sighting any Japanese at all. His SBDs, some burdened by 1,000-lb. bombs (despite Spruance's orders), had nagging fuel worries as they droned eastward into gathering darkness.

Meanwhile the *Enterprise* strike force departed at 1530 after the carrier rotated her CAP. Led by Shumway of Bombing Three, the attack group comprised thirty SBDs from the four squadrons (VB-6, VS-6, VB-3, and VS-5) then operating from the *Enterprise*. On the flight out, Shumway deployed planes from VS-6 and VS-5 into a scouting line abreast to widen the area of the search. By 1727, the group had flown 265 miles without turning up an enemy. Recalling the scouting line, Shumway headed for the contact reported by Ring. There she was, the tough little *Tanikaze*, but her wily skipper again avoided any hit and extracted a heavy price from the Americans. Anti-aircraft fire shot down the VS-5 SBD flown by Sam Adams, the man responsible for pinpointing the *Hiryu* the previous day.

By the time the first SBDs made it back to Task Force 16, darkness had fallen. The carriers had recovered their CAP fighters and anxiously awaited the return of the dive bombers. Spruance unhesitatingly ordered the carrier landing lights turned on, despite the real danger from Japanese submarines. The SBDs aloft comprise almost the whole of his remaining strike force, none of which he could afford to lose. Some of the pilots faced their first landing at night, but they performed admirably. There were no deck crashes, but VS-8's Lieut. Ray Davis had to ditch for lack of fuel. The *Enterprise* brought on board more aircraft than she had sent off: twenty-eight of her own SBDs and five more from the *Hornet*. On her part, the *Hornet* landed twenty of her brood and one from Bombing Six. Altogether it was a magnificent feat for the pilots, the LSOs, and Spruance himself. When the flattops shut down for the night, more than one pilot gracefully quaffed "medicinal" brandy, duly prescribed to help them relax.

The morning of 6 June, Task Force 16 held a westward course for what would be the final act of the Battle of Midway. By 0500, Spruance was more than 350 miles northwest of Midway, too distant to rely solely on searches sent from there. The *Enterprise* at 0500 launched a search mission of eighteen SBDs to cover the 180- and 360-degree semicircle to a distance of 200 miles. Also roused early for CAP were six F4Fs from each carrier. The first important contact flashed in at 0645, when a VB-8 SBD (which had taken off from the *Enterprise*) relayed the position of one battleship, one cruiser, and three destroyers, course 270 degrees, speed ten knots. Garbled in transmission, the message was received by Spruance as "one carrier and five destroyers." When plotted on the charts, their position was 128 miles southwest of Task Force 16. At 0730, another VB-8 aircraft appeared overhead and dropped a message on the *Enterprise*'s flight deck. This informed Spruance that the pilot had spotted two cruisers and two destroyers. When added to his chart, they were situated 52 miles southeast of the "carrier" contact, or even closer to Task Force 16 than the first group reported.

Two separate groups of Japanese ships, including one carrier, appeared to confront Spruance and his staff. Actually, the only Japanese ships in the area sailed together; they were the heavy cruisers *Mikuma* and *Mogami*, badly damaged in a collision with one another earlier on 5 June, and the destroyers *Arashio* and *Asashio*. They had been part of an abortive attempt to bombard Midway; now they limped westward. Midway-based aircraft had harried them the previous day. Now Task Force 16 swooped down upon them.

Not involved in the search, the *Hornet* was cocked and ready to go. At 0757, she began launching a strike of thirty-four planes.

Mitscher specifically provided the fighter escort in the event "previously undetected air opposition was encountered." Thach and the VF-3 refugees remained behind to fly CAP and give their VF-8 compadres their chance at the enemy. With Ring in the lead, the *Hornet* attackers started a slow climb toward 15,000 feet. Meanwhile, at 0815 the *Enterprise* and the *Hornet* began recovering SBDs from the search. The pilot who had made the first contact landed on board the *Hornet* and corrected the erroneous message. Spruance learned no carrier was out there, and at 0850 he advised Ring to that effect.

Ring located the little Japanese task force at 0930 and maneuvered his dive bombers into a good attack position. The *Mikuma* steamed into the lead; the Americans thought her a battleship. Compared with her maimed sister the *Mogami*, missing most of her bow, the *Mikuma* looked appreciably longer. The *Hornet* SBDs mostly concentrated on the two capital ships, although a few did take after the destroyers. Ring's pilots did well. They claimed three hits on the "battleship," and the *Mikuma* actually did take two or three bombs in her vitals. The crippled *Mogami* sustained two hits, and the destroyer *Asashio* took a 500-pounder on her stern.

Spiraling in with the SBDs, Ford led his eight F4Fs in a strafing run to support the dive bombers. In line abreast, his division of four ganged up on one destroyer, while Jock Sutherland retained a vivid recollection of angry Japanese sailors crowded on her stern, shaking their fists in hatred as the Grummans roared past at low altitude. Antiaircraft fire was active, accounting for two SBDs (one VB-8, one VS-6). The *Hornet* strike began landing on board their carrier at 1035 after the short hop back from the target. The *Hornet* air department rearmed the dive bombers for a second attack.

The *Enterprise* launched her strike planes at 1045. Taking off first was a relief CAP of eight VF-6 fighters, followed by thirty-one SBDs (from all four VSB squadrons) and twelve escort fighters from Fighting Six. Leading the stroke was VS-5's skipper, Wally Short. Short's orders before departure were to attack the same group of ships plastered by the *Hornet*, but once aloft, the *Enterprise* radioed new instructions to seek out and destroy the battleship reported 40 miles ahead of the other target. Almost as an afterthought, "the Big E" dispatched the three operational TBDs from Torpedo Six under Lieut. (jg) Laub. He departed with strict orders not to engage if any opposition appeared at all. Spruance would not lose any more torpedo planes if he could help it. On the slow climb to 22,500 feet, Short led the group into gentle S-turns to cut down the rate of advance and allow VT-6s TBDs to catch up. Unfortunately Laub never did establish contact with the dive bombers. Jim Gray, leading the escort fighters, briefly spotted the TBDs at 1211. He tried radioing the strike leader but failed to raise him.

Twelve minutes after Gray saw the TBDs, he observed the small Japanese task force. The SBDs pressed ahead to search another 30 miles for the mythical battleship, but Gray led his fighters away to look at the enemy ships below and offer support in case Torpedo Six attacked. Looking over the *Mikuma* and the *Mogami*, Gray likewise thought one of them was a battlewagon. At 1225 he radioed, "There is a BB over there!" Three minutes later he added impatiently, "Let's go! The BB is in the rear of the formation." On board the flagship, Spruance was anxious to get on with the attack. At 1235, the *Enterprise* radioed Short: "Expedite attack and return." He could find no ships ahead of the force already sighted, so he came back over the *Mikuma* and the *Mogami*. At 1245, he made ready to attack.

As briefed, Gray waited until the SBDs began to dive, then charged in F4Fs to strafe the destroyers. From 10,000 feet, Gray led his division of six F4Fs into a rapid 45-degree dive and barreled in from out of the sun. Responding to the threat, the Japanese tin can heeled over into a tight turn. In close succession, Gray and his pilots opened up with their .50-calibers as they descended below 2,000 feet and held their runs down to masthead level before pulling out. Chunks of metal flew off the destroyer as machine-gun tracers straddled the target and bullets struck home. They ignited a fire and set off a small explosion, visible as the last of the F4Fs rocketed by.

Tackling the other destroyer were six F4Fs led by Buster Hoyle. They approached from off her bow, as the destroyer tried desperately to maneuver out of the way. These VF-6 pilots likewise pressed their runs to within 100 feet of the waves, shot the destroyers full of holes, then in column swung sharply left to avoid the battered *Mogami*. Hoyle climbed to 5,000 feet, then brought his division around for a second try. Their heavy slugs punched more holes into the thin-skinned destroyer, igniting three fires and a satisfying explosion aft. None of the F4Fs sustained any significant damage, but the destroyers *Arashio* and *Asashio* bore souvenirs of the visit. Meanwhile, the SBDs left the *Mogami* and especially the *Mikuma* in a bad way, burning and shattered from more 1,000-lb. bomb hits.

While the *Enterprise* planes headed back to their carrier, Ring led a second *Hornet* wave with twenty-four Dauntlesses. Fighters were unnecessary for this attack, so they remained behind on combat air patrol. The task force had closed within 90 miles of the burning enemy vessels, and with the good visibility, Ring's crews at altitude simultaneously beheld the target smoking up ahead and their ships well astern. At 1415, the *Enterprise* recovered her strike group (except for three SBDs, which ended up on board the *Hornet*) and eight CAP fighters. Meanwhile the *Hornet* VSB pilots again gave a good account of themselves. They slammed as many as six 1,000-lb. bombs into the doomed *Mikuma*, besides securing another hit on the *Mogami* and a damaging near miss of the *Asashio*'s stern. In return the *Hornet* flyers took no losses. Spruance still did not know how many enemy ships were out there and what they were. At 1533, the *Enterprise* launched two SBDs for photo reconnaissance, and they secured superb shots of the bruised and burning *Mikuma* settling into the water. Spruance's analysts saw her for what she was, a *Mogami*-class heavy cruiser. So much for the battleship. They expected her to sink shortly, and she did. The battered *Mogami* and the two destroyers limped off to the west.

The *Enterprise* handled the dusk CAP; at 1629 she launched twelve F4Fs from the Fighting Six, two of which had to abort because of mechanical difficulties. The wear and tear of three long days of battle began to tell on airplanes and aviators alike. After sundown "the Big E" landed her ten fighters and the two recon SBDs. Now the Battle of Midway was over, as Spruance canceled any further pursuit. The task force had approached within 700 miles of Wake Island, making a Japanese air strike by land-based bombers highly likely the next day if Spruance continued to close on Wake. His destroyers were extremely low on fuel, and the aviators were exhausted. It was time to call it quits. Spruance at 1907 changed course northeast to head for a rendezvous with the fleet oilers *Cimarron* and *Guadalupe*. On board the carriers, the pilots finally realized the desperate battle had climaxed in a fantastic victory for the Allies. The night of 6 June was a time for relaxation and celebration. Liquor appeared from hidden recesses in surprising quantity, and on board the *Enterprise*, at least, the parties were quite lively.

The Loss of the Yorktown

During the night of 4–5 June, the *Yorktown*'s survival remained in jeopardy. His Task Force 17 jammed with *Yorktown* survivors, Fletcher had made contact with Task Force 16 and withdrew eastward. Listing steeply as she drifted across the dark seas, the *Yorktown* had only one companion, the *Hughes*, whose skipper had orders to sink the stricken flattop should the enemy appear. Still bouncing in the waves not far away was the partially flooded life raft of VF-3 pilot Harry Gibbs, shot down by a Zero fighter the previous afternoon. That terrible night Gibbs tried desperately to stay afloat. At dawn he perceived the flattop, also still afloat, and her faithful escort, and it gave him a new hope.

To the east, Task Force 17 that morning was busy transferring *Yorktown* survivors, including seven VF-3 pilots (Brainard Macomber, Bill Woollen, Tom Cheek, Harold Eppler, Van Morris, Milt Tootle, and Robert Evans), from the destroyers that had plucked them from the sea to the heavy cruiser *Portland*. On board Fletcher's temporary flagship *Astoria*, Buckmaster collected specialists to make a salvage team to reclaim the *Yorktown*. When he got them together—a lengthy process—he took the 170 men over to the destroyer *Hammann*. With the survivors crowded on board the *Portland*, Fletcher took the opportunity to fuel his thirsty destroyers from that vessel. Fueling took most of the day; at 1800, Fletcher sent the *Hammann*, *Balch*, and *Benham* to rejoin the *Yorktown*. The rest of the Task Force 17 headed south to rendezvous with the oiler *Platte* and also with the big submarine tender *Fulton* coming up from Pearl Harbor to take on the *Yorktown*'s crew.

After dawn that morning, Gibbs had paddled furiously in the direction of the drifting carrier. He tried to raise some response from the tin can's lookouts but without success. Floating close by was an empty raft that, although oil-soaked, was larger and more seaworthy than his own, so Gibbs switched over. Exhausted, he fell asleep. Later that morning, someone on board the *Hughes* noticed the raft, and she came over to investigate. Her crew recognized Gibbs and at 0938 brought him on deck. In all, he had rowed about six miles. Crewmen asked him how he was. He replied that he was all right—then promptly fainted! Gentle hands took him below deck for food, something to drink, a shower to wash off the saltwater, and a comfortable bunk. Gibbs slept until midafternoon, then strolled up on deck for a look around.

Around the drifting carrier, there was renewed activity. The fleet tug *Viero* had joined the little group, and at 1308, she began towing the carrier toward Pearl Harbor. The small tug and her tow could only make three knots or so, but it was a beginning. Gibbs remained on board the *Hughes* and thus became the only *Yorktown* fighter pilot to witness the carrier's curtain scene from start to finish. At 1606 the destroyers *Gwin* and *Monahan* (with Bill Warden on board) moved round the tug and her charge. Unfortunately the Japanese knew that the *Yorktown* still survived and roughly where she was. A Chikuma floatplane happened upon the carrier during the morning and disclosed her position. The Japanese high command gave the submarine I-168 the mission of finishing her off.

Fletcher on 6 June arranged to divest his warships of the burden of the 2,000-odd *Yorktown* survivors and also to complete fueling of all of the ships. At 0440, the overcrowded *Portland* and two destroyers peeled off to the southeast to meet the *Fulton*. The actual transfer of survivors took almost all day, delayed by a sub scare. Along with the other 2,000 or so Yorktowners, 6 pilots and 106 enlisted men from the Fighting Three went over in coal bags to the friendly sub tender. At the end of the day, the *Fulton* turned south for Pearl at 17 knots with her fill of *Yorktown* people. Meanwhile, Fletcher with the *Astoria* and two tin cans met the *Platte* and fueled. That evening he moved to reassemble his scattered task force, but by that time it was too late for the *Yorktown*.

Buckmaster in the predawn hours of 6 June arrived on the scene and started salvage work on board the *Yorktown*. His ad hoc crew initiated counterflooding to reduce the sharp list, attempted measures to restore power, pushed over the side anything reasonably portable (including the two faithful F4F-4s F-6 and F-23 lashed on the flight deck), and even cut away and jettisoned the port-side five-inch guns to decrease topside weight. By early afternoon, things looked much better for the brave flattop. The *Hammann* lay alongside her starboard side, while the *Viero* chugged away, moving her huge tow slowly but steadily.

Still a guest on board the *Hughes* in the screen, Gibbs around 1330 walked around the destroyer's bridge. Suddenly an alert sounded, and tremendous explosions erupted next to the carrier. With skill and daring, I-168 had infiltrated the antisubmarine screen and fired a spread of torpedoes. One fish slammed into the gallant *Hammann* and sank her almost instantly. Two others ripped into the *Yorktown*'s starboard side, wreaking fatal damage. The destroyers tried fruitlessly to hunt down the I-boat, while the salvage crew fought to overcome their shock and tried to stem the flooding. It was no use. The men abandoned ship for good at 1550. The *Yorktown* stayed afloat until shortly after dawn on 7 June, when she finally capsized to port. At 0501, with battle flag flying, the magnificent warship slipped beneath the waves. There was nary a dry eye among those who could bear to watch her go, including Ens. Harry B. Gibbs of Fighting Forty-two (temporary duty, Fighting Three).

THE *SARATOGA* BACK TO THE FRONT

The crucial spring of 1942, while the Pacific Fleet fought in the Coral Sea and braced for an onslaught directed against Midway, the *Saratoga* underwent repairs for torpedo damage and also general modernization at Puget Sound Navy Yard. Her air group split between Oahu and San Diego. Knowing he would soon have need of her, Nimitz on 12 May requested that the *Saratoga*'s repairs be expedited so she could sail around 25 May from Bremerton. Her new commanding officer, Captain Dewitt C. ("Duke") Ramsey, was to take her on a trial run to San Diego, there to pick up a cargo of airplanes. By 5 June he was clear San Diego, bound for Pearl Harbor. CinCPac the next day directed that Rear Admiral Fitch upon his return to the West Coast from the South Pacific shift his flag to the *Saratoga* as commander of Task Force 11.

If the *Saratoga* was the forgotten flattop that spring of 1942, the Fighting Two Detachment became the forgotten fighters, detailed as they were to act as her fighter force when she did leave the yards. In mid-February the VF-2 pilots had settled in at NAS San Diego, standing dawn alerts and trying to keep out of the way of fledgling carrier pilots of the advanced carrier training group operating out of North Island, as well. In March, they received orders to ferry aircraft from the East to the West Coast, traveling by commercial airliners from San Diego to New York and there picking up naval planes for the flights back to San Diego. Each VF-2 pilot made a couple of trips. In late March, during the midst of the ferrying, Jimmy Flatley left for parts west to take command of Fighting Forty-two on board the *Yorktown*. Taking his place in command of the VF-2 Detachment was Lieut. Louis H. Bauer, formerly Paul Ramsey's flight officer. A 1935 Naval Academy graduate, Lou Bauer had earned his wings early in 1939, reported to Fighting Two, and sharpened his skills as a fighter pilot under such greats as Truman J. Hedding, H. S. Duckworth, Paul Ramsey, and Jimmy Flatley. Likewise in March, the veteran VF-2 NAPs had received welcome promotions. Originally scheduled for warrant rank, Gordon Firebaugh, Theodore S. Gay, and Hal Rutherford obtained commissions as lieutenants (junior grade), while George Brooks became an ensign. Charles Brewer, Patrick Nagle, and Don Runyon fleeted up to warrant rank.

Bauer gradually exchanged his F4F-3As for new F4F-4s and also took one Wildcat, which seemed a strange bird indeed. On 24 April, the detachment received the first F4F-7 assigned to a West Coast fighting squadron. The F4F-7 was designed as an unarmed, long-range, photo reconnaissance version of the Wildcat. Fixed-winged, the F4F-7 featured a total 685 gallons of fuel stored in unprotected tanks, giving it a potential range of 3,700 miles! The prototype had flown nonstop from New York to California, unprecedented for a carrier aircraft. Bauer's new acquisition was the second of twenty-one to be produced for the Navy. It certainly was not a fighter—gross weight was 10,328 lbs.(!)—and Bauer likely did not know what to do with it.

The *Sara*'s repairs and facelift proceeded more smoothly than expected. Bauer received orders to fly north to be ready to rejoin the ship, and on 12 May the VF-2 Detachment headed for Seattle via NAS Alameda. Meanwhile, Don Lovelace had secured orders to reunite the squadron at Pearl Harbor and took ship for Oahu, unaware that the VF-2 Detachment was at NAS Seattle. On 22 May, the *Saratoga* departed Puget Sound for warmer water to the south, and Bauer's troops landed on board to serve as air defense if needed. Duke Ramsey made a swift run along the West Coast and reached San Diego early on the 25th. Bauer's pilots flew to NAS San Diego, while the *Saratoga* entered port. She was scheduled for several short cruises off San Diego, both for her trials and to permit carrier qualification landings for the ACTG pilots.

The afternoon the *Saratoga* arrived in port, several VF-2 pilots flew a glide-bomb practice mission to the exercise area about 15 miles south of San Diego. Fed Simpson rolled into his bomb run from about 10,000 feet and dived at 70 degrees. He released his practice bombs and started to pull out, but his dive had been too fast. Observers estimated his Grumman straining at 350 knots as Simpson tried to recover at 1,000 feet. Pulling 8 to 10 Gs, the F4F-4 broke up. First the left wing tore off, then the right. Simpson died on impact. One of the old-guard aviation cadets, Simpson had earned his wings in November 1937 and flew over three years with the Bombing Two. In March 1941, he had received a regular commission and his posting to Fighting Two. Fighting Two Detachment went to sea on board the *Saratoga* from 29 to 31 May, then returned to NAS San Diego.

Worried by the impending Japanese offensive against Midway, CinCPac on 30 May told Ramsey to sail as soon as possible for Pearl, even though Fitch, the task force commander, had not yet reached San Diego. Nimitz expected the *Saratoga* to clear Pearl on 6 June and get out to Midway about two days later, there to join Frank Jack Fletcher's Task Force 17 with the *Yorktown*. Ramsey got underway early in the morning of 1 June and nosed his newly designated Task Group 11.1 past Point Loma and into the Pacific. Already hoisted on board the *Saratoga* was a cargo of four F4F-4s, forty-three SBD-3s, and fourteen Grumman TBF-1 Avengers. At 1310, the *Sara* began landing her air group. Bauer's outfit had swelled in May to fourteen with the inclusion of six NAPs who had recently graduated from the ACTG, Pacific.

Other pilots, mostly fresh from advanced training, rode the *Saratoga* out to Pearl to join other squadrons. Ramsey set a westerly course at a steady 20 knots.

Missing his new command by a day and a half, Aubrey Fitch on board the *Chester* arrived at San Diego the afternoon of 2 June. The transports *Barnett* and *George F. Elliott* docked at the destroyer base inside San Diego harbor and disgorged the multitude of *Lexington* survivors. The fighter pilots split according to their orders. Paul Ramsey and the original

VF-2 hands waited for new assignments, while Scoop Vorse took charge of the VF-3 refugees, trying to get them back out to Pearl to rejoin the squadron. Noel Gayler headed east to become a test pilot. Jimmy Flatley happily reported to NAS San Diego and his nascent Fighting Ten, ready to implement the ideas he had so carefully thought out on the voyage back. Fitch waited until the *Chester* could be refueled and reprovisioned, so he could ride her out to Pearl.

The *Saratoga's* return to the war zone was uneventful except for some activity on 3 June. At 1026, a radar contact bearing 007 degrees, distance 26 miles, afforded an opportunity to practice a CAP scramble. Six VF-2 F4F-4s roared off the flight deck and checked out the bogey, which proved to be an Army B-17 Flying Fortress on a ferry flight to Oahu. At 1215, another contact activated the radar scope, and five fighters took off. A few minutes later, one of the five, NAP Tumosa, lost power at 5,000 feet and tried to get back to home plate for a deferred forced landing. The *Saratoga* was not prepared to recover him, and after circling three times, Tumosa had to put his Grumman into the water. The destroyer *Smith* quickly rescued him unharmed, offering practice of another sort but at the price of F4F-4 BuNo. 5182.

While the *Saratoga* ate up the miles toward Pearl Harbor, the Pacific Fleet slugged it out with the Japanese at Midway and triumphed in decisive victory. At 0545 on 6 June, the *Saratoga* dispatched her air group for fields on Oahu and headed in. She anchored at berth F-2 off Ford Island after an absence of nearly four months. The situation was not nearly as grave as it appeared two days before! With the victory, details of which were very sketchy, the CinCPac staff first thought to send the *Saratoga* out to join Task Force 16 for raids on the newly acquired enemy holdings in the Aleutians. With the second and fatal torpedoing of the *Yorktown* that afternoon, Nimitz decided not to risk an inexperienced carrier and ad hoc air group in combat. He assigned Duke Ramsey a new mission: ferry replacement aircraft to Spruance's carriers, then return to Pearl.

The *Saratoga's* cruise would provide carrier squadrons long based ashore the chance to stretch their sea legs. Alerted for duty on board the carrier were the outfits that had arrived at Pearl on 29 May: Roy Simpler's Fighting Five, Fighting Seventy-two under Mike Sanchez, and the Torpedo Eight Detachment with Grumman TBF-1 torpedo planes led by "Swede" Larsen. Given the news blackout on Oahu, Simpler's troops, who considered themselves the legitimate *Yorktown* fighting squadron, wondered what was happening to the old lady and were surprised at orders to embark on board the *Saratoga*. Also eager to go were those elements of the *Yorktown* Air Group left on the beach, the "real" Scouting Five and Torpedo Five. With all of the fighters now available, VF-42's Chas Fenton and Vince McCormack, unhappily waiting at Ewa, had to bide their time. They took custody of the sixteen rookie VF pilots who had come out on board the *Saratoga* and maintained a collection of battle-worn F4F-4s. Lou Bauer discovered on reporting in that his own superior, Don Lovelace, had gone out on board the *Yorktown*. Owing to radio silence, he did not know that Lovelace had died on 30 May. Bauer exchanged several of his F4F-4s and gratefully turned over to NAS Pearl Harbor the hybrid F4F-7 for the time being. He and eight pilots were to re-embark on board the *Saratoga*, relegating most of his rookies to Fenton at Ewa.

On 7 June, Ramsey's redesignated Task Group 11.2 set sail from Pearl with the *Saratoga*, five destroyers, and the oiler *Kaskaskia*. Jake Fitch missed the boat again. His temporary flagship *Chester* had departed San Diego on 4 June and was still en route to Pearl. Around 1100, the *Saratoga* began landing part of her improvised air group. All of those aircraft plus those previously hoisted on board the *Saratoga* totaled 107 (47 fighters, 45 dive bombers, and 15 torpedo planes). His aircraft safely tucked on board, Ramsey set course to the northwest.

"How Good Land Will Look This Time"

The seventh of June, the day the valiant *Yorktown* gave up the ghost, Task Force 16 with the *Enterprise* and the *Hornet* retired eastward for a vital fueling rendezvous. Other than for normal flight operations (search and inner air patrol), the aviator spent a quiet day trying to pick up the pieces. Spruance's two carriers had on hand a total of 131 aircraft (just over 100 short of the 4 June figure, including the *Yorktown*), of which 118 (54 fighters, 61 dive bombers, and 3 torpedo planes) apparently were operational. To the southeast, Fletcher spent the day completing his fueling, then headed out to meet Task Group 11.2 coming up from Pearl. That evening, CinCPac issued specific orders for the second phase of the Midway operation. He set a 10 June rendezvous between Fletcher's Task Force 17 (which by that time would include the *Saratoga*) and Spruance's Task Force 16 in order to transfer aircraft from the *Saratoga* to the other flattops. This completed, Fletcher was to turn south for Pearl Harbor.

For Ray Spruance's Task Force 16, Nimitz had other ideas. Concurrent with their assault on Midway, the Japanese had rampaged in the Aleutians and evidently intended to occupy a number of positions in the island chain. The enemy had used strong forces, including carriers, and Nimitz thought the enemy might be up to further mischief in northern waters. Thus Spruance with his two carriers, five cruisers, one light cruiser, eight destroyers, and a fleet oiler was to proceed north to "Point Blow" (Lat. 48° North, Long. 172° West), there on 12 June to rendezvous with elements of Rear Admiral Robert A. Theobald's overall command in order to "seek out and destroy enemy forces in the Aleutians." For the aviators, there boded uncomfortable, even perilous, flying conditions over cold Alaskan water renowned for fog, icing, and other noxious forms of bad weather.

The weather on 8 June round Task Force 16 seemed a foretaste of what the pilots could expect in the Aleutians. The *Hornet* lost two SBDs in the poor visibility, one of which found sanctuary on Midway. Good thing the weather was not that way on 4 June, when the Japanese first attacked! At 0430, Spruance's ships had begun fueling, destroyers first, from the oiler *Guadalupe*, and four destroyers joined up to hasten the fueling. The tin cans took the opportunity to transfer aviators they had fished out of the water the past several days. Bill Warden returned to Fighting Six on board the *Enterprise*, while VF-8's Jim Smith made it to the *Cimarron*. That day came definite word of the *Yorktown*'s demise, which saddened everyone and robbed the victory of some of its sweetness.

Fletcher's truncated Task Force 17 (the *Astoria*, the *Portland*, and three destroyers) at 1112 made contact with Ramsey's Task Group 11.2, and early that afternoon, he transferred his flag to the flattop. That accomplished, the reconstituted Task Force 17 steamed northwestward to contact Task Force 16. The *Saratoga* conducted the usual search and inner air patrols, but Ramsey kept his fighters under wraps.

The eighth of June also proved a red-letter day for the VF-8 pilots lost on the ill-fated 4 June escort mission. That day PBYs operating north-northeast of Midway finally happened upon some of the rafts and rescued their occupants. One Catalina bellied into the sea to recover the irrepressible John McInerny and section leader John Magda. The two had hoped for an early rescue on 5 June when they happened to see Task Force 16 pass by in the distance (as Spruance headed toward Midway that morning), but no one spotted them. Now flown to Midway, Magda and McInerny looked in good shape and high spirits as they clowned with John Ford's motion picture photographer at the seaplane base. McInerny, however, was deeply worried about the consequences of his turning the fighters back on 4 June, but nothing was ever said to him about it.

A second PBY that day found Frank Jennings and Hump Tallman not far from where the other picked up Magda and McInerny. As Tallman stepped out of his orange raft, a PBY crewman noticed its interior scribbled with a lengthy message. After ditching, Tallman had set down in detail his recollections of the mission, anxious that it be preserved. Both he and the crewman tried in vain to retrieve the raft, but it floated away and had to be left behind. Also rescued that afternoon was Johnny Talbot, weak from his lonely ordeal. Lieut. (jg) Francis M. Fisler's PBY from VP-51 spotted his raft and whisked him back to Midway for treatment. Still missing were five VF-8 pilots, but Talbot helped point out where they might be.

The morning of 9 June, one of Fisler's sharp-eyed crew spotted the two rafts containing Pat Mitchell, Stan Ruehlow, and Dick Gray. The three were emaciated, tired, sore, sunburned, hungry—and gloriously glad to be alive. The PBY picked them up at a point bearing 047 degrees, distance 131 miles from Midway, and one of the grateful castaways (evidently Ruehlow) presented the crew with a "short snorter," a ten-dollar bill upon which the details of the rescue were written.

For six days, the three VF-8 pilots had drifted slowly to the northwest, carried by the current. On 5 June, they had several times sighted search planes and tried signaling them with a hand mirror. After dark that day came a really big scare. In the blackness a shark repeatedly nudged both rafts. Finally the bump was violent enough to spill both Ruehlow and Mitchell into the water. Ruehlow actually brushed against the shark and gashed his right hand on its rasping skin. He lost no time in making it to Gray's raft, while Mitchell clambered into the now-vacant but damaged second raft. The skipper had to lie in the nearly swamped boat with his legs dangling in the water, but very fortunately the shark did not persist in its attacks. On 6 June, the three dipped into the survival rations so fortuitously saved by Gray. Even though severely rationed, the food and water did not go far. After another blistering day and cold night in the water-soaked rafts, they secured their first replenishment of fresh water from a rain squall, allowing them to refill their canteen. Rescue came none too soon, as far as they were concerned. The VF-8 pilots spent a few days at Midway; then they were flown back to the naval hospital at Pearl Harbor.

While the VF-8 pilots were recovered, other survivors of the Midway battle made it back to Pearl. At 1530 on 8 June, the submarine tender *Fulton* docked at the submarine base inside Pearl Harbor. There to greet the Yorktowners were Nimitz and the rest of the fleet brass, shaking hands and showing much good cheer. Headed ashore were Macomber and Woollen from VF-42, and from VF-3 came Cheek, Tootle, Eppler, Morris, and Evans. The seven traveled out to Ewa to join Fenton's contingent. Harry Gibbs came in the next day with the salvage survivors on board the *Gwin* and the *Benham*.

For the carriers, 9 June was a quiet day. The *Enterprise* had the duty, but the righters did not fly. Jim Smith got back to the *Hornet* while she refueled from the oiler *Cimarron*. Task Forces 16 and 17 made contact the morning of 10 June, for all the good it did them. It was "foggy, foul weather—a day in bed for all hands," recorded the VF-6 diary. Fletcher and Spruance marked time on a southerly course, waiting for the skies to clear. The *Enterprise* did not get a glimmer of the "floating drydock" (as her pilots unkindly dubbed the *Saratoga*) until late afternoon. The aircraft transfer finally took place the morning of 11 June. To the *Enterprise*, the *Saratoga* flew ten SBDs from Scouting Five (the "real" Scouting Five) and five TBDs from Torpedo Five. The *Hornet* received the nine replacement SBDs of the ferry detachment and the ten Grumman TBF-1s of Larsen's Torpedo Eight Detachment. The TBFs excited special interest, as this was the first time Task Force 16 had seen the big Grumman torpedo planes operate on a carrier. The reinforcements gave Spruance's two carriers a total of 163 aircraft on board (57 fighters, 87 dive bombers, and 19 torpedo planes, not all flyable).

Its mission completed, Task Force 17 by 1100 had turned south for Pearl, while Spruance shaped course north for the next day's rendezvous with Task Force 8 and further combat in Aleutian waters. A few hours later came a welcome reprieve. Nimitz relented and ordered Task Force 16 home. With the Japanese on the run in the Central Pacific, he had no need to risk the carrier in raids on the enemy toehold in the Aleutians. Also on 11 June, the carrier *Wasp* traversed the Panama Canal and reported for duty with the Pacific Fleet. With the loss of the *Lexington* and the *Yorktown*, however, that still left CinCPac with only four fleet carriers—but the Japanese did not have even that many big carriers after Midway!

Steaming southeastward into warmer waters, the two task forces gratefully enjoyed better weather on 12 June. The *Saratoga* that afternoon launched all of her operational fighters. Simpler's Fighting Five and Bauer's VF-2 Detachment (twenty-six F4Fs all told) flew a welcome gunnery training flight, while Sanchez led nineteen VF-72 fighters in squadron tactical drills. One pilot did not find the exercise much to his liking. At 1447, Lieut. (jg) Robert W. Rynd of VF-72 had engine trouble and ditched. The destroyer *Russell* recovered him unharmed. On board the *Enterprise*, VF-6 pilots handled the last two inner air patrols, but no one minded. They were on their way home!

The morning of 13 June saw a massive fly-in of carrier planes to fields on Oahu. Somewhat ahead of the rest, the squadrons of the *Saratoga* Air Group took off beginning at 0650 and made for NAS Pearl Harbor. Later that morning Task Force 17 entered port. Task Force 16's turn came a little later. The *Enterprise* Air Group flew to NAS Kaneohe Bay, pleased to find there "a band to meet us and free beer right on the field." The *Hornet* launched her squadrons for MCAS Ewa. Thach's VF-3/42/8 all took care to get into their own squadron's airplanes for the scheduled flight in. When they touched down, Thach and the VF-3 pilots taxied to one part of the field, Harwood's VF-8 troops to another, while Leonard led the VF-2 personnel to a homecoming at the hangar where Fenton, McCormack, and the company had set up shop. There was no formal good-bye between Thach and the VF-42 pilots who had served him well. There just was not time for that. He flew over to Kaneohe to reunite Fighting Three. Leonard personally did not see him again for two years. That was the way it went. The first phase of the Pacific War was over, but most of the work remained to be done.

CHAPTER FIVE

The Fiercest Battles

Marshall L. Michel III

BY MAY, THE MASSIVE AIR STRIKES HAD STRIPPED THE MAIN THRUST OF the North Vietnamese assault, and now the Americans turned their attention to destroying the supply chain. The North Vietnamese had large armies in the field that were in constant combat, and these forces had to be supported with a steady stream of supplies. Cutting this massive supply flow was expected to be much easier than before the invasion, when North Vietnamese forces simply refused to fight if supplies were low.

On May 9, 1972, the Nixon administration made its next move as the president decided to move the air campaign back into Route Package VI to seal off North Vietnam from China and destroy the supplies already there. This escalation of the air war was first called Rolling Thunder Alpha, but it was quickly renamed Operation Linebacker (Linebacker I), allegedly because of the president's fondness for football. It soon became clear that Linebacker was going to be different from Rolling Thunder and even Freedom Train. The first mission of Linebacker, called Pocket Money, was the dropping of delayed-action mines in Haiphong harbor and all of the other smaller harbors in North Vietnam; three days later they were activated, and the harbors were effectively closed for the duration of the war. Few events were as symbolic in showing the differences between Linebacker and Rolling Thunder, when the Joint Chiefs of Staff had asked for permission to mine the port of Haiphong and other ports on the North Vietnamese coast from the beginning of the war and the Johnson administration had denied it. Now, expectations were high that Linebacker operations would seriously cut the flow of supplies into North Vietnam.

Linebacker was in practical ways unrestrained, especially when compared to Rolling Thunder. In general, Nixon allowed the military to make all the decisions on targets once the general guidelines and rules of engagement were established. There was no policy of "gradual escalation" in Linebacker; most of the major targets in Vietnam were quickly put on the target list, and on the list there was no time limit; the target could be struck when tactically feasible. The commanders were given tactical latitude about how and when to strike targets on the list and were allowed to choose the weapons the wings thought were appropriate. The expanded target list not only allowed a more tactically flexible bombing strategy but also ensured that, when the weather over a target was bad, there was a list of lucrative alternate targets that could be struck. All this made Linebacker strikes much more effective—with many fewer casualties—than Rolling Thunder strikes.

In concept, the overall aim of Linebacker was the same as Rolling Thunder—interdiction of the North Vietnamese supply lines—but in execution it was very different. Linebacker's standing operations order was to disrupt transportation from the DMZ to the Chinese buffer zone (30 nautical miles wide to 106 E longitude, then 25 miles from the 106 line to the Gulf of Tonkin), but unlike Rolling Thunder, all of the North Vietnamese air defenses—SAM sites, most airfields, TCI radars—were included in targeting plans.

To keep the pressure on, one Air Force Linebacker strike was planned to the Hanoi area every day and flown if the weather permitted. The original list of Linebacker targets was intended to isolate Hanoi and Haiphong by neutralizing their defenses, destroying the rail and road links to the north and south, and then destroying all war material in storage or in transit. Still, not all of the restraints were removed. Fixed transportation targets (bridges, rail yards) within 10 nautical miles of Hanoi and Haiphong and the Chinese buffers zone needed Joint Chiefs of Staff approval, and the secretary of defense had to approve B-52 strikes above Route Package I. Linebacker bombing strikes were also instructed to avoid prisoners-of-war camps, churches/shrines, hospitals, and third-country shipping and to minimize civilian casualties. There were also occasional short-term restrictions. From May 21 through June 5, Hanoi was not bombed to avoid casualties during Nixon's visit to Moscow, and the Haiphong area was off limits from May 25 through 30 for the same reason. Following the president's return, strikes resumed.

But even with the restraints, Linebacker felt very different to combat aircrews. Approval for new targets was quickly granted, and as the operation continued, many of the rules of engagement were gradually or temporarily relaxed; in August and September, for example, there were twice the number of sorties into the upper route packages as there were from May to July. The military was quite pleased with the rules for Linebacker; the Seventh Air Force commander summed up their feelings when he said, "We were not constrained. In some of the sensitive areas, for example, I was allowed the take out all the power [major electric power plants] in a very short time with the exception of one power plant, and that was the thermal power plant for Hanoi itself."

LINEBACKER: THE FIRST DAY

On the morning of May 10, the Air Force launched its first strike of Linebacker against the Paul Doumer Bridge in Hanoi and the Yen Vein railroad yard. Oyster was the first Combat Tree MiGCAP in the area and was patrolling at low altitude when they picked up MiG activity on their Tree equipment. The F-4s turned toward the MiGs and set up a head-on pass, knowing that, since they were the only U.S. fighters in the area, they could fire their AIM-7s head on without visually identifying the MiGs. Oyster's radars showed there were four MiGs, and the F-4s locked on and closed; the F-4s were below the MiGs and seemingly undetected, in what looked like a perfect attack set-up. Once in range Oyster 1 fired his first Sparrow; it went about 1,000 feet in front of the F-4 and detonated prematurely, so Oyster fired a second AIM-7 at what he could now identify as four MiG-21s. The missile guided well and hit the second MiG in the flight. Oyster 2 fired two AIM-7s at almost the same time as the third MiG and also scored a hit. As the missiles hit, the first MiG flashed by, and Oyster 1 turned to pursue him; meanwhile Oyster 3 and Oyster

4 attacked the fourth MiG. As the MiG started a right turn, Oyster 3 fired two AIM-7s; the first went under the MiG without detonating, but the second hit the MiG amidships. At this point, all was going well for Oyster flight; three MiGs were fireballs, and Oyster 1 was behind the last MiG, maneuvering for the kill.

Oyster 1 was flying an F-4D without a cannon and found himself too close to the MiG to fire a missile. As he maneuvered to drop back far enough behind the MiG to fire, suddenly four MiG-19s appeared behind the F-4 (they apparently had been trailing the MiG-21s at low altitude).

The MiGs flew poorly; they overshot Oyster 1 and were slightly in front of and close off the left wing—in easy sight had the crew looked in that direction—but despite warning calls from Oyster 2, neither Oyster 1's pilot nor the WSO (who was temporarily distracted) saw the MiGs, and Oyster 1 continued his attack. The MiG-19s pulled back behind the F-4 and slid in close; as Oyster 1 fired and missed with an AIM-7 at the MiG in front of him, the MiG-19s opened fire with their 30-mm cannon. Oyster 2 saw the long flames from the MiG-19s' guns and again warned, "Hey lead, break right, break right, break right, they're firing." OT was too late; the MiGs hammered the F-4 with their heavy cannon, and it went into a flat spin. The back seater asked the front seater to bail out, but he demurred and said he would stay with the burning aircraft. The back seater ejected and, after several weeks on the ground, was eventually picked up. The front seater was killed in the crash.

A few minutes later, Cleveland, four F-4s escorting LGB flight, was attacked by a MiG-19 and was introduced to the maneuverability of the new fighter. The four F-4s saw the MiG crossing behind them perpendicular to their flight path at very high speed, and Cleveland 1 said to himself, "There is no way he can make that turn. . . . I just knew he couldn't make the turn, but he cranked in the bank, pulled it around, made square corner, and stopped" very close behind Cleveland 4. The MiG began to fire, hit Cleveland 4 in the wing, and the F-4 went down in flames. Cleveland 1 pursued the MiG, who apparently lost sight of the F-4. He pulled behind the MiG at low altitude and began to fire missiles, first an AIM-9 that went ballistic and then two AIM-7s. The first AIM-7 exploded off the MiG's wing, forcing the startled North

Vietnamese pilot to jerk back on the stick and snap his aircraft out of control into a spin. Cleveland 1 pulled off and "was going to watch him and see him hit the ground, just for the satisfaction of saying I got him. A kill is a kill." Just as the MiG was about to hit the ground, "He [the MiG-19 pilot] recovered the damn thing right in the weeds. When he came out of the spin, he was in a stall, just staggering along pretty close to the ground . . . still headed home." Overall that day the Air Force shot down three MiGs for two losses, both MiG-19s.

That same afternoon, after the Air Force strike, the Navy struck the Haiphong area with Alpha strikes, and a large number of MiGs attacked the strike force. The Navy was waiting for the MiGs and had two surprises: the Topgun-trained F-4 crews and a tactic that it had used successfully in the last engagements of 1968—communications jamming. Navy jammers, operating from close off shore, jammed the North Vietnamese communications, leaving the MiGs to fend for themselves, without GCI to warn them that the F-4s were attacking. Both tactics showed their effects; the well-trained Navy F-4 crews had a field day against the MiGs.

In the morning Silver Kite, two F-4Js on Target CAP (TarCAP), sighted two MiG-21s taking off and shot one down. During the afternoon strikes, the MiGs were up in force, and as the battle began, the Navy specialists began jamming the MiGs' communications with their GCI. Despite their loss of communication, the MiGs stayed to fight; it was a mistake. An F-4J on Iron Hand escort destroyed one MiG-17, and a few minutes later, two F-4Bs on MIGCAP engaged and destroyed another MiG-17. At almost the same time, another F-4 MIGCAP, Showtime, attacked a MiG-17 who was chasing an A-7. More MiG-17s poured in, and a large dogfight erupted; in the melee, Showtime 106 destroyed two MiG-17s. The MiGs kept coming. Another Showtime flight on a flak suppression mission on the Haiphong rail yard had just dropped their bombs when two MiG-17s attacked them from behind. Showtime 100 forced the first MiG to overshoot and fired an AIM-9 as the MiG flew in front of him, blowing it up. As the second MiG closed from the rear, Showtime 100 accelerated away to "drag" the MiG in front of his wingman. Unfortunately, his wingman had his hands full with two more

MiGs that had attacked him, so Showtime 100 outran the MiG and rejoined with his wingman, and the two F-4s turned back to the battle.

As they returned to the target area, the F-4s saw a low-altitude wheel of eight MiG-17s with three F-4s in the middle. Showtime 100 saw that one of the F-4s had three MiGs behind and dived in to help; as he did, he saw several MiG-21s in the area and was attacked from behind by two MiG-19s. Showtime 100 stayed fast—550 knots—to keep the MiGs from closing and continued toward the F-4 that was under attack. At first Showtime 100 was unable to fire because he was afraid his missile would home in on the F-4 instead of the MiG, but after several radio calls, the F-4 broke away, and Showtime 100 fired his missile. It hit the MiG, and the pilot ejected. As the missile hit, several MiG-21s began to attack Showtime 100; severely outnumbered and with no F-4s in sight, Showtime 100 broke off the engagement at high speed and headed for the coast.

On the way, Showtime 100 saw a single MiG-17 and turned for a head-on pass; as he passed, the F-4 went into a climb and turned back after the MiG, but to his surprise, the MiG began to climb with him. Showtime 100 thought this would be an easy kill if he just outclimbed the MiG and then dropped behind him, but before he could outzoom the MiG, it pulled behind him and opened fire, forcing the F-4 to dive away. The F-4 and the MiG went through several more vertical maneuvers; Showtime 100 took a chance in one of the zooms and slowed down rapidly; the MiG flew in front of him, and Showtime 100 had his fifth kill, which made the crew the first American aces of the Vietnam War.

Showtime 100 then turned and joined with another F-4 in the area and departed; on the way out, they passed very close behind several more MiGs, but low on fuel and without a gun for a quick kill, the F-4s had to continue out. At the coast Showtime 100 was hit by a SAM that knocked out its hydraulics, but he was able to get off shore and eject. The crew was picked up by a helicopter.

The Navy plan had worked to perfection; supported by the jamming of the North Vietnamese GCI, the well-trained Navy pilots shot down eight MiGs without losing an aircraft. In the melee several F-4s were very close to MiGs and reported they would have had several more easy kills if they had had a cannon. Most of the kills were in dogfights with the supposedly more agile MiG-17s, and all of the kills had come with AIM-9s; it was a stunning success for the Navy's post–Rolling Thunder training program.

At the end of the first day of Linebacker, six U.S. aircraft had been lost, two to MiGs. U.S. fighters had shot down eleven MiGs for their biggest day of the war, but the day had not been a good one for the Air Force. Despite their Tree equipment, they shot down only three MiGs for the loss of two F-4s. The loss of Oyster 1 had been especially disturbing; he had been a wing weapons officer at Udorn and was generally acknowledged as a "guru" of the 432nd tactics and the most knowledgeable pilot in the wing about the Combat Tree system. He had scored his third kill just before he was shot down, and he appeared to have been well on his way to being the first Air Force ace. After the back seater was picked up and explained how the front seater had deliberately ridden the aircraft down rather than take a chance on being captured and interrogated by the North Vietnamese, no one was surprised—"He was that kind of guy" was the common opinion.

The next day, May 11, the MiGs were active again, and the North Vietnamese tried new tactics. Tuna, a flight of four Iron Hand F-105Gs, was inbound into the target area when they were fired on by a barrage of unguided SAMs; distracted, the F-105s failed to see two MiG-21s attacking from below, and one of the MiGs shot down Tuna 4 with an Atoll. A few minutes later, a MiGCAP flight, Gopher 1 and Gopher 2, pursed an aircraft they could not identify. Gopher 1 closed to make an ID pass from the rear: as he approached he saw the target was a MiG-21, so he broke away and cleared Gopher 2 to fire an AIM-7. Seconds after Gopher 2 fired, he saw a missile hit Gopher 1 in the rear and down the F-4. This distracted Gopher 2's attention, and he did not see the result of his missile. During postmission debriefings the possibility was raised that Gopher 1 had been hit by the other F-4's malfunctioning AIM-7. (It was not until over two years later that the event was successfully reconstructed. Gopher 1 had been hit by an Atoll from a trailing MiG-21, unseen by either of the F-4s, and Gopher 2's AIM-7 had hit the lead MiG—probably a decoy—and destroyed him.)

The following day the F-4s continued to have missile problems but still scored. Harlow, a four-ship F-4D MiGCAP, was flying near Yen Bai airfield when they saw four MiG-19s taking off. Harlow 1 attacked the leader and fired four AIM-7s, but all missed. Harlow 2 attacked the other three and fired three AIM-7s at the fourth MiG; the last AIM-7 hit, and the MiG crashed. There was no more MiG activity until May 18, when the Air Force struck a large POL storage area just northeast of Hanoi; using LGBs, the strike flights destroyed more than 5.5 million gallons of fuel. The MiGs were active that day; two flights of F-4Ds on MiGCAP intercepted two MiG-21s and probably damaged one. Fifteen minutes later, four F-4s were engaging a MiG-21 when, in an attack reminiscent of May 10, they were attacked by two MiG19s, who shot down number 4.

Meanwhile, the Navy F-4Bs continued to set a fast pace. That afternoon a section of two Navy F-4Bs, Rock River, was on MiGCAP for an Alpha strike over North Vietnam when it received a call from Red Crown that there were MiGs airborne over Kep airfield. As the F-4s turned toward the airfield, they saw two silver MiG-19s in front of them, in trail at low altitude. Rock River 1 began an attack knowing the MiGs had been using decoys to set up trailing MiGs for attacks, and Rock River 2 went high to cover and look for these trailers.

As Rock River 1 began his attack, the MiGs saw him, jettisoned their external tanks, and began to turn into the F-4. The agile MiGs soon began to outturn Rock River 1, so Rock River 2 moved in to help and fired an AIM-9; the MiGs split up, one turning to defeat the missile and one heading off in the other direction. Each of the F-4s now was in a turning engagement with a MiG-19, and the MiGs were working toward an advantage when, inexplicably (perhaps they lost sight of one of the F-4s), both MiGs rolled out and one flew in front of Rocker River 1. As the F-4 began his attack, the second MiG-19 pulled behind him but in front of Rock River 2. Rock River 2 fired an AIM-9; the missile detonated about five feet behind the MiG and shot him down with an AIM-9.

Unfortunately for the Air Force, on May 20 another aspect of their poor training program reappeared. An F-4D MiGCAP was attacked by two MiG-21s; in a hard break to avoid the MiGs, one of the F-4s—untouched by MiG fire—went out of control because of adverse yaw and crashed. On May 23 MiGs were again very active and challenged both Air Force and Navy strikes. Balter, an Air Force flight of four F-4Es, was assigned as a chaff flight escort, then was supposed to convert to MiGCAP when the chaff flight completed its mission. After completing its escort role uneventfully, Balter was en route to a MiGCAP orbit when the F-4s passed a few miles north of Kep airfield and saw several MiG-17s, -19s, and -21s in the traffic pattern. Balter 1 turned to attack two of the MiG-19s but overshot his original pass and repositioned for a Sparrow shot, dropping low so his radar and missile had a "look up" angle to avoid ground clutter problems. Balter 1 fired two AIM-7s; the first hit and destroyed the MiG. Balter 1 then turned back and found that the MiG-19s had set up a wagon wheel; he made several passes on the wheel without results. As Balter 1 pressed the wheel, Balter 2 saw two MiG-21s attacking and turned to engage. He pulled his F-4 behind one of the MiGs and opened fire with his cannon; the MiG slowly came apart, rolled over to the left, and hit the ground.

The Navy scored well that same afternoon. Rock River, a section of two F-4Bs on the MiGCAP for an Alpha strike on Haiphong, received vectors for MiGs over Kep and turned toward the airfield. As they approached at 3,000 feet, the F-4s passed head on with two MiG-19s; they turned to engage, then found themselves surrounded by MiG-17s. The MiGs had been flying the trail of the MiG-19s, hoping to "sandwich" the F-4s, but they had been too close. The two F-4s were now in a low-altitude engagement with the two MiG-19s and about four MiG-17s. After several turns with the MiGs and after firing two AIM-9s, which the MiGs outmaneuvered, Rock River 1 found a MiG-17 close behind him, firing. The F-4 pulled into the MiG to try to make the MiG overshoot, but this simply allowed the very maneuverable MiG-17 to get in very close. As he closed, Navy training took over. Rock River 1 realized the MiG was pulling so much lead to fire his cannon that the pilot was in a position where he could not see Rock River 1 over his nose; he was simply expecting the F-4 to continue on and flew in front of the F-4, who fired a Sidewinder that blew off the MiG's tail.

Meanwhile, Rock River 2 had another MiG-17 behind him, so Rock River 1 called for him to accelerate away and fly toward him to "drag" the MiG in front of him. As Rock River 2 accelerated away with the MiG behind him, Rock River 1 pulled behind the North Vietnamese and fired his last missile, not expecting a good result because the missile had not worked in the pretakeoff ground checks. To his surprise the missile guided perfectly and hit the MiG; the MiG pilot ejected, and the F-4s departed the area.

CHAPTER SIX

The Night They Saved Vega 31

Darrel Whitcomb

ON MARCH 27, 1999, THE FOURTH NIGHT OF OPERATION ALLIED
Force, USAF Lt. Col. Darrell P. Zelko turned his F-117 to an outbound
heading, returning to Aviano Air Base in northern Italy. Zelko had
reached his objective, and both of his aircraft's precision guided bombs
appeared to have hit their target near Belgrade.

Zelko was flying with the call sign of Vega 31. It was his third sortie of the air war over Serbia. Deployed from the 49th Fighter Wing
at Holloman AFB, New Mexico, he was engaged in his second combat
operation. He was a veteran of the 1991 Gulf War.

However, Zelko was still deep in enemy territory. Vega 31 was
west-northwest of the target area when his routine suddenly was shattered by indications that Serbian air defense systems had targeted his
aircraft. The F-117 was not as maneuverable as most fighters, and Zelko
could only watch and press on as the enemy tried to find him.

Seeing the enemy fire as it approached his aircraft, he closed his eyes
as the brightness of the explosions temporarily blinded him and threw
deadly shards of jagged steel into his airplane. The aircraft began to pitch
and roll violently.

There were witnesses. Capt. Mark Baroni was the aircraft commander
of Frank 36, a KC-135 that had just refueled several other aircraft. Baroni
was looking toward Belgrade when he recalled that "all of a sudden, I saw
a series of airborne explosions and then one really big one."

Zelko's aircraft, a legendary stealth fighter, was hit. Realizing that his aircraft was dying, he reached down and pulled the ejection handles. The canopy separated from the aircraft, and the ejection seat fired, propelling him into the frigid night air.

Moonlight Ride

"My mom is not going to be happy with me," Zelko thought as he fell through the darkness. His parachute and life support equipment deployed. He quickly checked his chute, noting with some shock that the white and orange panels were clearly visible in the moonlight. Well-lit Belgrade was off to his right, and he sensed that enemy forces below would be alerted to capture him.

The propaganda value of shooting down and capturing an F-117 pilot would be enormous. The stealth fighter had until then seemed invincible. Zelko was determined to deny the enemy the second half of the prize—himself. It was about 8:45 p.m. local time. He was in for a long night.

Zelko took out his survival radio. "Mayday, mayday, mayday, Vega 31," he broadcast on the emergency "Guard" frequency.

The crew of Frank 36 heard the call, as did a NATO E-3 AWACS aircraft in an orbit not far away. Flight Lt. Frank Graham, a British officer onboard the AWACS, returned the call, "Vega 31, Magic 86 on Guard."

Zelko was not at that moment able to respond.

Graham and the other AWACS crew members began frantically to react. Digging through reams of data, they had to quickly determine who Vega 31 was and what he had been tasked to do.

At the same time, they were beginning to get calls from several other agencies as the word of Vega 31's troubles quickly spread.

Zelko made another radio call. "Roger, roger, out of the aircraft." He paused and then continued, "Vega 31 is out, beacon on now," as he switched his radio to transmit the emergency signal.

Knowing that the Serbs were probably monitoring the frequency, he stopped the beeper after three seconds, but it was critical that Zelko get a signal out quickly. Time was of the essence, and he knew that coalition rescue forces would respond.

The crew in Frank 36 acknowledged his call. Zelko put away his radio and oriented on the terrain. Still descending toward the Earth, he was only about 20 miles west of Belgrade.

At about 3,000 feet above ground, he passed through a cloud deck. The wind was from the southwest, and he could see that he was drifting down south of the town of Ruma in an area of open farm fields. There were many vehicles on the roads, and he was concerned that somebody would spot his parachute.

Zelko picked his landing spot and turned his canopy toward a plowed field about 50 yards west of a north-south rail line and a road with a "T" intersection.

In Enemy Territory

Zelko landed; quickly hid his parachute, harness, and life raft; and scanned the road. Seeing no activity, he moved to a hiding site he had noticed just before he landed. It was about 250 yards away.

There, he grabbed some of the rich Serbian dirt and smeared it all over his face, neck, and hands.

Fortunately, Zelko had worn several layers of clothes, and he had some extra insulation. Tucked inside his T-shirt, right over his heart, was a folded American flag. It belonged to the young airman who had prepared his target folder for this mission.

As he settled into his hiding site, Zelko anticipated that rescue forces were marshaling. The United States did not send its warriors into harm's way without providing the capability to rescue them.

In preparation for combat, Zelko maintained excellent physical condition and had spent long hours reviewing the rescue procedures as directed by the special instructions (SPINs) in the daily tasking orders for the aircrews. He had received combat crew survival and evasion training and worked with specialists in his unit to develop a workable escape plan of action for just such an occurrence.

Zelko assumed that enemy forces knew of his arrival and also were actively organizing a search operation. Instinctively, he knew that his actions would be critical to the success or failure of any rescue attempt.

The downed pilot was equipped with several items to help facilitate his rescue. Besides his radio, he had Global Positioning System location equipment, several signaling devices, and a 9 mm pistol.

Rescue forces were in the region. Before the start of the conflict, three special operations squadrons deployed to an airfield near Brindisi, Italy. They were joined there by pararescue jumpers (PJs) from the 720th Special Tactics Group.

All were attached to Joint Special Operations Task Force 2. Their helicopters could be called on to perform combat recoveries under the tactical control of the Combined Air Operations Center at Vicenza, in northern Italy.

The CAOC worked for Lt. Gen. Michael C. Short, the 16th Air Force commander and combined force air commander for this operation. Short had made combat search and rescue a high priority.

Brindisi was almost 250 miles from Belgrade. To reduce reaction time, several of the helicopters had been ordered to Tuzla, Croatia, and were on alert there.

The task force launched just before Zelko took off. It consisted of a lead MH-53M piloted by Capt. James L. Cardoso and Capt. John C. Glass, an MH-53J flown by Capt. Shawn Cameron and Capt. Mark Daley, and the MH-60G of Capt. Chad P. Franks and Capt. Matt Glover.

Lt. Col. Stephan J. Laushine, commander of the 55th SOS, flew in the lead aircraft as rescue mission commander.

Arriving at Tuzla, the alert aircraft proceeded to the hot refueling area, while Laushine went into operations for an initial orientation. The operations center was soon notified that the F-117 was down.

Their immediate concern was Zelko's location. Information coming in from several sources initially indicated that Vega 31 was down northwest of Novi Sad, along the aircraft's planned egress route. Based on that analysis, Laushine built a plan. The three helicopters would take off as a flight. Each would have a full complement of Air Force PJs and would be augmented with Army Special Forces.

As the rescue teams were getting ready to go, CNN showed scenes of the still-burning F-117 wreckage, footage being supplied by Serbian news services. The imagery sent a chill through the operations center at Tuzla.

Hunkered down in his hiding site near Ruma, Lt. Col. Darrell Zelko waited.

THE SEARCH AND RESCUE

CSAR doctrine calls for the formation of a task force composed of helicopters and A-10 attack aircraft. The escort aircraft would provide command and control and close-in air support for the helicopters.

For this operation, the A-10s from the 81st Fighter Squadron, Spangdahlem AB, Germany, had been deployed to Aviano. That evening, two A-10s were on rescue alert: Sandy 30, piloted by Capt. John A. Cherrey, and Sandy 31, piloted by Capt. John O'Brien.

Also orbiting—well to the south and at a safe altitude—was an EC-130E Commando Solo command and control aircraft. It had also monitored Vega 31's radio calls.

One of the team members, Capt. Ripley Woodard, an A-10 pilot from Spangdahlem, was monitoring intelligence reports. Strong enemy forces were in Zelko's area, and they were beginning to actively search for the F-117 pilot. Woodard knew that rescue forces had to move quickly.

Maj. Phil Haun, the A-10 weapons and tactics officer at Aviano, was in the operations center when it received the report that Zelko was down.

Another pilot delivered Zelko's vital isolated personnel report (ISO-PREP) information. This data, known only by the downed pilot, would give the Sandys the ability to authenticate the survivor and avoid being drawn into a trap.

The A-10s then took off. Arriving over the survivor, Cherrey would become the critical on-scene commander.

Using the same coordinates given to Laushine, Haun also began working with the intelligence section at Aviano to develop a battle plan. He met with representatives from the F-16 squadrons also at Aviano and suggested targets for them to bomb.

Haun intended to launch two more A-10s half an hour after Cherrey departed. These would be Sandy 41 and Sandy 42 and would be available to escort the helicopters for the run in and egress.

Then, 30 minutes after them, he would take off with another A-10, to be Sandy 51 and Sandy 52, able to swap out with Sandy 30 and 31. This should allow for continuous contact with Zelko.

Haun also calculated a rendezvous place and time for the helicopters to join up with the A-10s and had that location passed to the command center at Tuzla.

Unfortunately, the rendezvous time passed to Laushine was indicated in local time. Haun was doing all of his planning in Zulu time. In this theater of operations, local time was one hour ahead.

When Laushine got the message, he realized that his force would be late for the rendezvous, and he scrambled his crews to proceed to the meeting point, which was near the Serbian border west of Novi Sad.

COORDINATES AND CONTACT

Zelko could hear activity around him and stayed as still as possible. He took out his GPS and got a good readout of his position. He reported his position to the EC-130, using a special code directed by the SPINs.

Aboard the EC-130, the young sergeant who received the message from Vega 31 wrote it down and handed the message to Woodard, who knew immediately what it meant.

"He just gave us his position," Woodard said. "Plot it in the map." The sergeant did so. It showed that Zelko was down a few miles southeast of the town of Ruma, not northwest of Novi Sad. He was 30 miles closer to Belgrade than initially thought.

After more than an hour flying, Cherrey and his wingman entered Serbia northwest of Novi Sad. They tried to make radio contact with Laushine and his helicopters but were unsuccessful. Unknown to Cherrey at the time, he and the helicopters had been given different sets of CSAR frequencies. It took a few minutes to sort that out.

Cherrey proceeded into the rescue area, made voice contact with Zelko, and authenticated him using the ISOPREP data. Then Cherrey received a call from the AWACS, with an updated position passed by Zelko. He quickly plotted the new position on his map.

A-10 pilot Cherrey called helicopter rescue commander Laushine and gave him the survivor's updated location. To save fuel, Laushine had landed his force in a field.

The new coordinates voided the recovery plan. Laushine had to quickly develop a new one.

There was also another problem. All aircraft were now low on fuel. Flight Lieutenant Graham, up in the AWACS, scrambled to find tankers for all of the aircraft in the task force. Various Sandys would alternate as on-scene commanders.

The helicopters lifted off and rendezvoused with an MC-130P. They refueled from the tanker as it cruised 700 feet above the ground just three miles out of Serbian airspace.

After he had received his fuel, Cherrey and his wingman returned to the general area of the downed airman and reassumed the on-scene command role.

The helicopters were also now full of gas and had repositioned to a location west of Ruma along the Serbian border. The plan was for Sandy 41 and Sandy 42 to escort the helicopters as they proceeded in to the survivor at low altitude. As they approached, Sandy 30 and Sandy 31 would fly in over Zelko.

FROM BOTH SIDES

After receiving a report that the survivor had been captured, Cherrey called Zelko again to reauthenticate him. Zelko answered correctly, and the rescue was on.

The Serbs were closing in on him. In fact, it was later determined that a Serbian force of 80 troops and police were combing the nearby fields and had already found Vega 31's ejection seat and some boot prints.

Sandy 30 was ready to execute. He instructed the helicopter crews to call him when they were two miles from the survivor. Then Cherrey would direct Zelko to use a signaling device so the pilots could see him. Everybody acknowledged the plan.

Then another problem arose. A low cloud deck formed in the valley the approaching aircraft would use. The rescue helicopters could fly through such weather, but the escort A-10s needed to maintain visual contact with the helicopters to provide them any protection. It would be a helicopter-only rescue.

Additionally, Cherrey could no longer see the ground to assess the threat. This was critical because committing the helicopters for a pickup was his call. He could not fly down below the clouds for a look because the clouds were just too low. Thinking quickly, he called the survivor. "Vega 31, is it OK to come in there?"

Zelko was not ready for that question and did not answer. He knew that the enemy was all around but did not know how close or with what weapons.

After what seemed like an eternity, Cherrey called again. "Vega 31, if you don't answer, we're going to have to not do this now and come back later."

"Let's go for it," Zelko said, quickly figuring that if he then needed to abort the rescue effort, he could do it with his authentication data.

"Execute, execute," Cherrey said, and the helicopters committed to the rescue.

Then, Cherrey had to depart again because he was low on fuel. He quickly passed the on-scene command duty to Haun and his wingman, Capt. Joe Brosious, but Haun had a problem with his A-10.

His primary radio, UHF, could receive but not transmit. Haun had to call Brosious on a secondary radio and tell him what to broadcast on the primary. This was a critical step because the rescue helicopters, survivor, and Haun all needed to be able to instantaneously communicate during the pickup phase of the operation, and they had to do it on UHF. Brosious would have to be Haun's voice.

Into Serbian Airspace

Cardoso, in his MH-53, led the way with the second MH-53 and the MH-60 in trail formation on each side. Everyone aboard the helicopters was using night-vision goggles as they proceeded in at treetop level to avoid the Serbian radars, anti-aircraft guns, and searchlights, but there were other dangers. As Cardoso led the task force in, one of his crew members spotted power lines and screamed, "Wires! Wires! Wires! Climb! Climb!"

Instinctively, Cardoso yanked back on the controls, and the formation cleared the danger. They then descended back down to treetop level and continued in toward Zelko.

As the helicopters crossed into Serbian airspace, a surface-to-air missile site activated and began searching for allied aircraft. An F-16CJ overhead engaged it with a high-speed antiradiation missile.

Haun saw the missile streak down into the clouds. The site stopped radiating.

Below, the helicopters were rapidly approaching the survivor. The MH-60 would land and make the pickup, while the two MH-53s would orbit above and provide fire support.

The helicopter pilots called on the UHF radio that they were now two miles from the survivor. Zelko was ready. He was given the code word to turn on his signaling device. He complied.

Aware now that a rescue operation was going on, more Serbian missile sites in the area tried to track the intruding aircraft. The A-10 pilots received immediate threat indications on their radar warning receivers and employed their chaff dispensers, jamming pods, and maneuvered to evade the deadly missiles.

At the same time, the A-10 pilots were trying to maintain awareness of what was going on below them.

Cardoso announced that they were now overhead of the survivor's location—but he could not see Zelko's signaling device.

Zelko could hear the helicopters and tried to give them vectors. It did not help. He was becoming concerned and asked if the rescuers could see his signal.

Cardoso responded that they could not.

The moment was thick with tension as all realized that the opportunity was slipping away.

Zelko told the CSAR forces to stand by, informing them that he thought his signaling device was inoperative. Time for a successful rescue was running out.

Orbiting now in the pitch black above Zelko's position, Cardoso could see vehicles moving along the roads. There was no time to waste. "Just give me any . . . signal," he barked on the radio. Zelko lit one of his flares.

The flare lit up the whole area, and Cardoso immediately saw him.

"We are bingo, bingo, bingo. Kill the flare," he called on the radio. This caused some confusion. To the special operations forces, bingo means "we have the objective in sight."

However, to the fixed-wing pilots, bingo means "I only have enough gas to get back to base and must leave now."

It confused Zelko, too, but at least the rescue forces now had a visual on him.

So did everybody else in the vicinity.

Cardoso directed the MH-60 to land and make the recovery. Zelko was right in front of him, about half a mile away.

DISORIENTATION

The bright flash of the flare momentarily disoriented the MH-60 pilot, Franks. "It was like the sun coming up in my goggles," he said.

Zelko crushed the flare into the dirt with his boot. As he did, the MH-53s set up their protective orbit. Franks began a very steep descent and then settled on the ground. Zelko was 100 feet away. The PJs, SSgt. Eric Giacchino and SrA. John M. Jordan, dismounted and moved toward the survivor, rifles at the ready. In the helicopter, the gunners scanned with their mini guns for any close-in enemy activity.

Zelko was kneeling down as he had been trained to do. He used his radio to ask for permission to come aboard the helicopter. Then he noticed the dark forms of the PJs and raised his hands in a submissive pose. The PJs immediately identified him.

"How ya doin', sir?" one said. "We are here to take you home."

The orbiting MH-53 crews could see Serbian vehicles about 50 yards away.

When the PJs and survivor were safely aboard, Glover radioed the news that they were lifting off, survivor onboard.

They had been on the ground for 40 seconds. The rescue itself had taken a little over six hours.

The helicopters and A-10s headed west out of Serbia. Aboard the MH-60, the crew members did everything they could to make Zelko comfortable. The PJs gave him a quick examination and some water and food.

The helicopters proceeded directly to Tuzla. There, Zelko was more thoroughly examined by a flight surgeon and cleared to return to Aviano by MC-130.

Zelko personally tried to thank every one of the troops aboard all three helicopters. He received a pleasant surprise when he encountered Glover. Several years prior, Zelko had served at the Air Force Academy. Glover had been one of his cadets.

The MC-130 landed at Aviano at sunrise. The A-10 pilots had landed by then, and they and much of the base were out to greet Zelko. He tried to thank everyone.

"He was watery-eyed as he thanked . . . us for saving him," said Brosious.

The wing commander, Brig. Gen. Daniel P. Leaf, asked Zelko if he was ready to get a little rest. "Yes, sir," Zelko replied, but there was one more thing that he needed to do first: he had to present the young airman who had prepared his target folder with her flag.

CHAPTER SEVEN

Kanalkampf
The Battles over the Channel

Len Deighton

To begin, *Oberst* Johannes Fink, *Geschwaderkommodore* of the bomber unit KG2, was created the *Kanalkampfführer* (commander of the air fighting over the Channel). His task was to close the Channel to British shipping. To do it he was given command of two *Stukagruppen* and a *Jagdgeschwader* of fighters to add to his own bombers. Fink set up a command post on Cap Blanc Nez, five miles west of Calais, in a bus parked very near the statue of Louis Blériot, first man to cross the Channel by air.

There was sound reasoning behind the German attacks against coastal shipping in July and early August. It had been decided that the Luftwaffe would launch its major offensive only after Hitler gave the order. It was presumed that the Supreme Commander was coordinating the plans of the army and navy: timing the air offensive so that the invading army would find the British defenders stunned into the sort of paralysis that the Luftwaffe had produced in France and Poland.

Meanwhile, attacks against the Channel convoys were a "heads I win, tails you lose" proposition. If the RAF sent fighters to cover the shipping, they would be drawn into a battle of attrition and made tired before the Germans launched *Adlerangriff*. If RAF Fighter Command refused to be drawn, the bombers would sink the British ships.

Dowding had not calculated for shipping protection in his original plans, and now he warned the Air Staff, and the Admiralty, too, that he

93

could only protect shipping by committing a dangerously high proportion of his total force. So the convoys could have only minimal air support.

Britain's radar network was not very effective during this *Kanalkampf*, for fighters and bombers of the Air Fleets could climb to operating heights and get into formation out of "sight" of the British radar. To cross the Channel took only five minutes, but a Spitfire needed fifteen minutes to climb high enough to fight them.

As more and more ships were sunk, the pressure on Dowding increased, and it is typical of certain members of the Air Staff at this time that they felt able to offer Dowding advice. They told him to put his fighters onto the coastal airfields, so that they need only take off when the Germans were close. To a limited extent, this was being done, but it was very dangerous to be so near to the enemy formations before gaining equal—or better—height, for the German airmen were formidable.

Kanalkampfführer Fink was fifty years old and still flying operational bombing missions. The *Kommodore* of the fighter *Geschwader* assigned to him was also a veteran and an even more remarkable flier.

Oberst Theo ("Onkel Theo") Osterkamp was a slim, fastidious man, with a large forehead and pointed features that made him "gnome-like" to some. This impression was reinforced by anyone who had been on the receiving end of his quick mind, sharp tongue, or his machine guns. In the First World War, Osterkamp had been an outstanding ace, credited with thirty-two kills and awarded the *Pour Le Mérite*. A close friend of von Richthofen, he had trained alongside Oswald Boelcke, had survived an air battle with Charles Guynemer, and had been shot down by Albert Ball. He was one of the few such men to fly a fighter plane in the Second World War, and already the amazing "Onkel Theo" was becoming an ace all over again.

Until the last week of July, Osterkamp's JG 51 was the only single-seat fighter unit in the action across the Channel. The strength of this unit had fallen, until on 12 July, the third *Gruppe* of JG 3 was assigned to them to keep their serviceability up to the region of sixty or seventy aircraft.

Using their small force, the two colonels Fink and Osterkamp showed considerable skill as they probed the British defenses, discovered the response times, and found and hit the costal convoys, which were numerous along the southeast coast. Usually the fighter remained close to the bombers, but now and again "Onkel Theo" released them for fighter sweeps across Kent. These *"Freijagd"* (free-hunt) flights were of limited duration because of the Bf 109's short range.

Dowding's response was cagey. Park (group commander for southeast England) sent only small formations against the raids and let the *Freijagd* fly unhindered. In the radar stations, the girl operatives began to realize that they succeeded only by working quickly—by making "educated guesses" about enemy intentions while the bomber formations were still at the extreme edge of radar range.

9 July

Al Deere, from Wanganui, New Zealand, had traveled halfway across the world in order to join the RAF in 1937. By July 1940 he was a flight commander with 54 Squadron, and after a month of intensive air flight, he had got his DFC from the hands of the king at a ceremony held at Hornchurch airfield. By now he was as experienced as any fighter pilot that the British had.

On 9 July he was leading a formation on his fourth flight of the day when they found a German Rescue floatplane, painted white with eight large red crosses, flying at wave height. It was escorted by a dozen Bf 109s flying close behind it.

While one section attacked the floatplane, Deere dived upon the Messerschmitts, which split into two formations, climbing steeply to right and left, respectively, turning as they went. Deere remembered this tactic and later used it with some successes. Now Deere's fliers broke and individual combats started. Deere noted with satisfaction the way the new De Wilde bullets made "small dancing yellow flames" as they exploded against the enemy fighter. He found this valuable way of judging the effect of his gunfire.

I soon found another target. About 3,000 yards directly ahead of me, and at the same level, a Hun was just completing a turn preparatory

95

to reentering the fray. He saw me almost immediately and rolled out of his turn towards me so that a head-on attack became inevitable. Using both hands on the control column to steady the aircraft and thus keep my aim steady, I peered through the reflector sight at the rapidly closing enemy aircraft. We opened fire together, and immediately a hail of lead thudded into my Spitfire. One moment the Messerschmitt was a clearly defined shape, its wingspan nicely enclosed within the circle of my reflector sight, and the next it was on top of me, a terrifying blur which blotted out the sky ahead. Then we hit.

The crash snatched the control column out of Deere's hands, and the cockpit harness bit painfully deep into his shoulders. The engine was vibrating, and the control column was jumping backward and forward. As Deere watched, the engine gave forth smoke and flames, and before he could switch off the ignition, the propeller stopped. Now Deere could see that its blades were bent double: the Bf 109 had scraped along the top of his Spitfire.

Unable to get his hood open, Deere coaxed the aircraft into a glide toward the distant coastline, while he struggled to get out. With skill to match his amazing good fortune, he brought the wrecked aircraft down into a field, very near to Manston airfield. Still unable to open his hood, he smashed his way out of it, his "bare hands wielding the strength of desperation," he said. But he got clear of the wreckage, which burned brightly as the bullets exploded. "Won't you come in and have a cup of tea?" said a woman coming out of a nearby farmhouse.

"Thank you, I will," said Deere, "but I would prefer something stronger if you've got it."

Modestly Deere got back to his squadron expecting nothing more than a couple of days off. But they were so short of pilots that his commander asked him to fly again immediately. The squadron had lost two pilots to the Messerschmitts, and when Deere got to dispersal, there were only four Spitfires serviceable. "You needn't expect to fly this morning," he was told.

"I'm in no hurry," said Deere.

10 July

The Luftwaffe needed regular weather reports and more photo coverage of its targets. Not realizing what sitting ducks lone aircraft were for radar, the Germans came one at a time, flying out over the North Sea to what they hoped was an undefended landfall. Often it proved fatal for the German crew, but sometimes there were surprises. On 10 July, a Do 17 looking for convoy off the North Foreland had no less than an entire *Gruppe* of JG 51 flying escort on it. The other actions of the day were no more than skirmishes, but by the end of it, Fighter Command had flown over 600 Sorties.

11 July

On this day there was an endless stream of lone German aircraft. The RAF responded by sending lone aircraft to meet them. Often the squadron commanders reserved that job for themselves. Not long after dawn, for instance, Peter Townsend—the commander of 85 Squadron at Martlesham—was at the controls of his Hurricane VY-K, climbing out of ground mist into low gray cloud and heavy rain. The controller's voice took him up to 8,000 feet, where, in cloud, he made a perfect interception.

This Dornier Do 17M was Y5/GM from *Kanalkampfführer* Fink's own *Geschwader*, II/KG 2, the "*Holzhammer*." It came to England in a wide sweep out over the North Sea, reaching the coast near Lowestoft. Forbidden to bomb the mainland in the daytime, after what one of the crew described as a little "sightseeing," they dropped their ten tiny (50-kg) bombs over some shipping in the harbor.

The crew had mixed feelings about the cloud and rain; it made the pilot's job more difficult and reduced visibility for the bomb-aimer and gunner, but it was reassuring to think that any RAF fighters would be having the same sort of problems in locating them. The Germans were content, and as the nose of the Dornier turned for home, the crew began singing "Goodbye, Johnny." . . . The melody was interrupted by the sudden shout of a gunner, Werner Broner, "*Achtung, Jäger!*"

The *Jäger* was Peter Townsend, who could hardly see through his rainswept windscreen and so slid open the cockpit cover to put his head out into the rainstorm. He had not had to rely on visibility until the last few moments, for the single Dornier had provided the radar plotters with a blip on the cathode-ray tube no more difficult to interpret than the ones set up as prewar exercises.

Townsend was a peacetime pilot, a flier of great skill and experience. His eight Browning machine guns raked the bomber. Inside the bomber there were "bits and pieces everywhere: blood-covered faces, the smell of cordite, all the windows shot up."

Of the crew, the starboard rear gunner was hit in the head and fell to the floor. A second later another member of the crew—hit in the head and throat—fell on top of him. There was blood everywhere. But "our good old Gustave Marie was still flying," remembered one of the crew. Townsend had put 220 bullets into the Dornier, but it got home to Arras, and all the crew lived to count the bullet holes.

The German bombers were robust enough to endure terrible amounts of gunfire, especially small-caliber gunfire. Their strength did not depend upon bracing wires and wooden spars: these metal bombers had armor protection, with some of the vital mechanical parts duplicated. Even more valuable were the self-sealing fuel tanks. Of a very simple layered construction, they had a crude-rubber middle layer. As a puncture allowed fuel to spill, the crude rubber dissolved, swelled, and sealed the hole. The events of the day were to prove how effective these devises were in getting damaged bombers home.

Not only did Townsend's machine-gun bullets fail to shoot down his Dornier, but a lucky shot from one of its machine guns hit his Hurricane's coolant system. The engine stopped when still twenty miles from the English coast. Townsend took his parachute and was fished out of the ocean by a trawler that sailed into a minefield to reach him.

A little later, another squadron commander found another Dornier. This time the commander was the remarkable Douglas Bader. This peacetime fighter pilot had had both legs amputated after a flying accident, but when war began he had been allowed to rejoin the RAF and fly once more as a fighter pilot. Already he had caught up with his contemporaries, and at the end of June, he'd been made a squadron leader and assigned to command 242 (Canadian) Fighter Squadron. This squadron was flying old Mark I Hurricanes with two-blade fixed-pitch propellers. It consisted of Canadians who were serving in the RAF (it was not an RCAF unit) and had seen some air fighting in France. The squadron was deficient in equipment and morale when Bader arrived. He was now in the processes of remedying those defects.

On the morning of 11 July at about seven o'clock, Bader answered the phone in the dispersal hut near the aircraft. There was a single "bandit" flying up the coastline near Cromer, and the controller wanted a flight of Hurricanes to intercept it. Bader looked on the low cloud and decided that the Hurricanes would not be able to form up, so he would go alone. It was a significant decision from the man who later became the most enthusiastic proponent of "big wing," in which the fighters went to battle in large formations. It is interesting, too, to record that Bader (who was later to urge that the controllers should advise rather than order the fighter pilots about the enemy) this day found his victim without the assistance of the radar plotters.

His victim was a Dornier Do 17 of *Wetterkundungsstaffel* (weather reconnaissance unit) 261. It had already fought off two Spitfires. One of them—flown by the commander of 66 Squadron—had been damaged in the oil tank.

When Bader found his Dornier, it was just under the cloud base at about 1,000 feet. Methodically Bader closed without being spotted until he was about 250 yards behind; then the German rear gunner opened fire. Bader fired two bursts as the Dornier turned to face back the way it had come and made a shallow climb until disappearing into the cloud. Cursing, Bader flew back to the Coltishall and reported that his Dornier had escaped, but a few minutes later, the telephone told him that the plane had crashed into the sea just a short time after his action. Modestly Bader described this as "a lucky start for the new CO. of 242 Squadron," but there was no doubt that his success had come from skill and experience. There could be no such successes stemming from luck alone.

The fighting over the sea was an added worry for Dowding, for, unlike the Luftwaffe, his pilots had no dinghies, no sea dye, and no air-sea rescue organization. Landing fighters on the water was unwise: the radiators hit the water and tipped the aircraft upside down, in which position they sank. Yet, landing in the sea by parachute gave small chance of being found. But so far there were no complaints or even hesitation. This day's fighting showed the way in which his squadron commanders were determined to lead the action. To forbid them to do so would be a blow to morale, but how many such men could he afford to lose?

The RAF fighter pilots—like the regular officers that so many of them were—had tried to adapt the tight vee formations of peacetime to the needs of war. But tight formations require all a man's concentration and leave no spare moments for looking round. The modern high-speed monoplanes were more complex than the biplanes, and apart from watching the sky for enemy aircraft, pilots needed to attend to their instruments. In tight formations, each aircraft blocks a large sector of his neighbor's sky. Adding a "tail-end Charlie" to weave from side to side at the rear of the formation, and thus protect the tail, had resulted in the loss of too many tail-end Charlies. By the middle of July, weavers were seldom seen.

Before the war, the RAF had practiced "Fighting Area Attacks": carefully choreographed flight movements that, typically, provided a line of fighters with a burst of fire, as each took a turn at the victim. But the Germans would not readily play victim, and what had worked well enough at air displays was no tactic for modern war. Squadrons engaged in the Channel fighting soon saw the advantages of the loose *Schwärme* the Germans flew, and depleted squadrons gave the RAF an excuse for trying new formations.

The *Rotte*, or pair, was the basis of the formation that Werner Mölders, the German fighter ace, had started to evolve in the skies of Spain. The vee, a human triangle, is not psychologically stable, as any reader of romantic fiction knows. The *Rotte* consisted of a leader and his wingman. The leader was the senior flier and best marksman; his wingman stayed glued to him and was responsible for guarding the tail. When two *Rotten* joined to make a *Schwarm*, the senior pilot took charge, but the pairs remained effective. Wingmen were usually told that even if the leader flew into the ground, the wingman must follow. There were other subtle advantages to the German formations: for instance, the slightly different altitude of each aircraft was another way in which collision risk was reduced.

The RAF tried such formations unofficially. But, dogged by peace-time flying regulations, no Fighter Command formation was as loosely spread as were those of the Germans. Tight formations were easier to see in the sky. The sad truth was that no RAF unit could learn overnight the stalking skills that several years of combat had taught the Germans.

17 July

This fact was demonstrated on a miserable day of rain and cloud when twelve Spitfires of 64 Squadron flying out of Kenley were "bounced" off Beachy Head. The Germans came out of nowhere, knocked a Spitfire down, and disappeared so fast that no member of the RAF formation even got a glimpse of the enemy aircraft.

Still lacking any proper tactical directives—except a vague new order about attacking the British Home Fleet—the Luftwaffe brought more and more units into the fighting. As well as Air Fleets 2 and 3 in France and the Low Countries, Air Fleet 5 in Scandinavia was sending missions across the North Sea. *Küstenfliegergruppen* (coastal aircraft units) continued the exacting task of dropping mines into the Firth of Forth and the estuaries of the Thames and Humber and were at it almost every night. There were surprise attacks on factories as far apart as Glasgow and Yeovil, and after-dark experimental night-bombing units were flying over Britain testing their radio-guidance system.

18 July

Just as the Air Fleets lacked a common strategy, so they lacked a sound appreciation of Britain's defenses, upon which their tactical policy might have been based. Yet, on 18 July, a ruse devised by Air Fleet 2 suggested that someone on the staff realized how British radar worked. Shortly after eight o'clock in the morning, RAF radar operators saw a *Staffel* or so of aircraft circling for height and getting into formation for an attack on a coastal convoy that was moving through the Straits of Dover.

No. 616 (County of Chester) Squadron, from Biggin Hill, flew out to find the convoy. They kept just under low cloud until they found it. As these Auxiliary flyers got there, they were bounced by Bf 109s. One Spitfire was shot down. The Germans, who had formed up in the manner of bombing *Staffel*, were entirely fighters. They escaped without a scratch.

19 July

By now RAF loss rates were rising fast enough to draw on a graph and prove that Fighter Command would cease to exist within six weeks. This was before the promised *Adlerangriff* had even started. That no one at Fighter Command drew such a graph—as far as we know—must have been partly due to the exaggerated RAF claims. These persuaded even some senior RAF officers that the German Air Fleet were taking severe punishment. But on 19 July, those RAF optimists might have had second thoughts. Although the size of the air battle was very small, the casualty types were very significant. Of five German aircraft lost, only one was a fighter. The others were, in effect, stragglers, including one old He 115 floatplane. The RAF loss, on the other hand, was ten fighters. In fighter-to-fighter combat, the RAF were proving markedly inferior to the Germans.

This was the day when the RAF sent into battle the Boulton Paul Defiant two-seater. The Defiant was an updated version of the Bristol Fighter that had proved so successful in the First World War, but in 1940 it was a disaster.

Oberleutnant Hannes Trautloft, a veteran of Spain and an outstanding pilot, was leading the third *Gruppe* of JG 151. There were now only fifteen fighters left of his original forty. Trautloft saw nine strange-looking aircraft and noticed the gun turret behind the cockpits. He designed his attack accordingly. The Boulton Paul Defiant had no forward-facing armament. As one pilot put it, "The Defiant could only attack another plane after it had passed it." But with a power-operated turret that weighed three-quarters of a ton and an extra man, the Defiant didn't pass many other aircraft. Of the formation of nine, only three got back to Hawking, and one of those was so badly damaged that its gunner bailed out.

None of 141 Squadron's Defiants would have survived had 111 Squadron not arrived. This Hurricane Squadron was making a name for itself by using a new tactic. The German fighter pilots favored nose-to-nose, fighter-versus-fighter attacks. Now the Hurricanes were flying line-abreast, head-on through German bomber formations. Although this tactic usually succeeded in forcing the bombers to break formation, 111 Squadron was losing enough Hurricanes in head-on collisions with the enemy to make the pilots doubt its value.

24 July

Ever since "Dolfo" Galland had submitted his excellent reports about the employment of aircraft in the army-support role, he had been assigned to this specialization. Much to his disgust, he had been given a job at the Berlin Air Ministry. He returned to operational flying only in close-support units (*Schlachtgeschwader*). This meant flying antiquated biplanes, such as the Heinkel He 45 and Heinkel He 51. Even when Germany invaded Poland, Galland could not get an aeroplane any better than a Henschel Hs 123, a close-attack biplane with radial engine. Eventually, by conspiring with a friendly physician, he was able to get his medical records endorsed with a note to say that he should not fly in open-cockpit aircraft. What might have sentenced him to a short life with the Stukas got him a job with the fighters. But as operations officer with JG 27, paperwork left him little time for combat flying until, on 12 May, he flew as part of the great German thrust westward into France and the Low Countries. He shot down three Hurricanes in one day.

Galland was very conscious of the way in which Mölders—the subordinate who had taken over from him in Spain—was now recognized as Germany's ace fighter pilot. Galland was not too proud to ask Mölders for advice and now says, "Werner Mölders taught me how to shoot and bring down an aircraft." In June, as the Luftwaffe lined up for the air war against England, Galland was assigned to command III/JG 26. He shot down two enemy fighters on the first day with his new command. During July, says Galland sardonically, Hitler's creation of a dozen new field marshals in the Kroll Opera House, Berlin, filtered down as far as him. Galland was made major. This had no effect upon Galland's command of his *Gruppe* (about thirty fighters). In German armed forces, a new appointment gave no entitlement to new rank.

By now Galland was a well-known face amongst the fighter pilots. His jet-black hair, combed straight back from a high forehead, and the large Groucho Marx moustache and easy grin reassured the fighter pilots that their *Gruppenkommandeur* was still "one of the boys." So did the big black cigars, to which he was so addicted that he had an ashtray installed in the cockpit, enabling him to smoke right up until the moment he went on to oxygen. But only a fool would fail to see that behind the grin there was a cold, calm, and calculating fighter who, at this date, was determined to beat the score of Mölders.

His rival had claimed his twenty-fifth victim about seven weeks previously, over France, but afterward he was shot down and made a POW until the French armistice. Galland was determined to make the best of Mölders's setback. At midday on 24 July, Galland led his Messerschmitts into battle again, but Luftwaffe were beginning to find the Spitfire a tough one to down. This morning, as we shall see, the Spitfires handed out rather more punishment than they took.

July was a month of experiments. Kesselring discovered that attacking two coastal convoys at the same time forced the defense to divide. This worked well about 8 a.m. on 24 July, when two coordinated attacks were made: one on a convoy off Dover and the other on one that was entering the Thames Estuary. The defense—54 Squadron from Rochford—sent after one raid, saw both, and had to split up to attack them. The raiders escaped without casualties, but the bombing failed to hit any of the ships. About 11 a.m. two *Staffeln* of Do 17s returned to the Thames Estuary to attack a convoy. "Dolfo" Galland's Bf 109s were assigned as escort. Park sent 54 Squadron to attack them, and then, knowing that Galland's fighter escort would soon run short of fuel, he ordered 610 Squadron (Biggin Hill) to patrol Dover and so cut off their escape route. In fact, 610 ran into JG 52, who were coming north to help the returning Messerschmitts. There was a fight. The raid's escort—Galland's III/JG 26—and JG 52 each lost three fighters. The two RAF squadrons lost three Spitfires.

As the engagement ended, the elated Spitfire pilots dived upon another formation and shot down one of them. The victorious pilot reported that there had been no return fire and identified his victim as Chance Vought V.156. RAF intelligence thought the Germans were so short of aircraft that they were now using captured French ones, until the Royal Navy reported the loss of Blackburn Skua of 806 Squadron, Fleet Air Arm.

The fighter pilots were learning about their adversaries. The Bf 109, with its fuel-injection engine, not only dived without missing a beat or two (unlike the carburetor-fed Merlins) but could outdive the RAF fighters. Galland's Messerschmitts had dived out of combat and escaped that morning when their fuel ran low.

But the Luftwaffe had never before faced a fighter as good as the Spitfire. This was acknowledged by the disproportionate number of Messerschmitt fighter pilots who, on becoming POWs, insisted that they had been shot down by Spitfires. The Hurricane pilots, who sometimes had their claims disallowed because of it, called it "Spitfire snobbery."

RAF regulations said that eight Brownings should be adjusted so that the bullets converged at a point some 650 yards ahead of the aircraft. As one pilot of 54 Squadron said at the time, "All this guarantees is a few hits by the indifferent shot; the good shot on the other hand is penalized." The pilots who were prepared to get close were scattering gunfire all over the place.

Already the regulations were being ignored. Armament officers were having the guns adjusted the way the pilots wanted them (and eventually this was officially approved).

The courage to fly very close distinguished just about all the men who became aces, but without the skill of deflection-shooting, such a pilot could not make a kill. This aiming-off is not to be equated with the hunter shooting at a bird in flight. The fighter pilots were moving at three or four hundred miles an hour in three dimensions. So was the target. To hit it required an instant assessment of enemy speed, enemy size, angle between the two aircraft, and the distance. (Later in the war, there were gun sights that did some of this calculation, but in 1940 pilots on both sides had only a ring sight reflected on the windscreen.) The split-second judgment required for this kind of fighting was something that many superb pilots were never able to acquire.

In the First World War, some ace fighter pilots had become obsessional about the types of bullet they used, arranging them in the belts in certain set sequences according to personal taste. The provision of eight separate identical guns made varying the ammunition very simple. A common mix was four guns with normal bullets, two with armor-piercing, and two with the new De Wilde incendiaries. This later ammunition was very popular with the fighter pilots. Dowding said that they valued it far beyond its true worth, but he was not taking into account the way that, although it had no tracer or smoke trail as previous incendiary bullets had, it made a bright yellow flash on impact. This proved a valuable aiming device. Believing that his pilots should have what they wanted, Dowding made special efforts to increase supplies of the De Wilde bullets. "Sailor" Malan and Al Deere believed that the 250-yard harmonization and De Wilde bullets made the difference between damaging enemy aircraft and destroying them.

During July the fighter pilots rediscovered that aerial victory went to the formation that caught an enemy unaware. The old hands attacked out of the sun, and visibility was a paramount factor in the fighter pilot's war. German pilots, who had found their Emils good enough for Spain, Poland, and France, now demanded a better clear-view cockpit cover. RAF pilots were constrained by their Irving flying suits, gloves, and the seat's Sutton harness, which, one inspector said, "seemed specially designed to foul oxygen and wireless leads." The RAF flying helmets had earphones that tangled into the collar part of the "Mae West" life jackets. To relieve themselves of this tangle, many pilots adjusted the cockpit heaters and flew in uniform jackets or shirtsleeves.

But for the ground staff, there were few days suitable for shirtsleeves. July was a month of dull, wet weather: haze, drizzle, low cloud, electrical storms, and even fog. Often it was appalling visibility that enabled a convoy to get through the Channel intact. There was so much rain that some airfields on both sides were made unusable by flooding.

Then 25 July provided one of the rare breaks in the bad weather: the morning sky was blue.

25 July

Kesselring was playing cat and mouse with a convoy through the Dover Straits. CW8 (west-bound coal convoy number 8) consisted of twenty-one colliers and coasters. Only eleven passed Dungeness, and only two got to their destination undamaged. Just after noon, a force of Bf 109s headed for Dover, flying almost at sea level. They were a clear run to the Stukas. No. 65 Squadron went down to fight. All the aircraft were so low that, when one Bf 109—of JG 52—misjudged an attack, he hit the water and disintegrated.

Hurricanes of 32 Squadron from Biggin Hill and 615 Squadron from Kenley joined the fighting against forty Bf 109s. There is an old fighter pilot's maxim, "Never throttle back in combat," and maximum boost caused both sides to run low on fuel after only a few minutes. As the fighters disengaged, three *Stukageschwader* came in at medium altitude and dive-bombed the now-unprotected convoy.

The convoy's naval escort put up anti-aircraft fire and called urgently for fighter cover. Nine Spitfires of 54 Squadron hurried to their aid. When they arrived, they found that Kesselring had sent an overwhelming force of Bf 109s there to wait for them. Among 54 Squadron's losses was a flight commander. None of the German fighters was shot down.

The sector controller realized that if he answered the German attacks plane for plane, he would be bled dry. So at 2:30 that afternoon, when thirty Ju 88s came to bomb the convoy, he sent only eight Spitfires of 64 Squadron. They met a fighter escort of fifty Bf 109s. Undismayed, the newly appointed squadron commander called, "Tallyho!" and attacked. The controller sent the rest of 64 Squadron—three Spitfires—and 111 Squadron to the battle. The latter formed up line-abreast and did a head-on attack on the Junkers bombers, which broke formation and turned away. On seeing things, the Messerschmitts of the fighter escort also withdrew.

But it was still only afternoon: the men of the convoy had not yet earned their day's pay. As they passed Folkestone, the Bf 109s repeatedly strafed them at sea level, gaining the naval gunner's attention, so that about sixty Stukas could dive-bomb them out of the afternoon sun. The attack had been nicely timed between RAF patrols, and with unhurried precision they sank five ships and damaged four. At this moment, a force of German motor torpedo boats attacked the convoy, too. By nightfall two damaged destroyers moved into Dover harbor; one of them was under tow. The Admiralty concluded that coastal convoys should no longer try to get through the Straits of Dover except under the cover of darkness.

Although Fighter Command had lost only seven aircraft—against sixteen German raiders shot down—it had nothing to celebrate. No. 54 Squadron had lost five pilots killed—including a very experienced flight commander—and three pilots wounded. It had flown 800 hours, completed 504 combat sorties, and lost 12 aircraft. It was a warning of what could happen to the whole of Fighter Command if it was drawn into ever larger battles. Instead of canceling the coastal convoys—the cargoes were coal, which could have been moved by rail and later was—the Admiralty and Air Ministry pressed Dowding to commit more of his fighter force to protecting the shipping. Dowding resisted.

The U.S. ambassador in London—Joseph Kennedy, the father of the man who became president—had little faith in Britain's ability to survive, and he didn't mind who knew it. As early as 1 July, the British prime minister had written in his diary, "Saw Joe Kennedy, who says everyone in USA thinks we shall be beaten before the end of the month." Now there was only a week of it left. The British Foreign Office heard that Kennedy had summoned neutral journalists to a press conference in order to tell them that Hitler would be in London by 15 August. Such behavior infuriated Foreign Office officials—one wrote, "He is the biggest Fifth Columnist in the country"—but there was little they could do about him. Joseph Kennedy wielded great political influence in the USA (and had got the London embassy in recognition of past help). Now it was election year in the USA. President Roosevelt was running against Wendell Wilkie for an unprecedented third term. He needed Kennedy's support to win the election, and the British wanted Roosevelt to win. It was a dilemma for all concerned, not least for the Americans, who didn't want to send expensive war supplies to a nation just about to collapse.

To get a second opinion, Roosevelt sent another Irish-American to Britain. "Wild Bill" Donovan was ostensibly in England to study the extent of German espionage and the nature of British countermeasures. In fact, he was to report to Roosevelt Britain's chances of survival. Sending a man on an intelligence mission that was really a cover for a diplomatic function was a curious reversal of the usual way of doing such things.

28 July

A few days later, the storm clouds again gave way to a clear blue sky. At about 2 p.m., when most of England was sitting down to the ritual of Sunday lunch, something happened that was so unusual in the air war that this might have been unique: two ace pilots clashed in combat.

The South African "Sailor" Malan ended the war as one of the top-scoring aces on the Allied side. He was important, too, for the influence he had upon RAF tactics and formations.

Born in Wellington, South Africa, Adolphus Malan was a man of burly build with an amiable smile that made the men who met him unready for the deep and clinical hatred that he had for all his German opponents. He told one of his fellow officers that to badly damage enemy bombers—so that they arrived home with dead and dying aboard—was better than shooting them down: it had more effect on Luftwaffe morale. So that is what he tried to do.

Malan had been a merchant navy officer before volunteering for the RAF in 1935. He proved to be an exceptional pilot, according to his flying instructors. He was a flight commander by the time he saw action in May 1940. On the receiving end of his bullets this day was an even more revered master of the fighter pilot's trade: the legendary Mölders. Both men have been mentioned by their peers as possibly the greatest fighter pilots of the war.

Werner Mölders was a handsome young man, whose drawn face, deepset eyes, bony nose, and thin mouth were seldom captured on film in the act of smiling. He was an introverted man, and this serious demeanor earned him the nickname "Vati" ("Daddy"). So determined was he to be a fighter pilot that (like many others before and since) he endured the agonies and humiliation of constant air sickness.

Mölders took over Galland's command in Spain just as the new Bf 109 fighters replaced the old biplanes. This changed the odds, and he returned to Germany with fourteen destroyed enemy aircraft in his log book. He was a skilled administrator and dedicated teacher, as well as Germany's top fighter ace. Many Nazis took exception to the way that "Vati" Mölders made no secret of his Catholic religion, but Göring made quite sure that no harm came to him on that account. In 1940 it was decided that the coveted Knight's Cross of the Iron Cross would be given to a pilot who shot down twenty enemy planes. Mölders was the first fighter pilot to get it. He was to become the Luftwaffe's general of fighters before his twenty-ninth birthday.

Sunday, 28 July, was an auspicious day for Mölders. This was his first day as *Kommodore* of the entire JG 51. (The previous day "Onkel Theo" Osterkamp had gone to become *Jafü 2*, the commander of all the fighter planes in Air Fleet 2.) Concerned as he might be by his seven weeks out of action and the victories of Galland and *Hauptmann* Helmut Wick (the other two top German aces), Werner Mölders could this day reflect with satisfaction that he was the youngest *Kommodore* in the Luftwaffe.

With Mölders there were four *Staffeln* of Messerschmitts, and in keeping with Fighter Command policy, Spitfires were sent against them, while Hurricanes were vectored on to the German bomber formation. "Sailor" Malan was leading twelve Spitfires of 74 Squadron from Manston. As they closed, Malan chose a victim in the leading flight, fired, and watched him go down. Mölders was leading that formation; he turned and shot down a Spitfire. For Mölders this was his 129th combat mission of the war and his 26th victory (not including the 14 aircraft shot down in Spain). He came round again, looking for his 27th.

Both Mölders and Malan were fast, but Mölders was split seconds faster. Even as Malan was scoring his victory, Mölders was already on his tail. Malan turned in toward the attack—the classic reaction of the fighter pilot—and kept turning tightly enough to bring Mölders into his sights. His machine-gun bullets raked the Messerschmitt. Had Spitfires been armed with cannon, Mölders would not have been able to nurse his badly damaged machine back to his base at Wissant. When he landed, his leg wounds were bad enough to put him into the hospital. It was to be another month before Mölders could claim victory twenty-seven.

Enough Messerschmitt pilots failed to make it back across the Channel for German rescue floatplanes to be sent out to search for them. These large twin-engine rescue aircraft were painted white, with eight large red crosses in evidence. The Air Ministry had decided that any seen near Allied shipping or the English coast should be shot down. This instruction had been passed to all squadrons on 14 July, and in keeping with it, Hurricanes of 111 Squadron shot one down into mid-Channel and did considerable damage to another that was on the water ten miles west of Boulogne.

The resulting controversy was not confirmed to the rival propaganda industries. Some RAF pilots vowed that they would not obey such an instruction. Others wanted to see it in writing. Publication of this Air Ministry order, on 29 July, with its legalistic phrasing and vague talk of confining such attacks upon unarmed aircraft to "areas in which operations are in progress," did nothing to improve matters or even clarify them. For it was only where operations were in progress that drowning aviators would be found.

Mölders's badly damaged fighter plane provides an example of another problem. On this day alone, two Junkers Ju 88 bombers of 9/ KG 4, the *General Wever Geschwader* based at Amsterdam-Schipol, were damaged by anti-aircraft gunfire over the Thames Estuary. One did not get back as far as its base. Both crashed on landing and were completely written off. Almost all the survivors were wounded. Another Ju 88—of the *Edelweiss Geschwader*—had engine failure and forced-landed heavily enough to be severely damaged. Neither was Mölders's Bf 109 of II/JG 27 the only fighter that would not be ready to fly next day or for many days after that. Official Luftwaffe records show a Bf 109 of II/JG 27 crash-landed away from its base, with its pilot wounded. It was badly damaged, and two more Bf 109s were written off in crash landings, one of which killed the pilot. Two more fighters of JG 51 were damaged in forced landings that afternoon, and there was the Heinkel floatplane damaged near Boulogne and a Do 17Z of KG 2 that were written off in an accident that had nothing to do with enemy action.

It was like this almost every day: collisions during taxiing, takeoff, or landing, as well as curious entries that show aircraft that simply disappear, as a Ju 88 of II/KG 51, the *Edelweiss Geschwader*, had done on the night of 25 July. There is no record of its being encountered anywhere, by army, navy, or in air forces on either side of the Channel. These marginal losses sometimes account for the arguments that arise about the battles of 1940.

CHAPTER EIGHT

Hornets Get into the Fight

Jay A. Stout

THE CAMPAIGN'S KICKOFF HAD BEEN A FRENZIED REACTION TO A MUD-
dled mess for Heywood's Cobra squadron. Farther south, the war wasn't
getting off to a clean start at Al Jaber, either. Ross "Migs" Roberts was
the commanding officer of VMFA(AW)-533, a two-seat F/A-18D
squadron. He and the squadron operations officer—Major John "J. P."
Farnam—were supposed to be airborne as part of the scheduling kickoff
at 0300 on March 21. "I was in the rack [sleeping] when the first SCUD
alert sounded at around 1130 on March 20," he recalled. Roberts leapt
out of his cot and tore open the packaging that held his bulky NBC
(nuclear biological chemical) suit. The rest of his squadron, spread across
the air base, was doing the same. This was a standing procedure; U.S.
forces were not going to be caught unprepared in the event that the Iraqis
opted to use chemical weapons.

After what seemed an eternity but was actually only a minute or
so, Roberts had struggled into his NBC suit, masks, gloves, and boots
and clomped over to a bunker accompanied by Farnam. Through it all, a
female voice droned into the basewide loudspeakers: "This is not a drill,
this is not a drill." Crammed into the bunker, Roberts and Farnam hunkered down with a dozen or more other Marines. It was an odd feeling;
he probably knew every one of the other men in the bunkers with him,
but encased as all of them were in the black rubber masks and the rest
of the awkward ensemble that made up their protective NBC gear, he
couldn't have named a single one.

"We were all huddled in there, kind of staring at each other, when the all-clear sounded about an hour later." Immediately Roberts and the rest of the Marines reached up and pulled off their masks. After breathing through the masks, even the dusty air in the sandbagged shelters seemed refreshing. Roberts didn't delay long in the bunker. "I grabbed J. P., and we ran over to the MAG headquarters to see what was going on."

Like all of the leadership—up and down chain—the commander at the MAG was trying to react to various issues that often were at odds. Not least of them was the question of what to do with the aircraft and troops when a SCUD alert was sounded. For some, it made sense to get the aircraft airborne and out of harm's way. On the other hand, the short warning time that usually accompanied a SCUD launch meant that the jets could hardly get aloft before the enemy missiles hit—unless the aircraft were manned full time at the end of the runway. There was also the considerable risk of the Marines on the flight line in the event that the Patriot antimissile defenses were penetrated and the base was actually hit.

Roberts and Farnam left the MAG with no clear direction and headed to the ramp where the squadron's aircraft were parked. "On my own initiative, I took J. P. to the flight line—we were going to man a bird in case the order to launch was given. The MAG had four aircraft per squadron loaded with live weapons for this contingency. We had no sooner gotten into our flight gear when the alarm was sounded again." It was another SCUD alert. Everyone in the air group was getting frustrated as simply the threat of an enemy missile attack had essentially brought operations aboard the base to a halt.

The two fliers spent another hour in another bunker, this one on the flight line. Saddam had yet to hit Ahmed Al Jaber Air Base, and already the situation bordered on chaos. "I was getting exasperated," Roberts recollected. "J. P. and I went back to the MAG and found the CO, Colonel [Randy] 'Tex' Alles, and his operations officer, Lieutenant Colonel [Kevin] 'Wolfie' Williams. I suggested that, in this situation, fighters airborne were better than fighters on the deck." Alles disagreed with Roberts. He believed that shotgunning his jets into the air every time there was an alert was counterproductive and dangerous. He informed Roberts that during the confusion of the morning's SCUD alert, several of the jets that had been airborne had landed dangerously low on fuel. They had circled overhead waiting for a clearance to land that almost didn't come; the Marines who manned the tower were in a bunker.

It was while this discussion was going on that the MAG received a call from the First Marine Division's Air Officer (AO), Lieutenant Colonel Bruce "Iron" Shank. There was information that seventy to eighty Iraqi T-72 tanks were moving into position just beyond the earthen berm that demarcated the northern boundary between Kuwait and Iraq. The enemy tanks were supposedly digging in exactly opposite of where RCT-7 was scheduled to breach the border. If the report was true and the division was caught in a trap, the entire plan ran the risk of coming apart before it even began.

Roberts recounted, "I already had one crew on standby alert with their engines turning. Captain Jason 'Flamer' Pratt and Lance 'Puny' Muniz were ready to go. I recommended that we get them airborne to verify the report, and Tex agreed. We gave them a quick brief over the radio and launched them. Then Tex turned to me and said, 'Well, what are *you* waiting for?'"

It was all the prompting Roberts needed. Less than a minute later, he and Farnam were racing toward the flight line. "Once we got our engines up and running, we realized that in all the confusion we didn't have a call sign or an IFF squawk assigned," recalled Roberts. Both were important from a command and control standpoint in order to let everyone know who they were and what their mission was. Not to be stymied by a technicality, Farnam dug up a bogus call sign and identification friend or foe (IFF) squawk from the previous day's schedule, and the two fliers roared airborne. It was the tactical aviation equivalent of bullying past the maître d' at a fine restaurant.

Loaded with four Mk-20 cluster bomb munitions and eight 5-inch rockets, the F/A-18D's crew checked in with the DASC. It was the DASC's mission to track and direct air traffic to the ground units that needed supporting. On this day the DASC was just as confused as the rest of the air wing. Not sure of what Roberts and Farnam were doing, the DASC directed the two fliers to proceed to a CAS "stack" and await further instructions. It seemed that the center had not been informed of the Iraqi tank division that was reported to be on the other side of the berm.

Roberts wasn't having any of it: "The entire ground scheme of maneuver called for us to be out in front of the division looking for the enemy—not holding inside of Kuwait." In the two-seat F/A-18D, the back-seater—or WSO—runs the radio. Roberts remembered, "I told J. P. to do what we always did when DASC turned itself into a speed bump. We just 'rogered' their instruction and pressed on with what needed to be done." The crew started a descent and contacted Bruce Shank, the division's air officer. It had been Shank whom they had been talking with in the MAG headquarters only a short time earlier.

"Iron asked us to search Highways 6 and 8 directly to his front and then to look to the north along the highway that connects Umm Qasr and Basrah," Roberts said. It was getting late in the afternoon, and haze and smoke from the oil fires that were burning to the north made visibility poor. "We searched the roads twice and saw nothing—not even a car." Pratt and Muniz—who had launched before Roberts and Farnam—had also come up empty-handed. To their west the two airmen could make out the brilliant smoke trails that marked the paths of multiple volleys of U.S. Army ATACMS (army tactile missile system) missiles. Flying through their trajectory could have resulted in disaster, but the Marines were well to the east of where the missiles were ripping through the sky. Roberts and Farnam pressed on, intent on finding the Iraqi armored unit.

Just as the sun was about to drop below the horizon, they spotted a column of sixteen armored vehicles stopped on an overpass on RCT-7's route of advance. "J. P.," remembered Roberts,

did his magic radio stuff and got in touch with the division and the various RCTs to ensure that one of our guys had crossed into Iraq. We talked personally to Bruce Shank again and he was confident that one of the grunts had pushed past the LOD (line of departure). J. P. then contacted RCT-7's FSC (fire support center) and asked them to confirm that there were no friendly units at the coordinates where we had found the armored column.

The situation was still unclear, and the DASC declared the vehicles friendly. Not confident that anyone knew exactly what was going on, Roberts and Farnam headed toward the Iraqi city of al-Basrah to scout for enemy artillery units. Minutes later RCT-7 came back on the net and pronounced that the armored vehicles were positively hostile. Farnam responded, "You better be damn sure because we're going to kill them all." RCT-7 reiterated the declaration.

"All along," Roberts continued, "we were complying with the altitude restrictions that the wing had developed, and we were having no luck identifying the vehicle types from where we were at ten thousand feet." Farnam, in the rear cockpit, captured the lead portion of the column on the FLIR pod. Following the cueing that the FLIR displayed on his heads-up display, Roberts winged over to the west and dived toward the armored vehicles. There was no sign of enemy fire.

Only seconds earlier he had programmed the aircraft's weapons system to select two of the Mk-20 Rockeye cluster bombs that were slung under the jet's wings. The Rockeye canister is designed to separate into two halves prior to hitting the ground. When Robert's Rockeye came apart, they would each spread a wide-ranging, deadly shower of more than two hundred small, armor-piercing bomblets. Checking for the last time that his master armament switch was on, Roberts mashed down on the control stick's red bomb release button with his right thumb. Only a second or two later, as he guided the aircraft into the proper parameters, the jet automatically released the two bombs.

Roberts remembered, "We pulled off target, rolled left, and watched for the hits as we climbed back up above ten thousand feet." Instead of the football-field-sized pattern of sparling explosions he expected, there were two sharp flashes approximately a hundred feet south of his aim point. The Rockeye canisters had failed to open.

It was vexing in the extreme.

"J. P. backed me up," Roberts said, "and we rechecked our system and delivered parameters to make sure that we hadn't screwed anything up." They hadn't. Farnam found the targets with his FLIR again—it was almost dark now—and Roberts dropped the nose of the Hornet down for another run at the enemy armor. "This time one of the canisters opened, and we had effects on one of the vehicles. The other missed."

The only weapons that Roberts and Farnam had remaining were 5-inch rockets and the 20-millimeter cannon. These are primarily daytime weapons—unguided—requiring that the pilot visually aim them in order to have any effect. Still, with no other option in the smoky dusk, the two marines decided to make their attacks using the FLIR. Once more Farnam put the targeting diamond of the FLIR over a set of enemy vehicles. Roberts made two runs and shot all eight rockets; their motors burned a brilliant violet-white in the dim light. Each time the rockets went wide. It was later discovered that the FLIR was not properly "boresighted" to the aircraft. It was akin to trying to shoot straight with a rifle that had a bent gun sight. Nevertheless, Roberts and Farnam didn't give up easily. They made two more runs and sprayed the area with the aircraft's 20-millimeter cannon.

The confusion and bad fortune that had been their figurative wingmen all day were still in tight formation. Although they were out of weapons, they could still serve as airborne forward air controller or FAC(A) and bring other aircraft in to hit the target. "But we were getting low on gas," Roberts said, "and there were no tankers airborne. The DASC was still in reaction mode like everyone else, and evidently there weren't any aircraft available that could continue to prosecute these targets anyway." The pair had no good options. They passed the position of the enemy armor column to the DASC and returned to Ahmed Al Jaber.

After landing uneventfully and parking their jet, Roberts and Farnam climbed down onto the ramp to be greeted by many of the squadron's Marines, who were eager to hear how the mission had gone. "The first Marine to meet us was Sergeant Anderson, our plane captain," remembered Roberts. "He was anxious to find out what we had hit. I wished that I could have given him a more positive report."

The crew found out that the Marines working the flight line had been in and out of the bunkers three separate times while they were airborne. Now that they were out again, they were excited and angry and wanted to know if Roberts and Farnam "had kicked some Iraqi ass." The crowd of Marines continued to press the two fliers for more information.

Roberts reached inside his "nav bag" and pulled out his chart of southern Iraq. He dropped to a knee as he spread it out on the concrete. With Farnam shining his flashlight on the map, Roberts gave his Marines an impromptu debrief of the entire mission—warts and all. He was obviously displeased with the way the sortie had gone, and he could see the disappointment in the faces of the young men gathered around him. He recalled, "I could see that they were unhappy. They worked their hearts out every day so that I could do my job. Morale in the squadron moves up and down based upon the success of the aircrews." As the squadron commander—or "the Old Man"—Roberts was especially aware of their frustration. It stuck in him like a wooden knife.

Following the recap, Roberts and Farnam made their way to the MAG headquarters tent. Finding Tex, Roberts and Farnam recounted what they had found, and Tex directed them to report their mission to the tactile air command center (TACC) a few yards away. Roberts and Farnam found the atmosphere inside the command center calm but tense. Roberts recounted, "Major General Amos was there and waiting, as were Colonels Miclot, Sawyers, and Fox—all key players in the wing's operations. They were stern-faced—apprehensive about the prospect of our Marines running into the mysterious Republican Guard tank division." Amos, the wing commander, was working his chewing gum hard as Roberts and Farnam laid out a chart and reviewed the mission they had just flown. They pointed out that the steadily worsening visibility caused by the burning oil fires would make locating the tank division even more difficult. As to whether or not the Iraqi tanks even existed, Amos said that Mattis had emphasized that the original report came from a credible source.

The small group continued their discussion as they pored over the map. Areas where the Iraqis might be hiding, either in locations that Roberts and Farnam hadn't overflown or in areas that were obscured by smoke, were given particular scrutiny. "There was some concern as to what effect the smoke might have on our laser-guided ordnance—Mavericks, Hellfires, and LGBs," Roberts recollected. If it were too thick, it would keep the precision weapons from guiding to their targets. On the other hand, it would also be difficult to use the more traditional free-fall or dumb bombs if the aircrews couldn't even see the enemy. A decision was made to arm most of the aircraft with unguided ordnance. A few aircraft would stay loaded with thousand-pound GBU-16s; they would stay on alert to drop a bridge to the north of the division's advance in the event that the Iraqis attempted to attack or reinforce from that direction.

As the consultation wound down, Amos reported that the wing had already recorded its first "blue on blue" (friendly fire incident). An AH-1W Cobra from HMLA-169 had hit a Marine M1A1 tank just inside the northern Kuwaiti border. Roberts and Farnam collected their notes and exited. This was hardly the decisive, hard-hitting start to the aerial campaign that had been hoped for. But it was already in the past. Although the carefully plotted script was in disarray, the Marines on the ground were still being protected and supported from above. It could have been worse.

After his mission against the border ops, Lieutenant Colonel Steve Heywood led his flight to the Astrodome FARP in north-central Kuwait. (All the FARPs were named for major-league baseball stadiums—one of the planners was a baseball nut.) The horrendous visibility made him feel fortunate that all the crews had been able to land without incident. Now, only hours after the start of the war, the newly adjusted plan called for his squadron to continue the fight through the night in support of the regimental combat teams. However, smoke and worsening weather made that course of action seem unlikely.

"The wind was blowing out of the west-northwest," Heywood remembered. "The stuff that was rolling over our heads—oily smoke and dust and fog—was like black cotton. If I could have reached high enough, I think I could have torn pieces off of it." After checking on the status of his crews and their aircraft, he used his Iridium satellite telephone to make contact with Major Woody Lowe at the MAG-39 operations center. Lowe was busy trying to gather information about the friendly fire incident; it wasn't clear yet what had happened. Heywood reassured Lowe that his flight hadn't fired on any tanks.

"Aside from finding out who had shot up the tank," Heywood said, "Woody was anxious to get us airborne again to help out the grunts." Requests from the RCTs were coming in, and Cobra support was at the top of the list. Heywood was torn. He would never have launched in similar weather during peacetime, and he questioned if it was truly worth the risk at that moment. Because the Iridium wasn't encrypted, Heywood and Lowe couldn't talk about what was going on at the border except in generalities, but Heywood made the decision to stay on the ground until the weather improved.

Two more calls came in over the Iridium: The grunts needed help. Despite the atrocious flying conditions, Heywood reluctantly changed his mind and grabbed a copilot and two more Cobra crews. After a quick brief, they manned up, started their engines, and checked in over the radio. Heywood looked up at the oily scum that was passing only about a hundred feet over their heads and second-guessed his judgment one more time. He had thousands of hours of flight time, and the conditions were well beyond bad enough to give him pause; he could only imagine what the younger pilots he was about to lead into that goop were thinking.

"I had Jon Livingston on the controls in the front cockpit for this sortie," Heywood said. "I wanted him to fly because I wanted to keep an eye on the rest of the flight and coordinate our communications with the grunts." Heywood gave the command to lift off; at 2220 Livingston got the aircraft airborne and transitioned to forward flight. They had hardly gone half a mile when Livingston became badly disoriented in the swirling black smog.

"I've got vertigo—really bad," Livingston called over the intercom.

"Okay," Heywood answered. "Get on the instruments and just try to fly yourself out of it."

"No, I mean . . . I can't even fly the aircraft."

"I've got the controls." Heywood grabbed his set of flight controls.

"Roger, you've got the controls."

They had handled the situation by the book. Nevertheless, as soon as he began to fly the aircraft, Heywood started to wrestle with the same vertigo that had nearly overwhelmed Livingston. It took every bit of his training and experiences to set up an inside-outside that double-checked what little he could see through his night-vision goggles against what the instrumentation in his cockpit was telling him. Once, twice, three times the warning from his radar altimeter sounded, alerting him that he was too close to the ground. Each time he lifted the aircraft away from the desert floor only to settle back toward it again. On each side of the gunship, his two wingmen stayed tucked into formation as best they could.

Heywood turned the flight north along the east side of the main highway toward the RCTs clustered along the border. "We were basically doing the Helen Keller thing," he recalled, "only making about fifty or sixty knots and hoping not to run into anything while we felt our way along." A thin sliver of moon reflected against the airborne sludge and made visibility through their night-vision goggles worse rather than better. After a short time, the crews were able to make out flashes to their front where Eleventh Marines was putting preparatory fires downrange in front of the RCTs.

The bright flashes from the guns illuminated what looked to be a solid wall at the border. Heywood didn't believe it was possible, but the cocking black miasma they were chopping their way through was getting thicker. "By this time," he remembered, "I was totally task-saturated. I couldn't raise anyone on the radios, and it was all I could do to keep from flying the aircraft into the dirt." Just prior to the border, he eased his helicopter into a gentle left-hand turn.

Heywood weighed the risks of continuing against what little help his flight may have been able to provide the Marines on the ground. The Marines would have to do without his Cobras. "I made one of the hard decisions that I get paid for," Heywood said. "I was taking the flight back." As the flight leader, he was responsible for completing the mission but not at the expense of four aircraft and eight crewmen. And certainly not when it was doubtful that he would have been able to see well enough to help anyway.

━‿━

Heywood felt twice blessed when the last aircraft in his formation landed safely back at Astrodome.

━‿━

It was just past 0130 on March 21 when the commanding officer of MAG-39, Colonel Rich Spencer, received the latest intelligence update:

Enemy resistance on the Al Faw Peninsula was expected to be fierce. The report indicated that the Air Force AC-130 gunship assigned to prep the landing zone (LZ) had stayed on station longer than scheduled, as the defending Iraqis were more firmly entrenched than predicted. Despite the pounding the gunships had dealt the enemy positions, there was concern that they hadn't been hit hard enough. Spencer would have to discover the truth for himself when he got there. Around him he could see Marines making final preparations as the helicopters—sourced from several different air groups—were readied for the mission. In a very short time, he would be leading a flight of more than forty aircraft on the largest Marine Corps combat lift since Vietnam.

However, the troops that the Marine Corps was taking into battle that very early morning were not U.S. Marines. Rather, they were Royal Marines from the United Kingdom led by Lieutenant Colonel Buster Howe. Marines from both services had been planning and rehearsing the mission for several weeks. What had started as a company-sized insertion to capture a few key oil pumping stations had evolved into the operation that was about to unfold: when the helicopters touched down and the Royal Marines leapt out onto the desert, they would be charged with sweeping across the Al Faw Peninsula to the edge of al-Basrah. Now, despite the worsening weather, they were anxious to get airborne and start their part of the war.

Spencer was a Cobra pilot by training and would be leading the mission from the command and control ship—an HMLA-169 Huey piloted by Lieutenant Colonel Jim Braden, the commander of that unit. Spencer was in the main cabin, from which he could best monitor the mission's progress with the specially configured communications suite that had been installed just for this effort. At Spencer's side was the Royal Marine commander, Lieutenant Colonel Howe. The formation was made up of every helicopter type in the Marine Corps inventory: there were sixteen CH-46Es, ten CH-53Es, twelve AH-1Ws, and four UH-1s. Many of the ships—particularly the beloved CH-46E "Frogs"—were veterans of the war in Southeast Asia. Now the aged birds squatted in the dirt, their rotor blades drooping languidly in the dark. The aluminum skin that was riveted to their aluminum frames was patched and seemed to sag in places. The venerable aircraft looked every bit their age.

A few minutes before 0200, the last of the Royal Marines were aboard, and the helicopters whirled to life. Their once-floppy blades spun themselves into shadowy discs, and a cloud of dust whipped overhead the massive formation. Inside each cockpit the pilots completed their checklists, while the gunners and crew chiefs readied their weapons and gave the aircraft their final inspections. For their part, the Royal Marines double-checked and rechecked that their personal gear was strapped into place and that they would be ready for combat the instant they bounded from the helicopters.

It would be a short flight from where they were staged in northeast Kuwait to the Al Faw Peninsula. Over the radio Braden quickly checked the status of each division of aircraft. After he confirmed that the formation was ready, Spencer gave the order to lift off. Braden quickly checked that the area around him was clear, then coaxed the heavily burdened ship airborne amid a cloud of swirling dust. "Just as we climbed into the air," Spencer recounted, "Jim noticed a severe torque split—we had to land immediately." Braden quickly put the Huey back on the ground, and the rest of the ships pressed on without them.

Scrambling in the dust and the dark, the crew of the command and control ship hustled their gear and equipment to the backup aircraft. Minutes felt like hours, but before too much time passed, Braden and Spencer and the rest of the crew were airborne again. Braden wasted little time; instead of following the turns in the preplanned route, he raced directly toward a point where he hoped to intercept the formation.

⌐〜⌐

No one will know exactly what happened in the cockpit of the CH-46E where Major Jay Aubin and Captain Ryan Beaupre sat at their controls. Nevertheless, it is almost certain that they both fought against an enervating vertigo brought on by the blanket of smoke and sand and fog that the formation was flying through. But in the rear of the aircraft, it is likely that neither Staff Sergeant Kendall Watersbey nor Corporal Brian Kennedy knew that things were going bad. Neither is it likely that any of the eight Royal Marines—mentally and physically keen for combat—had any idea that disaster was imminent.

—◦—

Once he had the Huey on course, Braden called out over the radio for a communications check. It was then that Lieutenant Colonel Jerry Driscoll called out—very calmly—that his third aircraft was "down." Driscoll's remarkable composure led Spencer to believe that the aircraft in question had simply been left behind with mechanical problems. In fact, the helicopter had crashed.

At just this moment, Braden and Spencer flew into the shroud of black dust that the rest of the formation had been clawing through for the last several minutes. Spencer remembered, "I noticed that my goggles started to sparkle and that I could no longer see objects that had been clear only a few seconds before." Realizing that he was likely going to lose more aircraft and men if he continued to press the mission, Spencer called for an abort. The radio crackled as Braden made the transmission and got the rumbling mass of aircraft turned south. A short time later, Lieutenant Colonel Ron Radich called that he had flames from the downed helicopter in sight. Spencer cleared him to detach from the rest of the flight to assume duties as the on-scene commander.

The remainder of the aircraft returned to the start point without further incident. Once he was safely back on the ground, Spencer made his way to the Royal Marine command post and offered his apologies and condolences. It was a dreadful moment—he had lost four Marine crewmen, and the British had lost eight of their rock-hard Royal Marines. Regardless, there was still a war to be fought, and he and the commander post (CP) staff conferred on the merits of continuing the operation. It was decided that, weather permitting, another attempt would be made at first light.

As it developed, the weather at dawn was not permitting, and the joint effort was scrubbed. The Royal Marines planned to make another attempt later in the day with their own much smaller helicopter forces, and Spencer released his crews to support ongoing First Marine Division operations. In the meantime Spencer was still anxious about the crew he had lost. He and Braden got airborne and carefully felt their way through the morning fog toward the crash site.

After having flown much of the route at only fifty feet, Braden set the Huey down close to Radich's aircraft, and he and Spencer climbed out to talk to the other officer. "Ron met us and briefly tried to prepare us for what we were about to see." It was a hopeless effort—there was nothing to say to adequately prepare anyone for viewing the carnage that was still smoldering only a short distance away. "Simply put," Spencer said, "it was the most horrendous scene I had ever encountered—and that included two previous wars and twenty-seven years of service." There in the smoldering wreckage was the pride and love and hope of twelve different families. All were sons; some were husbands and fathers and brothers. All of them were gone. The sight shook Spencer and the other men to their cores.

Aside from the human tragedy, a very here-and-now concern was the ammunition that had been aboard the helicopter; it was cooking off sporadically and posed a real danger to the Marines from the other two ships. Spencer realized that there was little they could do. Dealing with the site would be "the grim task of the mortuary affairs and aircraft mishap teams." When Spencer and the other Marines left the crash site later that morning, it was with a sad sense of loss and helplessness. There was nothing they could do that would make right what had gone so badly wrong.

By the afternoon they were supporting other operations.

CHAPTER NINE

Thunderjets over Korea

Robert F. Dorr

THE F-84 THUNDERJET BEGAN ITS COMBAT ASSIGNMENT IN KOREA with a vengeance.

On January 23, 1951, while B-29 Superfortresses were bombing the North Korean capital of Pyongyang, Col. Ashley B. Packard, commander of the 27th Fighter Escort Wing, persuaded higher-ups to "frag" (assign) his F-84s to hit the airfield at Sinuiju, just south of the Yalu River. Thirty-three Thunderjets took off from the pierced-steel runway at K-2 Taegu Air Base in South Korea, flew north, and hit the airfield by surprise. The first eight F-84s, assigned a strafing role, began working the place. Only then, after Packard's force descended over Sinuiju like a tidal wave, did MiGs begin scrambling from Antung, their airfield on the Chinese side of the Yalu.

A furious battle ensued between F-84s and MiG-15s. First Lieutenant Jacob Kratt shot down two MiG-15s and captains. Allen McGuire and William W. Slaughter each bagged one MiG. All F-84s returned home safely. For pilot Kratt, who shot down a Yak three days later to rack up his third aerial victory, it was time to wallow in sweet triumph: In gunnery training back in the States, Kratt had "messed up," as he put it, and flown into a tow target. Only intervention by Packard with a skeptical Gen. Curtis E. LeMay had prevented the young airman from being grounded.

LeMay, of course, didn't want his 27th Wing in Korea. The wing was part of LeMay's strategic air command, and he wanted it back. He'd never liked fighters. He'd begrudgingly accepted the F-84 as an escort-fighter in SAC, almost certainly while biting into his famous cigar and twisting his face into a scowl. But as long as the planes were his, LeMay wanted them back and out of Korea. He was one of the architects of a policy that atomic war with the Soviet Union took priority over Korea: time and again, SAC and the air defense command received factory-fresh equipment denied to those doing the real shooting.

As for the F-84, it was the U.S. Air Force's final jet fighter to have straight wings, developed in the closing months of World War II. The Thunderjet had been built in part as "insurance" against failure of the more advanced Sabre, and pilots knew it.

Packard's 27th Wing flew 2,076 combat sorties in January 1951. At the end of the month, the wing moved from Taegu back to Itazuke. The F-84 offered somewhat more respectable range than the F-80, so the wing was able to continue flying combat missions against Communist ground targets. By July 30, 1951, the F-84E Thunderjet-equipped 136th Fighter Bomber Wing was in action with all three of its squadrons (111th, 154th, 182nd), made up largely of activated Air National Guardsmen. Soon, other F-84 squadrons, groups, and wings came to Korea—not from SAC but from tactical air command, which LeMay didn't own. The F-84 became a fixture in Korean fighting. One F-84 pilot was dubbed the "Junior Commando" by his squadron mates—not charitably—because he had a Thompson submachine gun strapped to his parachute harness and had to be shoved up the ladder to his airplane because of the weight of the .45-caliber ammunition in his survival pack.

The F-84 flew mostly air-to-ground missions, but there were times when air-to-air action was unavoidable. Six MiGs ambushed the F-84Es of the 8th Fighter-Bomber Squadron, 49th Fighter-Bomber Wing, intent on an air-to-ground mission near Sukchon, North Korea, on September 10, 1951. The Thunderjets' flight leader was 1st Lt. William Skliar.

William Skliar

We were on a rail-cutting mission. After our bomb runs, we were rejoining when the MiGs dove down on us. I called a break into the lead MiG, and when he saw us turn, he reversed his turn. At that moment, another

MiG came across my path in a rapid turn . . . about twelve hundred feet (371 m) in front of me. I laid my "Hog," as the F-84 was nicknamed, into as tight a turn as possible and managed to draw a lead. We were at near max range for our .50s, but I got some good long bursts in. After a quick glance around to check where the other MiGs were, my MiG just disappeared. Knowing that the enemy pilots often tried to decoy us into chasing them, I backed off in favor of getting everyone together again. At least I had the satisfaction of knowing that some of their decoys had almost bought the farm. I was credited with a "probable" kill.

OUT OF OXYGEN

On November 16, 1951, Thunderjet pilots lived through one of the most publicized occurrences of the conflict. F-84s of the 154th Fighter-Bomber Squadron, 136th Fighter-Bomber Wing, were slashing at railway targets in North Korea, led by Capt. John L. Paladino. The sky was free of MiGs, and the bombs seemed to be on target. Heading home to Taegu at 33,000 feet (10,216 m), Paladino's oxygen equipment malfunctioned. Flying nearby, 1st Lt. Wood McArthur and Capt. Jack Miller realized their flight leader was in trouble.

Jack Miller

We were headed south at altitude, when all of a sudden John's aircraft started to turn and then went into a steep dive to the left. I thought maybe he was practicing evasive action or something. After he had dropped down a few thousand feet, his ship did a "pitch up" that was characteristic of the F-84 when it goes through the speed of sound. After a few simple dives and sudden climbs, he was still on course, so we figured he was okay.

When I pulled alongside, I noticed that John was tugging at his oxygen mask. He said he was all right, so I told him to throttle back for the descent home. As we pulled closer, I saw that John's head was resting against the canopy. Before I could call to him, he slumped forward.

The F-84 flight leader had passed out from oxygen deprivation and could survive only if he could be gotten down to lower altitude, where he could breathe. I told McArthur to "put your wingtip under his wingtip on your side, and I'll do the same on my side."

Using the flow of air over our wingtips to keep Paladino's aircraft level between us, without any of the three aircraft touching each other, McArthur and I began the ticklish job of descending. After a hundred miles (161 km) and about fifteen minutes, we used this unusual feat of aerodynamics to lower the unconscious Paladino down to 15,000 feet (4,644 m). At 13,000 feet (4,024 m), Paladino became fully conscious and was able, now, to fly his Thunderjet home and land safely. Flight leader Paladino had a skull-grinding headache but no memory of the quarter-hour when his plane had been held aloft while he was out cold.

Tom Gill

The most difficult part of a mission is the anticipation. Once you're in the cockpit, you're too busy to think about it. I wanted jets. I didn't really have a preference as to what kind of jet, but I didn't want a reciprocating-engine airplane. I wanted to fly F-80s. At that time, I didn't even know an F-84 existed.

But once I completed pilot training and got into the F-84 Thunderjet, I was very glad to be flying that airplane. In the F-84, you were not in the glamour business. You were into reality.

The F-84 Thunderjet was a very good air-to-ground airplane. It was a very stable aircraft. It was an excellent gun platform. It had good fuel capacity, although at first it did not have the capability to receive air-to-air refueling. It was a good aircraft on instruments. On the negative side, I would have to say that both the F-84E and the F-84G were under-powered. We flew the F-84E and F-84G in Korea, and neither really had quite enough power. The Air Force didn't really have a fighter aircraft with sufficient power until the F-100 Super Sabre came along.

I was born in 1929 in Canton, Ohio. I started as a student at Ohio State University in 1947 and was studying there when the Korean War began. I was interested in flying. Dad's boss had a private aircraft, and I flew on it several times. I went to the recruiter in Canton in June or July 1950—the Korean War started on June 25—and the recruiter said, "Go home and graduate first." But I couldn't wait for graduation because I was about to be drafted.

I joined the Air Force on January 28, 1951. I joined at the same time as Dick Kempler, who was an all-American football player at the University of Michigan in Ann Arbor. Dick was in Flying Class 52-B, and I was in class 52-C. At the time I joined up, enlistments were frozen because the draft was being used to induct people, but my recruiter sent me a telegram that got me in.

I went first to Greenville, Mississippi, where I did primary training in the T-6 Texan from April to November 1951. From there, I went to Bryan Air Force Base near College Station, Texas, where I trained in the T-28A and the T-33A Shooting Star, as well as the single-seat fighter the F-80 Shooting Star. I pinned on my silver wings and became a second lieutenant on May 10, 1952.

I didn't have an aircraft preference, but I wanted fighters, and I wanted jets, not reciprocating-engine aircraft. I went to Nellis Air Force Base near Las Vegas, Nevada, for F-84 transition and gunnery training. They had F-84B and F-84C models at Nellis. I also remember flying an F-84G. Later in Korea, I flew mostly F-84E models but also flew the F-84G about 10 percent of the time.

I was assigned to the 428th Fighter Bomber Squadron, part of the 474th Fighter Bomber Group, at K-8 Kunsan Air Base in South Korea. We lived in Quonset huts that had been constructed by the Japanese. You had a cot, an air mattress, and three blankets.

I flew my first combat mission on October 4, 1952, from Kunsan. Like I said, the most difficult part of a mission is the anticipation. Once you're in the cockpit, you're too busy to think about it.

Before each mission, we had a briefing. In the briefing, they sometimes showed us photos of the target that had been taken just twenty-four hours earlier.

We frequently had large numbers of airplanes taking off on a mission. If you were in a 28-plane gaggle, you'd have to begin at your parking slow figuring out whom to follow when you taxi out. The runway ran from east to west. It was 10,000 feet long, with both ends over water. We took off two at a time, climbed out in a 270-degree turn, went back over the airfield, and turned to 90 degrees to fly north.

We flew north together, but it was a fairly loose arrangement. We maintained formation in pairs, but our two-ship formations didn't attempt to fit into larger formations. The number-one aircraft was the lead, of course, and it was his job to take us where we were going.

The number-two aircraft would look to the right and clear the right as we proceeded north.

We flew toward the target at 35,000 feet (10,668 m). I experienced air-to-air action on three occasions during my hundred missions. The F-86 Sabre boys who flew farther north were responsible for keeping the MiGs off of us, so we were not supposed to take them on. The MiGs flew through us, head on, and we saw their 37-mm cannons blinking.

They didn't worry us much. You can't hit a guy shooting at him from head on. They didn't have a lot of fuel and couldn't stick around to mix it up with us.

On a mission, we typically carried two 500-lb. (227-kg) or two 1,000-lb. (454-kg) bombs, one under each wing, plus six 5-inch high-velocity aircraft rockets, or HVARs, three under each wing, and of course we had six .50-caliber M3 machine guns, with 300 rounds per gun. The airplane had eight hard points for ordnance under the wings. All of that stuff weighs a lot, so the F-84 was a real heavyweight.

Bob James

We went in at low level to bomb and strafe, so we never intended to try to turn with the MiGs or maneuver against them. Once we'd dropped our bombs and pulled off the target, we were fighters, but by then the MiGs would be gone because they wanted to get us when we were vulnerable, going in with our bombs attached. The MiGs did get close enough to fire at me several times. The cannon in the nose of the MiG made smoke rings, so you could see it coming.

I got into the F-84 Thunderjet after being interested in flying as a kid. I was born in 1924 in Danville, Virginia, and went to Georgia Tech, where I was in Reserve Officer Training Corps, or ROTC. The training was an infantry-type deal, and I didn't like those rifles and marching. When I was a kid, my dad got me a ride in a Ford Tri-Motor. I built models. I wanted to fly planes, not carry a rifle.

I learned about the December 7, 1941, Japanese attack on Pearl Harbor that Sunday afternoon while in college. I had no idea what place the words *Pearl Harbor* referred to. We probably didn't know where Hawaii was.

Everybody was getting into the service. I wanted to fly. I went to the Navy recruiter and was close to being accepted for pilot training with the Navy. But I'm a pretty small guy, and they told me that at 119 pounds I didn't weigh enough to become a Navy pilot. I went to the Air Corps recruiter, and they said, (1) "If you want to come with us, you'll have to get yourself drafted in the next ninety days," and (2) "Once you're drafted, we'll make sure you get pilot training."

They later dropped the requirement to sixty days, and I got drafted on the fifty-ninth day. I was accepted into flying class 45-A, but they had too many pilots. So they sent me to become a bombardier and later to become a navigator. I was in A-26 Invaders in Valdosta, Georgia, when World War II ended.

I stayed in the Reserves and finished at Georgia Tech. Then they recalled me to active duty. This time I really was able to get pilot training in flying class 51-G. I got my pilot's wings in November 1951 and went to Nellis Air Force Base, Nevada, for gunnery training in F-80 Shooting Stars. Then, I went to Japan and from there to Korea to join the 182nd Fighter-Bomber Squadron of the 136th Fighter-Bomber Group, which was an activated Texas Air National Guard outfit. In July 1952, they changed the unit designations, and we became the 311th Fighter-Bomber Squadron of the 58th Fighter-Bomber Group. I had never seen an F-84 until I arrived in Korea, and they said, "Fly that."

In the F-84, we were the grunts, so to speak. Compared to other fighters, the F-84 was very stable. For a little guy with not much strength, it was a bit of a job, even though it had "boost" for the controls. It was very roomy, the cockpit being much less of a squeeze for me than the F-80, where my helmet was always hitting the top of the bubble canopy.

At Taegu airfield, we had about 7,500 feet of runway, so on hot days and when carrying heavy loads, we used jet-assisted takeoff, or JATO. That consisted of two bottles of compressed gas, one on each side of the fuselage. It gave you an extra push and created what looked like giant clouds of smoke. It was electrically operated from the cockpit. When it was working right, you could feel something, but it was not exactly like being pushed by a powerful rocket. If one of the bottles didn't work, your F-84 got into an asymmetrical situation, and you'd lose control.

We never seemed to have enough aircraft in service. Most of the Thunderjets in Korea were F-84E models, and they were joined eventually by some F-84Gs. We had the F-84D for a while, and they were not satisfactory. The Air Force pulled them out of training command units and sent them to Norton Air Force Base, California, for "disassemble, inspect, and repair," or DIR. When they arrived in Korea, they were supposed to be in good condition—but they weren't. They went kaput. They shed their wings in flight. If you overstressed an F-84D, the wings came off in flight.

This happened to Lt. Col. Sidney Weatherford, the newly arrived commander of the 182nd Squadron. He was in the middle of a combat run, and his wings folded. He was killed. Not long after that, the same thing happened to our operations officer. He lost a wing during a run on the Naktong firing range. After that, they removed the F-84D from service in Korea. The disruption from that change probably reduced the number of missions I got to fly. I flew eighty-three missions rather than reaching the goal of a hundred.

I liked the F-84E model 50 percent more than the F-84G. The F-84G was heavier on the controls and was not quite as agile.

I got hit on a mission in July 1952. I was in a two-ship formation that took off at daybreak to catch the North Koreans who'd been hiding out at night. We strafed trucks and pretty well beat them up.

The F-84 had a rather sophisticated gunsight for bombing and strafing. The truth is, I don't think we ever really learned how to use it. We were getting so much battle damage on our low-level runs that General Barcus, the head of Fifth Air Force, ordered us to stay above 3,000 feet. Before that, some guys were getting damaged from their own bomb detonations. Afterward, when we followed Barcus's rule, we were a lot less effective.

I think my truck-strafing mission took place while we still had no restrictions on our altitude over the target. I know we were pretty low.

When we were pulling off, I took a rifle round in my right tip tank. The tip tank exploded. It pulled the aircraft down. I brought it through the roll and got level, but it didn't want to fly with the damage. We had a T-handle to jettison the wing tanks. Normally, you didn't want to get rid of them, which is why you hardly ever see a photo of an F-84 flying without tip tanks. You can't get rid of one tip tank at a time. In this situation, I had to get rid of mine, so I jettisoned them, even though this made me low on fuel.

To my surprise, and contrary to everything they'd told us, my airplane handled perfectly well without tip tanks. In fact, it handled better. I discovered, however, that I didn't have radio contact. Apparently, my departing tip tank hit the fin and damaged the antenna.

After some difficulty regaining control, I was able to head south with no radio and land safely at K-14 Kimpo Air Base near Seoul.

Kenneth L. Skeen

My encounter with a MiG came on September 19, 1951, after I was forced to jettison my bombs and abandon an air-to-ground sortie. The entire 49th Fighter-Bomber Group, including my squadron, the 9th Fighter-Bomber Squadron, was going on this strike against a mail/rail complex located between Sinanju and Pyongyang. Each squadron used sixteen aircraft, and total ordnance was ninety six 500-lb. (227 kg) general-purpose bombs. Since I was one of the new pilots, I would be flying the number-four position in the last flight. My call sign was Purple 4.

As we passed east of Pyongyang, I heard the group leader call in MiGs at one o'clock high. For the past few minutes, we'd been listening to the controller calling out, "MiG trains heading south." We assumed the F-86s would be in a position to intercept them, but unknown to us, the Sabres were still on the ground at Kimpo, and we were on our own. There was a lot of radio chatter, with calls of, "MiGs at three o'clock high! They're coming in! Salvo your bombs! Get up some speed!" Then came the dreaded, "Break right, Purple flight!"

Being the last man in the flight, I was just hanging on as we went to full throttle. The MiGs overshot their attacking turn, and I pulled up high to our left, as Purple leader reversed the turn hard to the left into the

MiGs. Since I was on the outside of the turn, I started falling behind. As I cut across to the inside to catch up with Maj. Jim Sprinkle, my element leader, who was far ahead of me, a blue MiG-15 dropped down in front of me and locked onto Sprinkle's tail. The enemy pilot evidently never saw me, as he was busy lining up the F-84 in his sights. He was decelerating to get a better shot, while I was at full throttle to catch up. I lined the gunsight on him, took my feet off the rudder pedals to make sure the aircraft was flying true . . . and squeezed the trigger.

I gave him a long burst of .50-caliber (12.7 mm) armor-piercing incendiary. Immediately, pieces started flying off of the MiG, accompanied by smoke and flames. As he slowed, I saw he was on fire, and I pulled to his left to keep from running into him. He went into the thin undercast as I glanced to my left and saw another blue MiG right on the tail of another F-84. I yelled, "F-84! Break! Break! MiG on your tail! Break right!" I was hoping to bring the MiG into my sights. As the F-84 broke, the MiG pulled up high to the left. I looked back to my right as I entered the thin undercast.

I saw a parachute descending but not a single aircraft in sight. I climbed back on top, finding the sky deserted, where, just moments before, aircraft had been twisting and turning all over the sky. With my fuel showing well below bingo level, I headed south for the base at K-2. The rail-cutting mission had been unsuccessful, as we jettisoned our bomb loads, but all aircraft returned with only one damaged. Most important, the 9th Fighter-Bomber Squadron had gotten its first kill.

Tom Gill

Approaching the target, we let down to 20,000 feet (6,096 m) while following the number-one aircraft in the lead position. Exactly when we rolled in on the target was determined by where the enemy's antiaircraft guns were. The leader found the target and began the run-in. When you're ready to roll in, you push over the airplane to get it into trajectory to aim the bombs. We were supposed to pull out at 1,500 feet.

On my seventh or eighth night mission, going up to the bridges on the Yalu River, I got lost, became low on fuel, and couldn't use my radio transmitter, although I could receive. We went on these night missions by ourselves, so you were pretty much on your own except for the controller at Cho-do Island. The object was to harass the North Koreans and Chinese at night so they couldn't move stuff during the hours of darkness.

That was probably my most difficult mission. I couldn't transmit, but I used my "identification, friend or foe," or IFF equipment, to transmit—squawk—a signal to Cho-do. I squawked four on the IFF, which meant, "Mayday. This is an emergency." He came back to me with something like, "Aircraft squawking on IFF, if you can read me, turn to a heading of 090 degrees." I did that, and now we had communication of a sort. He said things like, "If your tip tanks are dry, turn to 180 degrees. Okay, got that, sir. Now, if you have your ordnance, turn to 170 degrees. Okay, thank you, sir." Using that kind of communication, he guided me, and I eventually landed safely at K-55 Osan Air Base, which was a little farther north than my base at Kunsan. It was the only time I ever went in there.

Landing the F-84 was a piece of cake. At Kunsan, we had 10,000 feet of runway, so there was plenty of space. There was water at both ends, so they didn't need to install Navy-style arresting gear, as they'd done at Taegu: If you got in trouble, you went into the water. For a period of time, we were told to practice landing with a brake on one side of the airplane only. Returning from one mission, my flight leader got shot up, lost one brake, skidded, went off the runway, and piled up. So he said, "We've got to practice that." So we got used to landing with one brake, almost as if we were being punished for what he did. When you landed with one brake, you would compensate with rudder and aileron: If you used the stick properly to compensate, you could keep the airplane straight on the runway.

To summarize my experience in the F-84, in a fast aircraft, you had to think ahead of the airplane. It helped if your only training was in jets. There were some guys who switched regularly from props to jets and back again. Some of them weren't thinking ahead, and they were getting killed. I flew a hundred missions. I got out of the Air Force after leaving Korea, mostly because I didn't want to fly a hundred more.

REPUBLIC F-84E/G THUNDERJET

The Republic F-84 Thunderjet was what many pilots saw as their second choice. It wasn't pretty. It wasn't glamorous. It didn't achieve much in air-to-air action. In Korea, Thunderjet pilots shot down only a handful of MiGs—including the one downed by Navy exchange pilot Lt. Walter "Wally" Schirra, later a Mercury astronaut—but they spent much of the war in the unglorious, unglamorous business of hauling bombs to the target. The F-84 was sturdy, which is why its maker, located at Farmingdale, Long Island, in New York, was sometimes dubbed the Republic Iron Works—and it could sometimes be sprightly, but many pilots found their way into F-84 cockpits only after not qualifying in the slimmer, prettier F-86 Sabre.

On November 11, 1944, the Army Air Forces authorized Republic to build three prototypes of a new jet fighter called the XP-84. Republic completed the first plane at Farmingdale and shipped it to Muroc, California—site of the future Edwards Air Force Base—where the XP-84 made its initial flight on February 28, 1946. By then, the swept-wing XP-86 Sabre was flying faster in its initial flight trials, and the P-84 remained on the U.S. Air Force's shopping list only as "insurance" against the catastrophic failure of the Sabre, which many believed was too advanced to have any practical use.

The XP-84's original engine was a 3,750-lb. (1,700 kg) thrust Allison TG-180 axial-flow turbojet, later redesignated J35-GE-7. The first production models of the new fighter, P-84Bs, began to reach squadrons in 1947. That year, the Air Force became an independent service branch. The following year, the P for "pursuit" nomenclature was dropped. The P-84 became the F-84. By then, the Air Force was receiving F-84D and F-84E models.

F-84s went into combat in Korea in 1951. They proved tough, able to absorb gunfire and return safely to base. By now, of course, the Sabre was making its mark as one of the great warplanes of all time, and an "insurance policy" was no longer needed. At this late juncture, the F-84 Thunderjet was a fine fighting machine and was beloved by pilots, but it was no longer on the cutting edge.

The idea of passing fuel from one aircraft to another in flight dated to at least the early 1920s, but two world wars had been fought without it being accomplished in battle. On May 29, 1952, the U.S. Air Force's 116th Fighter-Bomber Wing flew a mission as part of Operation

Hi-Tide; 227-kg bombs departed Itazuke Air Base, Japan; refueled aloft; bombed the North Korean city of Sariwon; and recovered at Johnson Air Base, Japan. Each F-84 carried a stiff probe that pointed forward from its wingtip fuel tank—plugging into a kind of funnel lowered by the KB-29M. This was called the "probe and drogue" refueling system. Except for a few missions flown by RF-80 photo planes, this was the first use of air-to-air refueling in combat: it pointed the way to a future in which all warplanes would be capable of taking on fuel in flight.

Straight-wing F-84D, F-84E, and F-84G fighters flew thousands of less dramatic missions in Korea and shot down a few MiG-15s. Others served as escort fighters with the strategic air command. The United States exported F-84s to many of its allies.

CHAPTER TEN

Sixty Squadron, R.A.F.

Group Captain A. J. L. Scott

SIXTY HAD NOT TO WAIT LONG FOR ITS FIRST TASTE OF SERIOUS FIGHTing. The "aerial offensive," which always precedes any "push," was already well developed when the squadron commenced war flying. Casualties were heavy, and on July 3, two days after the official commencement of the Somme battle, Ferdy Waldron was shot down and killed on the "other side." He considered it his duty to try and do one job per day over the line, and on this particular morning, he led "A" Flight's 80 h.p. "bullets" over at 4 a.m. in perfect weather. The other members of the patrol were Smith-Barry, Armstrong, Simpson, and Balfour. The last named thus describes the fight:

> Both Armstrong and Simpson fell out, through engine trouble, before we reached Arras. Armstrong landed by a kite balloon section and breakfasted with Radford (Basil Hallam, the actor), whose kite balloon was attacked a few days later and who met his death through the failure of his parachute. Waldron led the remaining two along the Arras–Cambrai road. We crossed at about 8,000 feet, and just before reaching Cambrai, we were about 9,000, when I suddenly saw a large formation of machines about our height coming from the sun towards us. There must have been at least twelve. They were two-seaters led by one Fokker (monoplane) and followed by two others. I am sure they were not contemplating "war" at all, but Ferdy pointed us towards them and led us straight in.

My next impressions were rather mixed. I seemed to be sur-rounded by Huns in two-seaters. I remember diving on one, pulling out of the dive, and then swerving as another came for me. I can recollect also looking down and seeing a Morane about 800 feet below me going down in a slow spiral, with a Fokker hovering above it following every turn. I dived on the Fokker, who swallowed the bait and came after me but unsuccessfully, as I had taken care to pull out of my dive while still above him. The Morane I watched gliding down under control, doing perfect turns, to about 2,000 feet, when I lost sight of it. I thought he must have been hit in the engine. After an indecisive combat with the Fokker, I turned home, the two-seaters having disappeared. Smith-Barry I never saw from start to finish of the fight. I landed at Vert Galant and reported that Ferdy had "gone down under control." We all thought he was a prisoner, but heard soon afterwards that he had landed safely but died of wounds that night, having been hit during the scrap.

About twenty minutes after I had landed, Smith-Barry came back. He had not seen us but had been fighting the back two Fokkers, which he drove east, but not before he had been shot about by them, one bullet entering the tail and passing up the fuselage straight for his back until it hit the last cross-member, which deflected the course of the missile sufficiently to save him.

This was the end of a first-class squadron commander and, coming so early in our fighting career, was a heavy blow. If he had lived, Waldron must have made a great name for himself in the R.F.C.

Smith-Barry now took over the squadron. He was a great "charac-ter"—an Irishman with all an Irishman's charm. A trifle eccentric, he was a fine pilot. He had crashed badly near Amiens in the retreat from Mons, the first Flying Corps casualty, breaking both his legs, which left him permanently lame. Although beloved by his squadron, his superi-ors sometimes found him a little trying officially. It is often said, half admiringly, of a man by his friends that "he doesn't care a damn for anyone." I believe this to have been almost literally true of Smith-Barry.

He could do anything with an aeroplane and delighted in frightening his friends with incredible aerial antics. He was a fine, if original, squadron commander, almost too original, in fact, even for the R.F.C., where, if anywhere in the fighting services, originality was encouraged. At a later stage (in 1917) in Smith-Barry's career, he rendered a very great service to the Corps and to the country by bringing his contempt for precedent and genius for instruction to bear on the question of teaching pilots to fly. It is no exaggeration to say that he revolutionized instruction in aviation, and having been given almost a free hand by General J. Salmond, he organized his Gosport School of Special Flying, which afterward developed into a station where all flying instructors were trained.

He has been seen to walk down the Strand in full uniform with an umbrella.

When promoted in 1918 to the command of a brigade, he, having come into conflict with authority, dispatched the following telegrams on the same day to his immediate superior:

1. "Am returning to Gosport. Smith-Barry, Brig.-Gen."

2. "Have arrived at Gosport. Smith-Barry, Lieut.-Col."

Smith-Barry's batman was a French boy named Doby, a refugee from Lille, whom Nicolson, sometime private secretary to General Seely and one of the early pilots of the R.F.C., had picked up during the retreat from Mons and taken back to England with him. When Nicolson was killed at Gosport, Smith-Barry appointed Doby as his batman and, in order to take him to France, dressed him in R.F.C. uniform and called him Air Mechanic Doby. This boy was most useful, being competent to bargain with his compatriots for the goods which the mess required. When a year had gone by and there had been several changes in command, nobody knew his history, and he was regarded as a genuine member of the Corps. History does not relate how he was eventually "demobilized."

This, then, was the kind of man who took over the squadron on Waldron's death—at a critical point in its career.

Those who were most conspicuous during the Battles of the Somme were Ball (who joined from 11 Squadron in August), Summers and Tower (two of the original flight commanders), Gilchrist, Latta, Grenfell, Meintjies, A. D. Bell Irving, Phillippi, Hill, Foot, Vincent, Armstrong, and Walters. Foot, as one of the most skillful pilots, was given a "Spad," on which he did great execution during the autumn.

The fighting was mainly over places like Bapaume, Courcelette, Martinpuich, Busigny, St. Quentin, Cambrai, Havrincourt, etc.

Ball began to show very prominently about this time, several times destroying two or more hostile aeroplanes, and hardly a day passed without at least one Hun being added to his bag. Much has been written about Albert Ball, so much that at this date it is difficult to add anything of interest to the accounts which are already so widely known, but this at least can confidently be said, that never during the war has any single officer made a more striking contribution to the art of war in the air than he, who was the first to make what may be called a business of killing Huns. He allowed nothing to interfere with what he conceived to be the reason of his presence in an aeroplane in France—the destruction of the enemy wherever and whenever he could be found. He was a man—a boy in truth—of a kindly nature, possessed by a high sense of duty and patriotism. These months (August and September 1916) saw Ball at his best, and though it is true that he was awarded the Victoria Cross after his death in an heroic fight in the spring of 1917, when he was a flight commander in 56 Squadron, yet it was in the summer and autumn of 1916 in 11 and 60 Squadrons that he began to show the Flying Corps what fighting in the air really meant. The copy of a report rendered to R.F.C. H.Q. is given below:

Lieut. Ball has had more than twenty-five combats since May 16 in a single-seater scout.

Of these, thirteen have been against more than one hostile machine.

In particular, on August 22, he attacked in succession formations of 7 and 5 machines in the same flight; on August 28, 4 and 10 in succession; on August 31, 12.

He has forced 20 German machines to land, of which 8 have been destroyed—1 seen to be descending vertically with flames coming out of the fuselage, and 7 seen to be wrecked on the ground.

During this period he has forced two hostile balloons down and destroyed one.

(Sgd.) *J. F. A. Higgins,*
Brigadier-General,
Commanding 3rd Brigade R.F.C.
In the Field,
Sept. 1, 1916.

Of the others, Latta became a wonderful pilot; Gilchrist, a gallant South African, commanded 56 at the end of the war and became one of the very best instructors under Smith-Barry at Gosport; Roderick Hill, a fine pilot, is also an artist of no small reputation; A. D. Bell Irving worthily upheld the traditions of an heroic Canadian family whose name will always appear prominently in any history of the Air Force; while Meintjies, also a South African, though young, himself displayed an infinite patience, together with a wisdom far beyond his years, in the introduction of new pilots to the hazardous game of aerial fighting as practiced on the Western Front, of which he himself was a first-class exponent.

As for D. V. Armstrong, a South African who was killed in a crash just as the war had ended and who after leaving 60 became a brilliant night-flying pilot, the following letter from Col. Small will give some slight idea of the work done by him in 151 Night Fighting Squadron:

At 10.40 on the night of September 17/18, whilst on patrol east of Bapaume, Capt. Armstrong observed a Gotha biplane caught in a concentration of searchlight at 8,500 feet, with a Camel machine behind it.

Seeing the Camel was not engaging the E.A. (enemy aeroplane) from a sufficiently close range, this officer dived down, coming in on the E.A.'s right. He closed right up under its tail and fired 100 rounds into it. The E.A. then burst into flames and dived to the ground, where it burst into pieces just east of Bapaume.

On the night of September 10/11, 1918, on receipt of a report that E.A. was over the 4th Army front, Capt. Armstrong volunteered to go up, although the weather was practically impossible for flying, the wind blowing at about fifty miles an hour, accompanied by driving rain storms. In spite of this, Capt. Armstrong remained on his patrol 1 hour, 5 minutes, although his machine was practically out of control on several occasions. On landing, his machine had to be held down to prevent it being blown over.

On the night of August 6/7, 1918, Capt. Armstrong attacked Estrées-en-Chaussée aerodrome. After dropping three Cooper bombs on the hangars from 600 feet, he observed an E.A. coming in to land. Capt. Armstrong then closed under the E.A.'s tail and opened fire from 15 yards' range when at 700 feet. The E.A.'s observer answered the fire and then suddenly ceased altogether. Capt. Armstrong continued firing until the E.A. suddenly turned to the right with nose down and crashed on its aerodrome, bursting into flames as it struck the ground. This officer then dropped his fourth bomb on the wreck and fired a further burst into it, returning to his aerodrome with all ammunition expended.

On the night of August 8/9, 1918, although the clouds were at about 500 feet, this officer flew to the same hostile aerodrome, but finding no activity there and seeing no lights whatever, he flew to Cizancourt Bridge, dropping his four bombs upon it from 500 feet.

On this night he was unable at any period to fly at over 800 feet, owing to low driving clouds and a very strong wind.

Capt. Armstrong attacked aerodromes as follows on the dates shown:

Moislans, 3.15 a.m. to 3.30 a.m. on August 21/22, 1918, dropping two incendiary and two Cooper bombs from 400 feet on hutments and tents, although subjected to the most accurate and fierce machine-gun fire from the ground and his machine being brightly illuminated in the glare of the incendiary bombs.

Estrées-en-Chaussée, on the night of July 31–August 1, 1918, dropping four bombs on landing lights from 500 feet.

Capt. Armstrong took part in the defence of London against all but three raids by E.A. between September 1917 and June 1918.

This officer has been the right hand of his squadron commander since the formation of his squadron and has, by his wonderful flying, taught the pilots of 151 Squadron more than any other instructor could possibly have done. He has demonstrated to all pilots daily the only successful method of attack at night against E.A. by personal supervision of their flying.

As a flight commander, I cannot speak too highly of him and his wonderful spirit at all times. His bravery as a pilot at all times and in all weather conditions cannot be surpassed, and I am unable to recommend him too strongly for this decoration.

B. C. D. Small,
Lieut.-Colonel,
Commanding 54 Wing R.A.F.
Sept. 19, 1918.

Three Le Prieur rockets of the ordinary type were attached to the interplane struts on each wing; these were fired by means of an electric bell-push in the nacelle (or pilot's seat) and, if they hit the hostile kite balloon, were guaranteed to send it down in flames. The effect of this extra load was to make the machine singularly unhandy when fighting, but it must be admitted that they did effectually set hostile kite balloons alight if the pilot was sufficiently resolute to restrain himself from pressing the button until he was within 150 yards of the object balloon. This sounds much easier than, in fact, it was, as hostile balloons were usually found as low as 2,500 feet, and the wretched pilot had to contend with heavy gunfire from the ground, while always remembering that he was some considerable distance over the line and had sacrificed his height in order to approach the balloon. The aeroplane of those days would glide about one mile per 1,000 feet in still air, and remembering that the balloons were usually at least two miles behind the line and that the wind was almost always from the west, it will be obvious that, if the engine was hit, there was very little chance of gliding back over the trenches. Hence it will be readily understood that balloon strafing was not enormously popular among junior flying officers.

Nevertheless, Gilchrist, Bell Irving, Summers, Phillippi, and Hill all successfully brought down hostile kite balloons during the Somme battles (September 1916).

Later, in 1917, Buckingham incendiary ammunition was used for destroying balloons. This change was greatly appreciated by the R.F.C. because the handiness of the machine was not impaired, as was the case when the Le Prieur rockets were carried.

From Vert Galant the squadron moved to St. André on August 3, 1916, to refit, having only five pilots left. There the first flight of Nieuport scouts was received, and after a fortnight, another move was ordered to Izel le Hameau on August 16. This was an aerodrome we were destined to occupy again during the Arras battle. We here became a homogeneous unit completely equipped with Nieuport scouts and moved three miles away to Savy, midway between Arras and St. Pol, early in September. Here, during November, little flying was possible, owing to continual rain and fog, and the squadron settled down, almost in the Roman manner, into winter-quarters. Savy Aerodrome stood just above the village of that name, and while "C" Flight were accommodated in huts on the aerodrome so as to be near their machines in order to deal quickly with any Huns who were bold enough to cross the line, the remainder of the squadron were billeted in the mayor's château in the village itself, some half a mile away. Here pigs and turkeys were kept, out of which the mess made a good profit and which, in addition, provided both an excellent Christmas dinner for the men and the material for the farewell banquet to Smith-Barry, who was posted to Home Establishment early in December. This dinner was somewhat memorable. The guests included General Higgins (the brigade commander), Pretyman (the wing commander), Col. Lewis and Barnaby of the "archie" gunners, Robert Loraine, and several other squadron commanders. The squadron band, organized by Vincent, performed during dinner with great vigor. Led by Sergt. Nicod at the piano and conducted by Vincent himself, it helped to enliven the evening very considerably.

In addition to the band, the squadron ran at this period both a rugby and an association football team. The rugby side was for a time invincible, the leading players being Middlemas, the wing machine-gun officer, an old Cambridge Blue, and a fine three-quarter; D. Bell Irving and Giles, a first-class pair of halves; and Meintjies, a tower of strength at full back. The soccer team also won many matches, captained by the "Great Man," Sergt. Maj. Aspinall; while the stores sergeant, a league player, was the star performer at center forward. Matches were very difficult to arrange, as they had to be postponed if the weather was fine and could only take place, therefore, on thoroughly "dud" days, to use the inevitable R.F.C. expression.

Smith-Barry was succeeded by Major E. P. Graves, a regular gunner, young in years, who had crashed a Gnome Martinsyde scout at Netheravon early in 1915 and spent many months in hospital, emerging toward the end of that year permanently lame but quite fit to fly. He had been staff captain and brigade major to General Higgins at home when recovering from his injuries but, as soon as he became fit, gave his general no peace until he was allowed to go to France in a fighting unit. He got posted to 20 Squadron as a flight commander early in 1916 and had been sent home again on promotion to command a training squadron after six months of very good work in France. Soon after he had taken over, the squadron was moved from Savy back to Izel le Hameau, the correct name of the station being Filescamp Farm. Here, with the aid of the local R.E. and thanks to Graves's tireless efforts, an almost ideal little station was created in the orchard adjoining the great gray walls of M. Tetus's demesne.

This was a very old and picturesque house, half farm and half château, and was removed some two miles from a main road or railway line, a circumstance which prevented the aerodrome being bombed at night for a very long time, as it was hard to see from the air. An admirable mess, with a large brick fireplace, corrugated-iron hangars, together with Nissen huts for the officers and N.C.O.s and good accommodation for the men, were all built by the sappers. At this station in M. Tetus's orchard, the squadron found a quiet retreat when not actually engaged with the enemy. It is, perhaps, appropriate here to observe that every pilot at this time did, on the average, three patrols in two days over the line and seldom returned to the aerodrome without a brush of some kind with the Boche.

The contrast between our quarters and those occupied by the infantry and gunners in the line was striking. We had cream at every meal and a hot bath—made by digging an oblong hole in the turf and lining it with a waterproof sheet—whenever we felt inclined. That the mess was good was largely due to Dobson, a 19th Hussar, partly paralyzed as the result of a fall when riding in a steeplechase before the war, who was the recording officer at this time, having vainly tried to qualify as an observer in spite of his disability.

During the early months of 1917, there was a very hard frost, which made it difficult for the Germans to start their engines, most of which were water-cooled stationaries, but did not affect 60's air-cooled rotaries, though both sides found that their machine guns were almost useless, owing to the extreme cold. This frost lasted till mid-February.

Below will be found the first of a series of letters written by Molesworth, who joined the squadron at this time. They have been inserted as far as possible whenever the narrative reaches the events which they describe.

60 Squadron R.F.C.,
B.E.F., France.
March 1917.

It has been snowing hard all day, so at last I have a chance of sending you a scrawl.

Well, old bean, I had my first trip with my flight commander over the lines on the 2nd. My word! It was some trip, too, I can tell you. I was posted to "A" Flight and allotted a machine. Having interviewed my C.O. with much fear and trembling, I was told that he would take me up to the lines to have a look round. My job was to watch and follow my leader, look out for any Huns, and get a good idea of the ground. By this time I had got well acquainted with my machine, or "grid," as it was generally called by one of our colonial flight com-

manders, and felt quite confident that, if we met any Huns, I could give them a pretty hot time.

We started off late in the afternoon, climbing to about 8,000 feet. The view was wonderful—the ground covered with a thin coating of snow, while far away one could see the incessant flashing of the guns near the battered old town of Arras. White clouds floated in the ground mist over the eastern horizon like great icebergs, their tops tinged with a wonderful pink which one only sees in the air.

I shall never forget that first impression of the battlefield from an aeroplane; it was so different to the sights of war on the ground. No Huns were on view, but a few of our artillery machines were still working. We turned home and landed in the dusk.

I don't think I told you about a Boche we brought down last week. We got him quite near the aerodrome—apparently he had lost his way in the clouds. He appeared out of them at about 3,000 feet over our heads. Of course, every available machine dashed off in pursuit and caught him up in a few minutes, as he was forced to turn from the lines by some old F.E. Birds. They all went for him, and he had to land in a ploughed field nearby. He put the machine down quite well, without crashing anything, but one of his pursuers, who belonged to the squadron next to us, turned upside down in his excitement when landing. However, he did not hurt himself and managed to prevent the Hun from setting his machine on fire by holding a Very pistol at his head.

Afterwards I had a chat with the prisoner in French and found out that he was a star pilot, having a number of our machines to his credit and the inevitable Iron Cross.

I am all out for getting a Hun now and hope to be able to tell you, when I next write, that my name has appeared in Comic Cuts.

The Nieuport scout deserves a short description, as it was on the successive types of this aeroplane that nearly a year's work was done, from September 1916 to July 1917. This single-seater fighter was a French machine and one of the most successful in its day which our allies ever produced. The various types of this make with which the squadron was at different times equipped—15, 16, 17, 21, 24, and 29—showed a continuous improvement in performance, though all had the same engine, 110 h.p. Le Rhone, which itself was modified slightly and converted into a 120 h.p. engine by the substitution of aluminum for cast-iron pistons. Through all the modifications introduced in each successive type, the machine preserved its essential characteristics. It was a biplane, but its lower planes were nonlifting and only operated to stabilize the machine to some extent in flight; the top planes were streamlined with the pilot's eyes, giving him the free view which is essential in a fighting scout. It may be said that it was mainly this characteristic, that it was good to see out of, that made the Nieuport, in 1916, the best fighting machine on either side. Strong in construction and very handy, it could turn inside any German aeroplane we ever encountered. It was not very fast, but with an exceptionally good climb to 10,000 feet, it was no bad "grid" on which to go Hun-hunting between the sea and the Somme. It was armed with a single Lewis gun carrying a double drum with ninety rounds of .303 ammunition and two spare drums. The gun was mounted on the top plane and fired over the propeller at an angle slightly above the horizontal. The earlier Nieuports were all treated with a bright silver-colored "dope"—the substance used to tighten the fabric—and when properly turned out had a very smart appearance.

Another characteristic of all types was the V-shaped interplane strut, which, although the Germans also used them in their D3 Albatros, made the machines easy to recognize in the air.

In conclusion, the silver Nieuport was a good machine to fight in but a bad one either for running away or for catching a faint-hearted enemy, as its best air speed, even near the ground, rarely exceeded ninety-six or ninety-seven miles per hour.

Arras

With the beginning of March 1917, the Boche became very active in the air. The D3 V-strut Albatros appeared in numbers on the 3rd Army front, and about the same time, a squadron of red-painted machines of this type, known to the R.F.C. as "the Circus," did a good deal of damage to British machines and annoyed us very much. One aeroplane in particular, called the "Pink Lady" on account of an absurd story that it was flown by a woman—the machine itself was colored bright red—was often seen between Arras and Albert. It is thought that the pilot was Freiherr von Richthofen, the elder. This machine it was that, venturing well over our side of the line on March 6, 1917, crashed an F.E. and went on and engaged and shot down Evelyn Graves, whose machine caught fire. When picked up, he was found to have been shot through the head, so that he was spared the pain of death by burning.

After Evelyn Graves's death, A. J. L. Scott, of the Sussex Yeomanry, was appointed to succeed him. He was a flight commander in 43—a Sopwith two-seater squadron—and was also lame as the result of a crash during the early part of the war, being the third lame squadron commander in succession appointed to 60.

Scott took up his appointment on March 10, 1917, about the time that the aerial offensive precedent to the Arras battle began to develop.

There had been, on the 3rd Army front, a lull during January and February, and by a lull is meant that pilots were doing one job a day instead of the two that they were almost certain to be called upon for when business was good. The casualties lists show this clearly, as, though E. O. Grenfell and Gilchrist were wounded in December, there were only two more casualties until Evelyn Graves's death in March—R. Hopper, killed on January 11, and E. G. Herbert, wounded on the 28th. February passed without the loss of a single officer. This was due mainly to the month of hard frost referred to above, which kept the Hun machines on the ground. Even when machines did meet in the air at this time, it was very difficult to get the guns to fire, so that on several occasions the pilots, after maneuvering round one another for a while, waved hands and went home. A nonfreezing gun oil was brought out before the next winter, which put an end to these not altogether unwelcome interludes to the sterner business. Mention of Grenfell's wound calls to mind the occasion on which he received it. An O.P. (offensive patrol) led by him and consisting of Caldwell, Daly, Whitehead, Weedon, and Meintjies, met a two-seater Albatros over Dainville on our side of the line. All our machines opened fire, and the Hun hurriedly landed. Grenfell, anxious to get down and claim him, crashed and broke his leg, while all the other five machines landed, and three of these also crashed, not so seriously as to injure the pilots but enough to prevent them taking off again. Thus the Hun in one field was flanked by a crashed Nieuport in every adjoining enclosure, while, to make matters worse, the Boche observer—who, unlike the pilot, was not wounded—set fire to his machine to prevent it falling into our hands. The machine shortly exploded, seriously injuring the observer and several of our own infantry, who by that time were standing by. If these had grasped the situation a little more quickly, they could easily have prevented the destruction of the machine, which it was important to preserve.

The Battle of Arras, as it came to be called, was now imminent and would probably have commenced before April 10 but for an unexpected move on the part of the enemy. On March 30, the first clear day after a spell of bad weather, the first patrol to land reported thirty or forty fires in the tract of country east of the Arras-Albert sector. Every village for ten or fifteen miles back was alight. At first we could not understand what it meant—for although an R.F.C. squadron knew a good deal more of what was happening than a battalion in the line, still we did not always fully comprehend the meanings of the incidents we reported, which the G.H.Q. Intelligence Staff could, no doubt, interpret with the help of reports from their numerous other sources of information.

The German retreat of March 14 came, therefore, as a complete surprise to us. For, even at this stage of the war, we had become so used to hearing that the enemy's *morale* was undermined and that their troops were unwilling to fight, etc., that we had ceased to take much notice of these stories, the truth of which—for they were true—only became manifest nineteen months later.

The next two days, the 14th and 15th, were days of stormy weather, in spite of which patrols were continually sent out to try and ascertain the depth of the withdrawal and to locate the new German positions. The rough-and-ready way in which this was done was to fly low until we came under fire from antiaircraft guns or rifles and machine guns on the ground. Molesworth, in a letter, gives quite a graphic account of this retreat as follows:

60 Squadron R.F.C.,
B.E.F., France.
March 1917.

No luck for me in the Hun line yet, although the beggars seem to be running on the ground all right.

Three of us went out the other day and had the most hectic time. The clouds were about 3,000 feet and very dense, with gaps here and there. We crossed the lines and expected to get it pretty hot from Archie, but strangely enough, nothing happened. Heading towards Croisille, we came out of a thick cloud and saw a most extraordinary sight. For miles around every village was a blazing mass with smoke columns, like great water spouts, ascending upwards to the clouds. Along the roads one could see lines of retreating men making for the Hindenburg defences, which we could plainly distinguish, owing to the amount of barbed wire entanglements round them. Suddenly we were met by a perfect tornado of bursting "archies" and so were forced to turn into a cloud. This cloud was so thick that we all promptly proceeded to lose ourselves. I looked at my compass and saw that it was pointing west, so carried on. At last, after about half an hour's flying, I found myself alone in an opening in the clouds. Below me were dozens of shell holes filled with water; round about, black clouds and sheets of driving rain. I knew I was somewhere near the lines and yet could not decide in which direction to turn. Trusting to the compass, I still pushed on west, and at last the shell holes disappeared. Just as my petrol was giving out, I spotted some hangars. There was nothing for it, so I decided to land. Coming down to about 200 feet, I did a half circle to get into the wind and, to my utter disgust, saw a large party of Germans on the ground. I therefore made up my mind that it must be a Hun aerodrome. No machines were out, owing to the "dud" weather, so I landed, jumped out of the machine, seized the Very pistol, and was just going to fire it into the grid when I saw, to my amazement, two mechanics in khaki coming across to give me a hand. I tell you, I have never been so bucked to see anyone in khaki before. Evidently the party I had seen were German prisoners. When the old kite had been filled up, I pushed off again and got home after about an hour's run. On arrival I heard that the other two had lost themselves as well but had managed to get back. In future I shall take jolly good care to get to know the country better before playing about in clouds.

On the 17th and 18th, the weather became too bad to fly, and an "excursion" was organized in tenders to the nearest points of the old front line, Ransart and Monchy-au-Bois, near Adinfer Wood; this last named had been the home of a peculiarly accurate enemy "archie" gun for many months past. At the latter place, skeletons of French soldiers still hung in the wire, where they had been since September 1915 at least.

The systematic and deliberate devastation of the evacuated country made a great impression on all our pilots, who were also thrilled to see the very trenches which the enemy's troops had occupied only a few days earlier. It seemed wonderful to see the marks in the muddy sides of the trenches made by German feet and elbows, and the clips of rifle cartridges laid on the fire steps by their sentries less than a week before. Absorbingly interesting, too, to explore their dugouts and to trace the routes by which their troops came up into the line from the rest billets behind. All the roads had been blown up, and every house in each abandoned village was most efficiently destroyed, except in a few cases, like Bapaume town hall, where delay action mines had been prepared.

One of the most impressive sights was the German cemetery, which was to be found in almost every hamlet, carefully laid out and extremely carefully tended, with monuments, cement steps, and ornamental shrubs symmetrically disposed amid the ruins of the houses among which it stood.

There were souvenirs enough for an army, let alone a squadron, and we were fortunate when collecting them not to fall into a single "booby trap," such as a helmet which exploded when picked up. This expedition is also described by Molesworth in another letter:

60 Squadron R.F.C.,
B.E.F., France.
March 1917.

The rumour about leave is true, so my turn ought to come in a few days, as my name is next on the list. The weather has been hopeless lately for aviation. Yesterday some of us decided to go and have a look at the old Boche trenches. We chose the ones west of Adinfer Wood, as they were less likely to be mined than those further north.

Having seized a tender, we pushed off after breakfast towards the line. We got to our front trenches at about ten o'clock and left the tender here, as the road was still in pretty bad repair. No Man's Land was dotted about with shell holes. A few broken stumps of trees lined the road—war-worn veterans that had stood the test of battle. (Amongst other souvenirs, I am bringing you back a walking stick made from a branch of one of these.) There was a wood, or what remained of it, to our right front, as this part of the line had been very quiet and was nothing compared to the utter desolation of the Somme or "Arras" battlefields.

The German system of trenches consisted of thick belts of barbed wire, behind which was a trench about 10 feet deep, with platforms and machine-gun emplacements to shoot from. About every 50 yards or so, square openings led down to the underground dugouts. The old Hun seems to have lived fairly comfortably, as there were beds and tables here and there, with storerooms and passages connecting each dugout.

We went about collecting souvenirs very gingerly, as warnings of booby traps were posted up everywhere we went. But luckily no one was caught out. We managed to collect some tin hats, bombs, Very pistols, and a few other odds and ends, which we loaded into the tender.

I am bringing some of these home.

Orders have just come through for us to go on another balloon strafe, so I will finish this when we come back if old Fritz doesn't stop me.

* * * * *

(Two hours later)

Here I am back again, with a Hun and a "sausage" added to my bag. I am fearfully bucked with life, as the major has just told me that I have been made a "flight commander." No time for any more, as I

*am just off to have a cheery time with the other lads, who seem to have
done pretty well too.*

That the enemy knew that the British intended to attack was evident
because the numbers of the aforementioned V-strut Albatros scouts had
obviously increased on this front. The performance of these machines was
considerably better than the Nieuport, and they had two Spandau guns
firing through the propeller, and moreover, the circus of red machines led,
so they said, by Richthofen, was functioning freely throughout the month
of March 1917. It is perhaps unnecessary to repeat that the offensive in
the air commences always before the push on the ground, and though the
latter was timed to commence on April 10, 60 had a hard month to go
through before this date arrived.

We were short of scout squadrons at this time, and though 48, the
first Bristol fighter squadron, and 56, another new squadron equipped
with the S.E.5s, had arrived from England, these were to be kept as a surprise for the Boche and were not to cross the line until "zero day," as the
day fixed for the first assault was called. With 56 Ball had come out again
from England, and it was during this battle that he was killed, on May 7,
1917, after a severe engagement in which Meintjies, who also had been
posted to 56 after a period of rest at home, was badly wounded; the latter
is one of the best pilots and almost the most popular officer 60 ever had.

The flight commanders at this time, mid-March 1917, were K. L.
Caldwell, who when on leave fell sick and did not return till June. He
was a New Zealander, a great friend of Meintjies, and was beloved by
everyone. He was a curious instance of a fine and fearless fighter but a
bad shot at this time, who in consequence did not get many Huns; he
afterward remedied this defect and made a great reputation both in 60
and when commanding 74 in 1918. The other two were Alan Binnie, an
Australian who had fought with the 9th Division in Gallipoli, and Black,
who went sick and was subsequently posted away.

At the beginning of this month (on the day before Graves's death,
to be exact), W. A. Bishop joined. The son of a well-known family in
Montreal, he had passed through the Royal Military College and had
joined the Canadian Cavalry, coming over with his regiment with the

first Canadian contingent. On arrival in England, he very soon applied to join the Flying Corps and was posted as an observer to No. 7 Squadron. After a tour of duty in France in this capacity, he went home to learn to fly and was posted to us almost as soon as he had got his wings.

It was curious to notice how quick the mechanics of the squadron were to recognize Bishop's quality. Only a few days after his arrival at the squadron, the sergeants gave a musical evening to which the officers were invited, and it was observed that one of the very few toasts which were proposed by them was that of Bishop's health, although at this time he had only destroyed one enemy machine, and none of his fellow officers had, as yet, any idea of the brilliant career that was in store for him. This occasion, on which he got his first Hun, was remarkable for the fact that his engine failed and forced him to land very near the frontline trenches. He only, in fact, just succeeded in scraping over. The failure of the engine was due to his inexperience in allowing it to choke while diving. Having landed in a very unhealthy spot, he got rapidly into a dugout occupied by some field gunners and, with their help, moved his machine every half hour to prevent the German artillery shelling it. During the night he borrowed a toothbrush from the gunner officer and with this contrived to clean the sparking plugs of his engine. Having heard nothing of him, the squadron had already reported him missing, when he succeeded in getting a telephone message through to say that he was safe.

Our Corps machines, the eyes of the artillery, were being shot down every day in the valley of the Scarpe, despite our efforts and those of 29 (also with Nieuports) and 11, an F.E.2B. squadron. The ground on both sides of the river was littered with B.E.s. The scouts, whose losses were much heavier, fell usually far over the lines in hostile territory.

The work at this time still consisted mainly of offensive patrols (whose business it was to operate east of the artillery machines and to keep the air clear of hostile scouts), reconnaissances, and sometimes escorts to bombing and photographic patrols. On April 7 M. B. Knowles, C. S. Hall, and G. O. Smart—the latter was originally an N.C.O. pilot who had but lately been commissioned for gallantry in the field—all failed to return after an engagement with a much superior force of the enemy. At this time it was very hard to get all the photographs wanted by the army, owing to the enemy's activity in the air, and when special information about some point was required, 60 was sometimes given the job of taking the photographs. It was thought that the Huns would not expect a scout to be doing photography, and they were not overkeen, even at that time, on attacking a scout formation. It was no easy task this, to fly a sensitive single-seater, look out for Huns, and expose plates at the same time, but it was done with some measure of success. Here follows Molesworth's description of a fight:

> *60 Squadron R.F.C.,*
> *B.E.F., France.*
> April 1917.
>> *A Hun at last!*
>> *We started out this morning, led by our new squadron commander, who seems one of the best. Our late C.O. was brought down in flames, this side of the lines, in a scrap. He was a very great loss to the squadron, and we buried him, with full military honours, in a little village cemetery nearby.*
>> *There were five of us on the patrol, my position being the rear one on the left. We got to the lines at about 10,000 feet and crossed them, making towards Douai. Soon we sighted a small patrol of Sopwith two-seaters, northeast of Arras, flying towards the lines as hard as they could go, with a large pack of Huns chasing them. The latter managed to get the last machine in flames, the poor devils going down burning like a furnace.*
>> *The major immediately dived for the Huns, and I knew that I was in for my first real big scrap. The leader saw us coming and turned east with his nose well down; however, we soon caught him up and started scrapping. Then ensued the usual dogfight. I managed to get well behind a Hun two-seater which was a little way out of the scrap. He didn't seem to mind me plugging him a bit and went calmly on. In my excitement I lost my head and started spinning madly to the ground. Coming out, I saw an Albatros scout about 50 yards ahead, so loosed off at him and saw him spin and crash on the ground, much to my delight.*

Having lost the rest of the formation, I headed for home and found out, on landing, that we had accounted for three Huns. The two-seater which I had been trying to worry was known as the "Flying Pig," owing to the likeness of the observer to that rotund animal.

Talking about casualties, we have had a pretty hot time the last few days. However, twenty Huns have been accounted for during this time, and many more sent down out of control, so we hope to put up a record in the R.F.C.

From the last week in March to the last week in May, our losses were very severe; in fact, counting those who went sick and those injured in crashes on our side of the line, we lost thirty-five officers during these eight weeks, almost twice the strength of the squadron, which consisted of eighteen pilots and the squadron commander. One weekend in April, the 14th, 15th, and 16th, was especially unlucky, as on Saturday "A" Flight went out six machines strong (full strength) and only one returned. Binnie was leading and was hit in the shoulder when trying to extricate two of his patrol from a cloud of enemies. The blood from his wound spurted all over the nacelle, obscuring the instruments, and in addition his machine caught fire. He extinguished the flames and then fainted when gliding homeward. The machine must have turned west after this, for he woke up in a little park in Lens, having hit the ground while still unconscious, without further serious injuries. He lost his arm at the shoulder and was a prisoner till the spring of 1918, when he was repatriated and immediately commenced flying again. He was a very great loss to the squadron, as he was a first-class flight commander, who had already destroyed several Huns and would have got a lot more. On the next day, Sunday, "B" Flight, five strong, lost two pilots: one, Milot, a French-Canadian major, who was killed; the other, Hervey, who had already gained two Military Crosses as an observer and promised very well, was forced to land on the other side by antiaircraft fire. On this patrol Bishop, who had just been promoted captain, got two Huns and a balloon, having had five or six combats. On Monday "C" Flight (Bishop's) went out without the flight commander, and only one, Young, returned; this meant that in three days, ten out of eighteen pilots were lost and had to be replaced from England by officers who had never flown this particular type of machine because there were none in England. Our new machines were collected from Paris, and the chance of a trip to fly one back was eagerly looked forward to by every pilot.

Some of these new machines were not well built and began—to add to our troubles—to break up in the air. Lieut. Grandin's fell to bits while diving on a hostile two-seater, though this may have been due to injury from machine-gun fire. Caffyn's and Brackenbury's collapsed when practicing firing at ground targets on the aerodrome, and the former was killed, while Ross's wings folded upwards when pulling out of a dive after firing a burst; he was badly injured but has since recovered. A good show was that put up by Penny, who, when his left lower plane came off while diving on a Hun, contrived to fly the machine back and to land at one of our aerodromes and quietly reported to the squadron commander as follows: "My lower plane came off, so I thought I had better land. Sorry I left the patrol, sir." The reason for these accidents was that badly seasoned wood was being used by the French manufacturers, who also allowed a lot of little screws to be inserted in the main spars, thus weakening them considerably. H.Q. were informed, and the matter was put right.

During this battle the R.F.C. began to take a hand in the ground operations by machine-gunning support troops during an attack. "C" Flight led by Fry, who was given an M.C. for this, did well on May 11 by shooting up the enemy in a cutting east of the chemical works at Roeux, in the valley of the Scarpe. These pilots came back, having exhausted their ammunition, refilled with petrol and 300 rounds, and dashed off again to the chemical works without waiting for orders. One of them, E. S. Howard, who was killed seven days later on an escort to machines doing photography, thus described this adventure:

May 13, 1917.

On Friday night the infantry made an attack east of Fampoux, and we were told off to assist them. When they went over the top, we dived down and emptied our machine guns into the Hun trenches. Our people put up a wonderful barrage; it was good to see but not at all nice to fly over, as the bursts from the shells threw the machines about. We have just come back from a show, chased four Huns away over their lines, and then flew round keeping our eye on them so they could not come back.

This "low flying," as it was called, became more popular with the higher command, though not with the pilots, as the war went on, and in fact, during the German offensive of March 1918, it was said to have very materially helped to stop the Boche advance on the 5th and 3rd Army fronts.

Hostile balloons also were constantly attacked during April and May, and Bishop, Ross, Molesworth, and Penny did considerable execution. Others who were doing well at this time were Langwill, Hall, J. Elliott, Smart, and F. Bower; the last named on April 2 pursued, with his patrol, six hostile scouts a long way east of Douai in a very strong westerly wind, and though shot through the stomach and with his intestines hanging out, he flew west and landed his machine near Chipilly, completely undamaged except from enemy bullets. He died next day, and his machine was flown back to the squadron without having had to be repaired by another pilot. A fight as a result of which R. B. Clark, an Australian, was killed on April 30 is well described below:

60 Squadron R.F.C.,
B.E.F., France.
April 1917.

We are all feeling rather down in our luck today, as news has come through that one of our chaps has "gone west" in hospital. He put up an awfully "stout" show against the Hun.

It was on one of our big balloon shows. He was attacked by three Hun scouts just after firing at the "gas-bag." He scrapped them all the way back to the lines, crashing one of them and holding the other two off. As he crossed the trenches, one of them plugged him in the petrol tank, and his grid caught on fire. As he was only about 50 feet up, he managed to get her down in the shell holes, or rather a strip of ground between them, without burning himself badly. Luck was all against him, however, as he just tippled over into a trench at the end of his run. A few men who were in an advanced dressing station nearby quickly came to his rescue and hauled him clear of the burning wreckage, but the poor devil was by this time badly singed about the legs. He insisted on giving his report before allowing the doctor to attend to his burns, and the men told me afterwards that he was extremely plucky.

The day after this occurred, I was detailed to find the machine and see if it could be salved. The weather was absolutely vile. We started for Arras with a tender and trailer, got there about noon, and commenced making inquiries as to where the machine had crashed. One place was pointed out to us where there was an old "quirk," which had obviously been brought down doing artillery work. Then we were sent off in another direction, only to find the remains of an old Boche two-seater. At last, after an hour's wading in trenches with mud up to our knees and shells bursting near us, we arrived at the advanced dressing station. Here we were given a full description of the fine way in which our pilot had fought.

The machine, needless to say, was a total wreck, and so, after a cup of tea with a drop of gin in it to warm us up, we pushed off home, followed by some heavy shells which we knew meant the commencement of the "evening hate."

Hardly a day passed during April and May without Bishop destroying at least one Hun machine, and on June 2, 1917, he visited an enemy aerodrome near Cambrai—a long way over—by himself at dawn and found seven machines on the ground with their engines running. They began to take off, and he destroyed four, returning safely with his machine considerably shot about by machine-gun fire from the ground. For this exploit, after three months of remarkably fine work, he was awarded the Victoria Cross. Others who were prominent during the Battles of Arras and Vimy Ridge were Pidcock, "Red" Lloyd and "Black" Lloyd (the latter, a fine officer, was unfortunately shot down and killed), and Fry (who drove down a Hun on our side and found in the pilot's pocket a ticket for a box in Cambrai theater dated the day before). Molesworth also was doing well; he afterward went to 29 on a second tour of duty with the R.F.C. in France (he had already seen service overseas with the infantry), where he did most brilliantly during the winter of 1917–1918. His account of a successful balloon attack is given here in full:

60 Squadron R.F.C.,
B.E.F., France.
April 1917.

Still more excitement! I tackled my first balloon yesterday and consider it even more difficult than going for a Hun; at least, I think one gets a hotter time. We had received orders a week ago that all balloons had be to driven down or destroyed, as they were worrying our infantry and gunners during the advance.

We had been practising firing the Le Prieur rockets for some time—a most weird performance. One dives at a target on the ground and, when within about fifty yards of it, presses a button on the instrument boards. Immediately there is a most awful hissing noise, which can be heard above the roar of the engine, and six huge rockets shoot forward from the struts, each side towards the target.

We did not think these were much of a success, owing to the difficulty of hitting anything, so decided to use tracer and Buckingham bullets instead. These are filled with a compound of phosphorus and leave a long trail of smoke behind them.

On the morning we were detailed to attack the balloons, the weather was so "dud" that none of them were up, although we went across twice to have a look. We got a pretty hot time from Archie, as we had to fly below the clouds, which were about 2,000 feet, and dodge about all over the shop. Next day the weather cleared, and we decided to carry out our strafe.

We all went off individually to the various balloons which had been allotted us. I am glad to say most of us managed to do them down. I personally crossed the trenches at about 10,000 feet, dropping all the time towards my sausage, which was five or six miles away. It was floating in company with another at about 3,000 feet and reminded me of that little song, "Two Little Sausages."

I started a straight dive towards them, and then the fun began. Archie got quite annoyed, following me down to about 5,000 feet, where I was met by two or three strings of flaming onions, luckily too far off to do any damage. Then came thousands of machine-gun bullets from the ground—evidently I was not going to get them without some trouble. I zigzagged about a bit, still heading for the balloons and, when within 200 yards, opened fire. The old Huns in the basket got wind up and jumped out in their parachute. Not bothering about them, I kept my sight on one of the balloons and saw the tracer going right into it and causing it to smoke.

As our armament consists of a Lewis gun, I had to now change drums. This is a pretty ticklish job when you have about ten machine guns loosing off at you, not to mention all the other small trifles! However, I managed to do it without getting more than half a dozen or so bullet holes in my grid.

By this time the second balloon was almost on the floor. I gave it a burst, which I don't think did any damage. The first sausage was in flames, so I buzzed off home without meeting any Huns. On the way back, a good shot from Archie exploded very near my tail and carried away part of the elevator. Don't you think this is the limit for anyone who wants excitement? I must say I prefer it to the infantry, as one gets decent food and a comfortable bed every night, if you are lucky enough to get back.

I am afraid these letters are awfully full of my own "shows," but none of the other chaps will tell me about theirs, so I can't describe them to you; however, it's much the same for all of us. Please forgive me, and don't think it's swank!

There are rumours that leave is going to start again soon, so I hope to see you in a few weeks.

One day in early June, General Allenby, then commanding the 3rd Army, was to inspect the squadron at nine o'clock in the morning. The squadron commander had gone out by himself in his Nieuport at dawn, unshaved, in pajamas, a Burberry, bedroom slippers, and snowboots, a costume which many of us used to affect on the dawn patrol. The line was unusually quiet that morning, so he ventured almost to Douai and on turning west saw a formation of eight or nine machines over Visen-Artois, near the front line, well below him at about 8,000 feet. They turned and, the sun glinting on the fuselage, showed a bright flash of red. This meant that they were Huns, and not only Huns but "the Circus." Having the advantage of height and as the formation was very near the line, he determined to try and do a little damage. He flew toward them from the east and from the sun and, diving on the top machine, fired a burst and pulled sharply up, being careful to retain his height. After a few dives of this kind without doing much apparent damage, an S.E.5 patrol of 56, which had seen the scrap, bustled up, and a very pretty "dog-fight" ensued, in the course of which one of the Huns detached himself from the mêlée and appeared to be going home. This was the Nieuport's opportunity, so, hardening his heart, he dived right in, making good shooting. The Albatros appeared to take no notice but flew straight on. (In parenthesis it may be observed that this is a good sign, as it usually means the pilot is dead, for if the opposing machine begins to perform frantic evolutions, the pilot is as a rule very much alive and not in the least "out of control.") Flushed with excitement, the Nieuport man put the stick (control column) between his knees and, going down on the tail of the Albatros, began to put a fresh drum of ammunition on to his Lewis gun, with which alone this type of machine was armed. While thus busily engaged, something made him turn his head to see about twenty yards behind him the white nose of a grim-looking Albatros. Swifter than thought, the Nieuport was wrenched to the right, and even as she turned, the Albatros's Spandau guns spat out a burst, which riddled the engine and cut the bottom out of the petrol tank, allowing all the remaining petrol to pour onto the pilot's feet. The height of both machines at this moment was about 5,000 feet, the locality just east of Monchy-le-Preux, and but for the attentions of the Boche machine, it would have been comparatively easy for the Nieuport to glide back to Arras and perch on one of our advanced landing grounds or on the race course; but with a bloodthirsty Hun on one's tail and a dead engine, the problem, however, was not such a simple one.

Twisting and turning like a snipe, the Nieuport began to descend, taking care to make his turns as much as possible toward our side of the line. Mercifully the wind was from the east. Close behind followed the

Albatros, firing short bursts at frequent intervals but always wide because it is not easy to hit a machine whose pilot knows you are there. It was a stout Hun, however, who would not be denied but continued the chase down to 300 feet, a few hundred yards west of Monchy-le-Preux, when he suddenly turned and flew home to report, no doubt, a British machine destroyed. With a gasp of relief, the Nieuport pilot turned his attention to the ground and, seeing nothing but shell holes beneath him, made up his mind that a crash was inevitable. Suddenly a strip of ground about a hundred yards long and very narrow but free from shell holes caught his eye, and putting in a couple of "S" turns, he made a good, slow landing. The machine ran on and had almost stopped when a shell hole appeared, and she ran very gently into it without doing any damage whatever.

A couple of dusty gunners walked up and before speaking produced a packet of Woodbines, one of which the Nieuport pilot greedily took and lit. Inquiries showed that an advanced antiaircraft section was nearby, where the officer in charge gave the airman breakfast and, better still, produced a telephone, with the help of which he got into communication with his squadron and ordered a car to come straight through Arras and up the Cambrai road. It was getting late, and an army commander's inspection was not a thing to be treated lightly. Further inquiries disclosed an artillery ammunition column in a little valley who lent him a horse and an orderly. There was no saddle, but the pilot climbed gratefully onto the animal, which had very rough paces and a hard mouth, and set out toward the road. In a short time, he met the car and drove furiously through Arras and back to Le Hameau, only to see Allenby, the R.F.C. brigade commander (General J. R. Higgins), and George Pretyman arriving at the station. His costume being hardly that prescribed for inspections, the wretched officer dived into his hut, did the quickest shave on record, and timidly approached the glittering cortège.

Everyone was furious with him except General Allenby, who was rather amused and very kind. He got, however, a well-deserved and proper "telling-off" from the brigadier and wing commander and saw the troupe depart with a feeling of profound relief.

The account of this scrap has been given at some length, but it should not be assumed that it was in any way exceptional. It should be remembered that during the squadron's history there have been about 1,500 distinct combats in the air, all of which deserve a detailed description. Within the limits of a book of this kind, however, it cannot be done.

We made a hard tennis court in Tetus's orchard with red *pierre de fosse* from the Bruay mines and discovered that Caldwell, Molesworth, Horn, and both Lloyds were all good tennis players. With the beginning of June, things quietened down on the 3rd Army front. Colonel Pretyman, O.C. 13th Wing, put the squadron onto wireless interception. This term needs, perhaps, a little explanation. Everyone knows, of course, that both German and British artillery observation machines were fitted with wireless sets, by means of which the pilots corrected the shooting of the gunners for whom they were observing.

These wireless messages were "tapped" by our compass stations, and it was discovered that two of these stations could get a cross-bearing on any machines registering for the enemy artillery. By linking up the compass station with an aerodrome by telephone, it was possible to send off a patrol of scouts to chase off or destroy the artillery machine as soon as he began to send down fire signals; i.e., as soon as he was actually directing the fire of the enemy batteries. This was useful though exhausting work for pilots, for the Hun, who did his registration chiefly in the morning, when the sun was behind him in the east, usually saw the scouts coming before they saw him and turned and dived three or four miles back behind his own lines, where it was very difficult to attack him, even if he was visible, which usually he was not, as our scouts were looking for a machine at 5,000 or 6,000 feet in a certain place, whereas it was probably at that moment at a height of 1,500 feet some five miles east of the bearing given. As soon, therefore, as the scouts, seeing nothing, turned back to return to the aerodrome, the Hun swung up again and resumed his registration.

The British pilots, on returning to their aerodrome, would find an irate squadron commander who had just got a telephone message from the compass station to say that V.K., or whatever the call sign used by that particular machine might be, was working again quite happily and, "What the devil was 60's patrol doing, anyhow?" Off the wretched patrol had to go again, only to go through the same performance. It is only fair to say, however, that they did get a good many two-seaters in this way, though the main result was, perhaps, seen rather in the enormously decreased amount of artillery observation the Germans were enabled to do than in hostile artillery machines shot down by us.

This work, however, was genuinely exhausting, as in order efficiently to answer the compass calls, as they were termed, three or four pilots always had to be standing by to leap into their machines and be off the ground, in formation, inside of two minutes. Nevertheless, they became extraordinarily smart at this maneuver and answered to the hunting horn—doubled blasts of which were the signal at that time—as keenly as a fashionable pack of foxhounds. Only those who know how irritating a thing an aero engine can be when you are in a hurry to start can appreciate the high standard of efficiency attained by 60's mechanics, which made it almost a certainty that the 120 seconds' limit would not be exceeded.

The next few paragraphs will show how this maneuver struck one of the pilots at this time:

60 Squadron R.F.C.,
B.E.F., France.
July 1917.

The tennis court we made three months ago is now in topping condition, so we decided to get up a tournament amongst ourselves. Yesterday we drew lots for partners. The unlucky lad who drew me is a "coloured troop"; that is, he hails from South Africa. He is quite good at the "Willies," and so I think we have got a fair chance. I expect you wonder where all these weird names come from. They are invented by one of our flight commanders, who is also a "coloured troop" and one of the leading lights of the squadron. All jobs are washed out today as the weather is "dud," so two of us are going over this afternoon to the village nearby to purchase articles of furniture for the "Hôtel de Commerce."

You will be pleased to hear that we are getting a new kind of grid. It is supposed to be a good deal faster than the Hun and can dive to 300 miles an hour, so I'm told. We shall probably have a quiet time while we are getting used to them and only do "line patrols" for the first fortnight or so. A French "ace" landed here today; he says the Huns are getting a pretty bad time down south. Jolly glad I'm not a Hun airman these days, with men up against me like some of our chaps. Most of them are fairly old hands at the game now, and we are really beginning to properly annoy our friends across the way. The work has been fairly hard lately: two patrols in the morning, one generally at dawn and the other about noon, with "wireless interruption" in the afternoon. The latter is rather a strenuous job. This is how we work it: When a Hun two-seater begins to register on any part of our front, a telephone message, giving his height and locality, is immediately sent through to the wireless squadron. Each scout squadron in the wing takes it in turn.

As soon as the recording officer receives the message, he sounds a horn. Three of us who are standing by in readiness immediately jump into our machines, and the leader gets hold of the position and height of the Hun. Then we push off as quickly as possible to the lines and a sort of "hide-and-seek" begins. We try if possible to hide in the clouds and approach the Hun when he is off his guard. He, on the other hand, departs hurriedly into Hunland when he spots us, and as soon as we go, he comes back to carry on his job. We then turn on him again, but he is off like a flash, and so it goes on until the next three machines relieve us. It is really quite amusing at times, and although we do not often bring our man down, we give him such a devil of a time that he hasn't much of it to spare for his companions on the ground. Our "stunt merchant" is good at this game and continues to add to his score, seldom coming back without firing his red light. He works by himself a lot now, preferring to surprise the Hun by hiding rather than by trying to get him in a scrap. Wish I could do the same. I always feel so fagged after a patrol that I haven't got the energy or the patience to sit up in the clouds waiting for a chance to bag a "lone Hun."

You remember the petrol tank which was so shot up the time I was brought down? Well, I am having it made into a topping inkstand. The souvenirs are coming in in fine style, and I hope to have quite a good collection by the time I see dear old "Blighty" again.

After the battle had died down, the sorely tried pilots were given, whenever possible, one day's rest in three, and the following letter shows that the device was appreciated:

60 Squadron R.F.C.,
B.E.F., France.
June 1917.

> *It is funny hearing the war again after being on leave so long. We had quite a good crossing, although I had a deuce of a time getting onto the boat at Folkestone. The silly ass of a porter had carted all my baggage onboard, including the leave warrant, which was in my British-warm pocket. I had to persuade the A.M.L.O. I wasn't a Hun spy, and after a long discussion, he let me on.*

> *The major seemed pleased to have me back, and they all had great stories to tell about our "stunt merchant," who had been putting up a jolly good show by bringing down umpteen Huns. His star turn was the shooting up of an aerodrome. He started off at dawn by himself and arrived over the aerodrome he had planned to attack. Finding that there was nothing doing here, he pushed off to look for trouble elsewhere. Suddenly he saw the hangars of another aerodrome. He attacked these with much gusto, and when the Huns came up to do him down, he crashed two of them and drove another into the trees. He also managed to flatten out a large number of mechanics and put pukka wind up the rest. You can imagine how the fat old Huns ran, as nothing like this had ever happened to them before. I believe his name has been put in for something big in the decoration line.*

> *It has been arranged that we get one day off in every three, which gives us a bit of spare time. We had ours off today. Four of us aviated over to Paris-Plage, near Etaples, this afternoon and tested our grids by firing into the sea. Afterwards we landed opposite the Hôtel Continental and left our machines there under a guard. We wandered about the village for a bit and then started for home, stunting about to amuse the populace, which had collected on the front to see us off. We all got home safely just as it was getting dark.*

LIST OF OFFICERS WHO HAVE SERVED IN 60 SQUADRON

Together with the decorations gained by them, not necessarily in the squadron; all officers are shown in the highest rank to which they attained during the war.

Name	Casualty	Date
2/Lieut. A. R. Adam	Missing	July 1917
Lieut. J. R. Anderson	Killed	Aug. 1918
Capt. D. V. Armstrong, D.F.C. (151 Sqdn.)	Killed	May 1916
Lieut. J. L. Armstrong.	—	Jan. 1918
Lieut. (A/Capt.) F. L. Atkinson	Injured	April 1917
2/Lieut. W. R. Ayling	—	Nov. 1918
Lieut. J. Baalman	—	Aug. 1917
Lieut. D. H. Bacon	Missing	Nov. 1916
Lieut. C. G. Baker	—	Jan. 1917
Major H. H. Balfour, M.C. and Bar, Croix de Guerre (French)	—	May 1916
Capt. A. Ball, V.C., D.S.O., and 2 Bars, M.C., Order of St. George (Russian, 4th Class), Croix de Chevalier (French)	Killed	Sept. 1916
Lieut. A. C. Ball	Missing	Feb. 1918
Lieut. H. J. O. Barnett	—	Jan. 1918
Lieut. J. N. Bartlett	—	June 1918
F/Officer H. F. V. Battle	Wounded	Sept. 1918
Capt. A. Beck, D.F.C.	—	June 1918
Capt. J. D. Belgrave, M.C. and Bar	Missing	April 1918
Major A. D. Bell-Irving, M.C. and Bar, Croix de Guerre	Wounded	May 1916
2/Lieut. I. Bigood	—	May 1916
Capt. A. Binnie, M.C.	Missing	April 1917
Lieut. Col. W. A. Bishop, V.C., D.S.O. and Bar, M.C., D.F.C., Croix de Chevalier, Legion of Honour, Croix de Guerre with Palm (French)	—	April 1917

Name	Casualty	Date
Capt. C. T. Black	—	March 1917
Capt. C. L. Blake	—	June 1917
Lieut. R. C. W. Blessley (U.S. Air Service)	Wounded	Sept. 1918
2/Lieut. F. Bower	Killed	April 1917
Lieut. H. S. Brackenbury	Injured	March 1917
Capt. N. A. Browning-Paterson	Killed	May 1916
Capt. W. E. G. Bryant, M.B.E.	Wounded	May 1916
Lieut. H. E. W. Bryning	—	June 1918
2/Lieut. H. Buckley	Wounded	Aug. 1918
2/Lieut. E. A. Burbidge	—	Sept. 1918
2/Lieut. C. M. H. M. Caffyn	Killed	March 1917
Major K. L. Caldwell, M.C., D.F.C. and Bar, Croix de Guerre (Belgian)	—	Jan. 1917
Lieut. K. T. Campbell	Died	June 1918
Lieut. L. H. T. Capel	—	Feb. 1918
Capt. C. W. Carleton, A.F.C.	—	Dec. 1916
2/Lieut. W. M. Carlyle	Missing	Oct. 1916
Lieut. A. Carter, M.M.	—	Sept. 1917
2/Lieut. W. E. Cass	Died	Aug. 1916
Lieut. G. F. Caswell	Missing	Sept. 1918
Capt. J. C. A. Caunter	Missing	Oct. 1917
2/Lieut. L. C. Chapman	Missing	April 1917
Capt. L. S. Charles	Missing	July 1916
Capt. R. L. Chidlaw-Roberts, M.C.	—	Sept. 1917
2/Lieut. E. W. Christie	Missing	April 1918
Capt. S. Clare, M.B.E.	—	Jan. 1918
Capt. F. W. Clark, A.F.C.	—	Jan. 1918
2/Lieut. L. L. Clark	Killed	May 1916
2/Lieut. R. B. Clark	Died of Wounds	April 1917
Major A. C. Clarke	—	Aug. 1918
Lieut. J. H. Cock	Missing	April 1917
A/Capt. E. S. T. Cole, M.C.	—	Sept. 1916
Capt. J. Collier, D.F.C. (80 Sqdn.)	—	July 1917
Capt. W. H. K. Copeland	—	March 1918

Name	Casualty	Date
Lieut. G. F. Court	—	Nov. 1917
2/Lieut. G. B. Craig	Missing	Feb. 1918
Lieut. F. D. Crane	—	Jan. 1918
Capt. K. Crawford	Missing	April 1918
Lieut. H. D. Crompton	—	Sept. 1917
Lieut. (A/Capt.) J. B. Crompton	—	Sept. 1917
Major C. M. Crowe, M.C., D.F.C.	—	July 1918
Lieut. C. F. Cunningham	—	Jan. 1918
F/Lieut. A. P. V. Daly	—	Nov. 1916
Capt. I. Meredyth Davies	—	April 1918
Lieut. W. B. Day	—	Oct. 1918
Capt. G. C. Dell-Clarke, M.C.	Killed	July 1918
2/Lieut. E. W. C. Densham	—	Sept. 1918
F/Lieut. G. W. Dobson, O.B.E.	—	Oct. 1916
Capt. J. E. Doyle, D.F.C.	Missing	Sept. 1918
Lieut. L. Drummond	—	Aug. 1916
Capt. J. M. Drysdale	Wounded	Aug. 1916
Lieut. G. L. Du Cros	—	June 1918
Capt. G. M. Duncan, D.F.C.	—	Aug. 1918
Capt. W. J. A. Duncan, M.C. and Bar	—	Nov. 1917
2/Lieut. (Hon. Lieut.) J. Elgood	—	July 1916
Lieut. G. F. Elliott	—	Sept. 1917
Lieut. J. McC. Elliott	Missing	April 1917
Lieut. C. D. Evans	—	Jan. 1918
2/Lieut. J. J. Fitzgerald	Missing	Oct. 1917
2/Lieut. H. T. Flintoft	—	July 1918
2/Lieut. J. H. Flynn	Killed	Sept. 1917
Major E. L. Foot, M.C.	—	Oct. 1916
2/Lieut. C. V. Forsyth	—	Nov. 1918
Lieut. C. W. France	—	Aug. 1918
Capt. W. M. Fry, M.C.	—	Jan. 1917
Capt. P. E. M. Le Gallais, A.F.C.	—	Aug. 1916
Lieut. W. P. Garnett	Missing	March 1917
Lieut. F. O. Gibbon	—	July 1917
Major E. J. L. W. Gilchrist, M.C., D.F.C.	Wounded	Dec. 1916

Name	Casualty	Date
Lieut. W. Gilchrist	Missing	May 1917
Capt. G. A. Giles	—	Jan. 1917
Lieut. H. Good	—	May 1916
Capt. F. E. Goodrich, M.C.	Killed	Sept. 1916
Lieut. H. A. Gordon	Missing	July 1918
2/Lieut. R. J. Grandin	Missing	July 1917
Major E. P. Graves	Killed	March 1917
Hon. Capt. D. B. Gray, M.C.	—	May 1916
F/Lieut. E. O. Grenfell, M.C., A.F.C.	Wounded	Dec. 1916
F/Officer J. S. Griffith, D.F.C. and Bar, Order of St. Vladimir, 4th Class	Wounded	July 1918
2/Lieut. W. H. Gunner, M.C.	Missing	July 1917
Capt. H. W. Guy, Croix de Guerre (Belgian)	—	June 1917
Lieut. C. S. Hall	Missing	April 1917
Lieut. J. G. Hall	Missing	Nov. 1918
Lieut. H. Hamer, A.F.C.	—	Feb. 1917
Capt. H. A. Hamersley, M.C.	—	Sept. 1917
Lieut. H. T. Hammond	Missing	Sept. 1917
2/Lieut. L. P. Harlow	—	Nov. 1918
Lieut. H. Harris	—	May 1916
2/Lieut. R. M. Harris	Killed	June 1917
2/Lieut. J. J. A. Hawtrey	Missing	Sept. 1917
Lieut. J. Headlam	Killed	May 1918
Major J. N. D. Heenan	—	June 1916
Capt. H. G. Hegarty, M.C.	—	Jan. 1918
Lieut. G. W. Hemsworth	—	Jan. 1918
Lieut. C. R. Henderson	—	March 1918
Lieut. N. P. Henderson	Wounded	April 1917
Capt. E. G. Herbert	Wounded	Jan. 1917
Lieut. H. E. Hervey, M.C. and Bar	Missing	April 1917
2/Lieut. F. A. Hickson	—	Sept. 1918
Sqdn. Ldr. R. M. Hill, M.C., A.F.C.	—	Aug. 1916
Capt. C. Holland, M.C.	—	Dec. 1916
2/Lieut. R. Hopper	Killed	Jan. 1917
F/Lieut. S. B. Horn, M.C.	—	Sept. 1917

Name	Casualty	Date
2/Lieut. E. S. Howard	Killed	May 1917
2/Lieut. G. D. Hunter	Missing	May 1917
2/Lieut. W. E. Jenkins	Killed	Nov. 1917
Lieut. O. P. Johnson	—	July 1918
Lieut. B. S. Johnston	—	Aug. 1918
Lieut. R. N. K. Jones, M.C.	—	July 1916
Lieut. P. S. Joyce	Missing	March 1917
Capt. R. C. Kean	—	Jan. 1917
Capt. G. D. F. Keddie	—	May 1916
Lieut. S. W. Keen, M.C.	Died of Wounds	Aug. 1916
Lieut. C. M. Kelly	—	Aug. 1916
2/Lieut. W. M. Kent	Missing	Feb. 1918
Lieut. J. F. M. Kerr	—	Aug. 1918
2/Lieut. J. L. Kight	—	Aug. 1916
2/Lieut. R. E. Kimbell	Missing	April 1917
2/Lieut. C. H. M. King	Killed	Sept. 1916
Capt. A. N. Kingwill	—	Feb. 1917
Lieut. R. A. Kirkpatrick	—	April 1918
Capt. H. Kirton	—	Jan. 1917
Capt. M. B. Knowles	Missing	April 1917
Lieut. R. H. Knowles	—	—
Lieut. T. Langwill	Missing	April 1917
Capt. J. D. Latta, M.C.	—	Nov. 1916
2/Lieut. J. Laurie-Reid	—	May 1916
Lieut. (Hon. Capt.) J. K. Law	Missing	Sept. 1917
2/Lieut. L. H. Leckie	—	April 1917
Lieut. H. M. Lewis	—	July 1917
Lieut. R. G. Lewis	Missing	March 1918
Lieut. D. R. C. Lloyd	Missing	June 1917
Capt. E. A. Lloyd	—	Jan. 1917
Major G. L. Lloyd, M.C., A.F.C.	—	June 1917
Lieut. L. B. Loughran, American Air Service	Killed	July 1918
2/Lieut. J. C. Louw	—	March 1918
Lieut. (Hon. Capt.) R. J. S. Lund	—	Sept. 1918

Name	Casualty	Date
Capt. J. D. McCall	—	Nov. 1917
Lieut. W. F. McCarthy	Wounded	Nov. 1918
Lieut. E. J. C. McCracken	Missing	Aug. 1918
Major J. B. McCudden, V.C., D.S.O. and Bar M.C. and Bar, Croix de Guerre, Mil. Medal	Killed	July 1918
F/Lieut. B. McEntegart	—	Aug. 1918
Lieut. I. C. MacGregor	Injured	Sept. 1917
2/Lieut. C. W. McKissock	Missing	May 1917
2/Lieut. R. D. McLennan	Killed	Dec. 1917
Lieut. J. E. C. MacVicker	Killed	June 1918
2/Lieut. N. C. Mackey	—	Sept. 1918
2/Lieut. H. E. Martin	Killed	Nov. 1916
F/Officer S. J. Mason	—	Sept. 1918
Major H. Meintjies, M.C., A.F.C.	—	May 1916
Capt. P. Middlemas, M.B.E.	—	Feb. 1917
2/Lieut. S. C. Millar	—	July 1918
Major J. A. Milot	Missing	April 1917
Capt. W. E. Molesworth, M.C. and Bar, Italian Medal (Silver) for Military Valour	—	March 1917
Capt. H. A. S. Molyneux, D.F.C.	—	March 1918
Lieut. Col. B. F. Moore	—	Jan. 1918
Lieut. A. W. Morey, M.C.	Killed	Jan. 1918
Lieut. D. H. Morris	—	Oct. 1917
Capt. F. J. Morse, Croix de Guerre (French)	—	Dec. 1918
Lieut. A. W. M. Mowle	Injured	July 1917
Lieut. D. C. G. Murray	Missing	June 1917
2/Lieut. W. B. Newth	Killed	Sept. 1918
2/Lieut. H. J. Newton	Missing	May 1916
Lieut. B. Nicholson	—	Sept. 1917
Lieut. J. I. M. O'Beirne	—	May 1916
Lieut. A. R. Oliver	—	Aug. 1918
Lieut. J. A. N. Ormsby	Missing	July 1916
Lieut. H. C. M. Orpen	—	Sept. 1918

Name	Casualty	Date
Lieut. E. R. Ortner	—	March 1918
Lieut. F. H. Osborne	—	Sept. 1918
Lieut. G. E. Osmond	—	March 1917
Lieut. C. F. Overy	—	May 1916
Capt. G. A. Parker, M.C., D.S.O.	Missing	Nov. 1916
Major S. E. Parker, M.B.E., A.F.C.	—	Aug. 1916
2/Lieut. F. C. Parkes	—	June 1917
Lieut. G. A. H. Parkes	Missing	July 1917
Capt. C. Parry, D.F.C.	Wounded	July 1918
Major C. K. C. Patrick, D.S.O., M.C. and Bar	—	Aug. 1917
Major C. Patteson, M.C., A.F.C., Croix de Guerre (French)	—	May 1917
Capt. A. R. Penny, M.C.	—	June 1917
Lieut. E. W. Percival	—	May 1917
2/Lieut. R. M. Phalen	Missing	May 1917
Capt. G. Phillippi, M.C.	Wounded	Sept. 1916
F/Officer G. A. H. Pidcock, Croix de Guerre (French)	—	Jan. 1917
F/Officer S. L. Pope	—	May 1917
Sqdn. Ldr. C. F. A. Portal, M.C., D.S.O. and Bar	—	May 1916
2/Lieut. O. Price	—	June 1918
Lieut. J. O. Priestley	—	Nov. 1917
Lieut. H. N. J. Proctor	—	March 1918
Capt. E. B. A. Rayner	—	Jan. 1917
Capt. J. W. Rayner	—	Aug. 1918
Lieut. F. K. Read, American Air Service	—	June 1918
F/Lieut. C. A. Ridley, D.S.O., M.C.	Missing	May 1916
2/Lieut. D. M. Robertson	Missing	April 1917
Lieut. N. McL. Robertson	Killed	Oct. 1916
Lieut. H. G. Ross	Injured	May 1917
Lieut. J. A. Roth, United States Air Service	—	Oct. 1918

Name	Casualty	Date
Capt. B. Roxburgh-Smith, D.F.C. and Bar Croix de Guerre (Belgian)	Injured	Feb. 1917
Lieut. N. C. Roystan	Injured	Feb. 1918
Lieut. W. O. Russell	Missing	April 1917
Capt. W. J. Rutherford	—	May 1917
Lieut. A. W. Saunders, D.F.C.	—	Feb. 1918
Capt. O. J. F. Scholte, M.C.	Killed	July 1918
Grp. Capt. A. J. L. Scott, C.B., M.C., A.F.C.	Wounded	April 1917
Capt. J. Seabrook, A.F.C.	—	Oct. 1916
Capt. F. H. B. Selous, M.C., Italian Silver Medal	Killed	Sept. 1917
Lieut. W. B. Sherwood	Missing	Oct. 1917
Lieut. R. G. Sillars	—	May 1917
F/Lieut. J. H. Simpson	—	May 1916
2/Lieut. M. D. Sinclair	—	June 1918
2/Lieut. G. O. Smart	Missing	April 1917
Sqdn. Ldr. H. G. Smart	—	May 1916
Lieut. J. E. Smith	Missing	Sept. 1918
2/Lieut. L. H. Smith	Missing	Oct. 1918
Lieut. R. H. Smith	—	Sept. 1918
Lieut. Col. R. R. Smith-Barry, A.F.C., Chevalier de l'Ordre de Leopold	—	May 1916
F/Lieut. F. O. Soden, D.F.C.	—	July 1917
2/Lieut. L. V. Southwell	Injured	March 1918
Sqdn. Ldr. W. Sowrey, A.F.C.	—	Nov. 1916
Lieut. J. M. J. Spencer	Missing	Oct. 1916
Lieut. F. Stedman	Missing	April 1917
2/Lieut. R. B. Steele	Injured	Sept. 1917
2/Lieut. L. G. Stockwell	Missing	Oct. 1918
T/Capt. V. A. Stookes, M.C.	—	Oct. 1916
2/Lieut. H. S. Stuart-Smith	Missing	Sept. 1918
Lieut. E. A. Sullock, A.F.C.	—	March 1918
Capt. A. S. M. Summers	Missing	Sept. 1916
2/Lieut. H. E. Talbot	—	Dec. 1918
Capt. H. S. Taylor	—	Aug. 1916

Name	Casualty	Date
Capt. G. J. Temperley	Injured	Oct. 1917
Lieut. G. E. Tennant	—	Sept. 1918
Lieut. O. Thamer	Missing	Jan. 1918
2/Lieut. S. A. Thomson	Missing	Sept. 1918
F/Officer E. Thornton	—	Jan. 1918
Capt. H. C. Tower	Missing	May 1916
F/Lieut. E. J. D. Townesend	Missing	April 1917
Lieut. J. W. Trusler	—	Feb. 1918
2/Lieut. F. E. Upton-Smith	—	Feb. 1918
Capt. S. F. Vincent, A.F.C.	—	July 1916
Lieut. B. M. Wainwright	Missing	July 1916
Major F. F. Waldron	Killed	May 1916
Lieut. Walker	—	Aug. 1916
Lieut. A. M. Walters	—	Sept. 1916
Capt. L. S. Weedon	—	Sept. 1916
2/Lieut. A. N. Westergaard	—	June 1918
2/Lieut. M. West-Thompson	Killed	Sept. 1917
Lieut. A. D. Whitehead	Missing	March 1917
Capt. L. E. Whitehead	Wounded	June 1916
Lieut. J. O. Whiting	Missing	Sept. 1917
Lieut. R. K. Whitney, D.F.C.	Wounded	Aug. 1918
2/Lieut. R. C. R. Wilde	—	Oct. 1918
Lieut. C. Williams	Missing	May 1916
2/Lieut. V. F. Williams	Missing	April 1917
2/Lieut. J. Winslow	—	Oct. 1918
Lieut. C. O. Wright	—	Aug. 1917
Lieut. G. C. Young	—	May 1917

CHAPTER ELEVEN

The Red Baron Remembers

Captain Baron Manfred Freiherr von Richthofen

MY FIRST ENGLISHMAN

WE WERE ALL AT THE BUTTS TRYING OUR MACHINE GUNS. ON THE previous day, we had received our new aeroplanes, and the next morning Boelcke was to fly with us. We were all beginners. None of us had had a success so far. Consequently everything that Boelcke told us was to us gospel truth. Every day, during the last few days, he had, as he said, shot one or two Englishmen for breakfast.

The next morning, the seventeenth of September, was a gloriously fine day. It was therefore only to be expected that the English would be very active. Before we started Boelcke repeated to us his instructions, and for the first time, we flew as a squadron commanded by the great man whom we followed blindly.

We had just arrived at the front when we recognized a hostile flying squadron that was proceeding in the direction of Cambrai. Boelcke was of course the first to see it, for he saw a great deal more than ordinary mortals. Soon we understood the position, and every one of us strove to follow Boelcke closely. It was clear to all of us that we should pass our first examination under the eyes of our beloved leader.

Slowly we approached the hostile squadron. It could not escape us. We had intercepted it, for we were between the front and our opponents. If they wished to go back, they had to pass us. We counted the hostile machines. They were seven in number. We were only five. All the

Englishmen flew large bomb-carrying two-seaters. In a few seconds, the dance would begin.

Boelcke had come very near the first English machine, but he did not yet shoot. I followed. Close to me were my comrades. The Englishman nearest to me was traveling in a large boat painted with dark colors. I did not reflect very long but took my aim and shot. He also fired, and so did I, and both of us missed our aim. A struggle began, and the great point for me was to get to the rear of the fellow because I could only shoot forward with my gun. He was differently placed, for his machine gun was movable. It could fire in all directions.

Apparently he was no beginner, for he knew exactly that his last hour had arrived at the moment when I got at the back of him. At that time I had not yet the conviction "He must fall!" which I have now on such occasions, but on the contrary, I was curious to see whether he would fall. There is a great difference between the two feelings. When one has shot down one's first, second, or third opponent, then one begins to find out how the trick is done.

My Englishman twisted and turned, going crisscross. I did not think for a moment that the hostile squadron contained other Englishmen who conceivably might come to the aid of their comrade. I was animated by a single thought: "The man in front of me must come down, whatever happens." At last a favorable moment arrived. My opponent had apparently lost sight of me. Instead of twisting and turning, he flew straight along. In a fraction of a second, I was at his back with my excellent machine. I gave a short series of shots with my machine gun. I had gone so close that I was afraid I might dash into the Englishman. Suddenly, I nearly yelled with joy, for the propeller of the enemy machine had stopped turning. I had shot his engine to pieces; the enemy was compelled to land, for it was impossible for him to reach his own lines. The English machine was curiously swinging to and fro. Probably something had happened to the pilot. The observer was no longer visible. His machine gun was apparently deserted. Obviously I had hit the observer, and he had fallen from his seat.

The Englishman landed close to the flying ground of one of our squadrons. I was so excited that I landed also, and my eagerness was so great that I nearly smashed up my machine. The English flying machine and my own stood close together. I rushed to the English machine and saw that a lot of soldiers were running towards my enemy. When I arrived I discovered that my assumption had been correct. I had shot the engine to pieces and both the pilot and observer were severely wounded. The observer died at once and the pilot while being transported to the nearest dressing station. I honored the fallen enemy by placing a stone on his beautiful grave.

When I came home, Boelcke and my other comrades were already at breakfast. They were surprised that I had not turned up. I reported proudly that I had shot down an Englishman. All were full of joy, for I was not the only victor. As usual, Boelcke had shot down an opponent for breakfast, and every one of the other men also had downed an enemy for the first time.

I would mention that since that time no English squadron ventured as far as Cambrai as long as Boelcke's squadron was there.

The Battle of the Somme

During my whole life, I have not found a happier hunting ground than in the course of the Somme Battle. In the morning, as soon as I had got up, the first Englishmen arrived, and the last did not disappear until long after sunset. Boelcke once said that this was the El Dorado of the flying men.

There was a time when, within two months, Boelcke's bag of machines increased from twenty to forty. We beginners had not at that time the experience of our master, and we were quite satisfied when we did not get a hiding. It was an exciting period. Every time we went up, we had a fight. Frequently we fought really big battles in the air. There were sometimes from forty to sixty English machines, but unfortunately the Germans were often in the minority. With them quality was more important than quantity.

Still the Englishman is a smart fellow. That we must allow. Sometimes the English came down to a very low altitude and visited Boelcke in his quarters, upon which they threw their bombs. They absolutely challenged us to battle and never refused fighting.

We had a delightful time with our chasing squadron. The spirit of our leader animated all his pupils. We trusted him blindly. There was no possibility that one of us would be left behind. Such a thought was incomprehensible to us. Animated by that spirit, we gaily diminished the number of our enemies.

On the day when Boelcke fell, the squadron had brought down forty opponents. By now the number has been increased by more than a hundred. Boelcke's spirit lives still among his capable successors.

BOELCKE'S DEATH (28TH OCTOBER, 1916)

One day we were flying, once more guided by Boelcke against the enemy. We always had a wonderful feeling of security when he was with us. After all, he was the one and only. The weather was very gusty, and there were many clouds. There were no aeroplanes about except fighting ones.

From a long distance, we saw two impertinent Englishmen in the air who actually seemed to enjoy the terrible weather. We were six, and they were two. If they had been twenty and if Boelcke had given us the signal to attack, we should not have been at all surprised.

The struggle began in the usual way. Boelcke tackled the one and I the other. I had to let go because one of the German machines got in my way. I looked around and noticed Boelcke settling his victim about two hundred yards away from me.

It was the usual thing. Boelcke would shoot down his opponent, and I had to look on. Close to Boelcke flew a good friend of his. It was an interesting struggle. Both men were shooting. It was probable that the Englishman would fall at any moment. Suddenly I noticed an unnatural movement of the two German flying machines. Immediately I thought: Collision. I had not yet seen a collision in the air. I had imagined that it would look quite different. In reality, what happened was not a collision. The two machines merely touched one another. However, if two machines go at the tremendous pace of flying machines, the slightest contact has the effect of a violent concussion.

Boelcke drew away from his victim and descended in large curves. He did not seem to be falling, but when I saw him descending below me, I noticed that part of his plane had broken off. I could not see what happened afterwards, but in the clouds he lost an entire plane. Now his machine was no longer steerable. It fell, accompanied all the time by Boelcke's faithful friend.

When we reached home, we found the report "Boelcke is dead!" had already arrived. We could scarcely realize it.

The greatest pain was, of course, felt by the man who had the misfortune to be involved in the accident.

It is a strange thing that everybody who met Boelcke imagined that he alone was his true friend. I have made the acquaintance of about forty men, each of whom imagined that he alone was Boelcke's intimate. Each imagined that he had the monopoly of Boelcke's affections. Men whose names were unknown to Boelcke believed that he was particularly fond of them. This is a curious phenomenon which I have never noticed in anyone else. Boelcke had not a personal enemy. He was equally polite to everybody, making no differences.

The only one who was perhaps more intimate with him than the others was the very man who had the misfortune to be in the accident which caused his death.

Nothing happens without God's will. That is the only consolation which any of us can put to our souls during this war.

MY EIGHTH VICTIM

In Boelcke's time eight was quite a respectable number. Those who hear nowadays of the colossal bags made by certain aviators must feel convinced that it has become easier to shoot down a machine. I can assure those who hold that opinion that the flying business is becoming more difficult from month to month and even from week to week. Of course, with the increasing number of aeroplanes, one gains increased opportunities for shooting down one's enemies, but at the same time, the possibility of being shot down one's self increases. The armament of our enemies is steadily improving, and their number is increasing. When Immelmann shot down his first victim, he had the good fortune to find an opponent who carried not even a machine gun. Such little innocents one finds nowadays only at the training ground for beginners.

On the ninth of November, 1916, I flew towards the enemy with my little comrade Immelmann, who then was eighteen years old. We both were in Boelcke's squadron of chasing aeroplanes. We had previously met one another and had got on very well. Comradeship is a most important thing. We went to work. I had already bagged seven enemies and Immelmann five. At that time this was quite a lot.

Soon after our arrival at the front, we saw a squadron of bombing aeroplanes. They were coming along with impertinent assurance. They arrived in enormous numbers as was usual during the Somme Battle. I think there were about forty or fifty machines approaching. I cannot give the exact number. They had selected an object for their bombs not far from our aerodrome. I reached them when they had almost attained their objective. I approached the last machine. My first few shots incapacitated the hostile machine gunner. Possibly they had tickled the pilot, too. At any rate he resolved to land with his bombs. I fired a few more shots to accelerate his progress downwards. He fell close to our flying ground at Lagnicourt.

While I was fighting my opponent, Immelmann had tackled another Englishman and had brought him down in the same locality. Both of us flew quickly home in order to have a look at the machines we had downed. We jumped into a motor car, drove in the direction where our victims lay, and had to run along a distance through the fields. It was very hot, therefore I unbuttoned all my garments, even the collar and the shirt. I took off my jacket, left my cap in the car, but took with me a big stick. My boots were miry up to the knees. I looked like a tramp. I arrived in the vicinity of my victim. In the meantime, a lot of people had of course gathered around.

At one spot there was a group of officers. I approached them, greeted them, and asked the first one whom I met whether he could tell me anything about the aspect of the aerial battle. It is always interesting to find out how a fight in the air looks to the people down below. I was told that the English machines had thrown bombs and that the aeroplane that had come down was still carrying its bombs.

The officer who gave me this information took my arm, went with me to the other officers, asked my name, and introduced me to them. I did not like it, for my attire was rather disarranged. On the other hand, all the officers looked as spic and span as on parade. I was introduced to a personage who impressed me rather strangely. I noticed a general's trousers, an order at the neck, an unusually youthful face, and undefinable epaulettes. In short, the personage seemed extraordinary to me. During our conversation I buttoned my trousers and collar and adopted a somewhat military attitude.

I had no idea who the officer was. I took my leave and went home again. In the evening the telephone rang, and I was told that the undefinable somebody with whom I had been talking had been His Royal Highness, the Grand Duke of Saxe-Coburg Gotha.

I was ordered to go to him. It was known that the English had intended to throw bombs on his headquarters. Apparently I had helped to keep the aggressors away from him. Therefore I was given the Saxe-Coburg Gotha medal for bravery.

I always enjoy this adventure when I look at the medal.

Major Hawker

I was extremely proud when, one fine day, I was informed that the airman whom I had brought down on the twenty-third of November, 1916, was the English Immelmann.

In view of the character of our fight, it was clear to me that I had been tackling a flying champion.

One day I was blithely flying to give chase when I noticed three Englishmen who also had apparently gone a-hunting. I noticed that they were ogling me, and as I felt much inclination to have a fight, I did not want to disappoint them.

I was flying at a lower altitude. Consequently I had to wait until one of my English friends tried to drop on me. After a short while on, the three came sailing along and attempted to tackle me in the rear. After firing five shots, he had to stop, for I had swerved in a sharp curve.

The Englishman tried to catch me up in the rear while I tried to get behind him. So we circled round and round like madmen after one another at an altitude of about ten thousand feet.

First we circled twenty times to the left and then thirty times to the right. Each tried to get behind and above the other.

Soon I discovered that I was not meeting a beginner. He had not the slightest intention of breaking off the fight. He was traveling in a machine which turned beautifully. However, my own was better at rising than his, and I succeeded at last in getting above and beyond my English waltzing partner.

When we had got down to about six thousand feet without having achieved anything in particular, my opponent ought to have discovered that it was time for him to take his leave. The wind was favorable to me, for it drove us more and more towards the German position. At last we were above Bapaume, about half a mile behind the German front. The impertinent fellow was full of cheek, and when we had got down to about three thousand feet, he merrily waved to me as if he would say, "Well, how do you do?"

The circles which we made around one another were so narrow that their diameter was probably no more than 250 or 300 feet. I had time to take a good look at my opponent. I looked down into his carriage and could see every movement of his head. If he had not had his cap on I would have noticed what kind of a face he was making.

My Englishman was a good sportsman, but by and by the thing became a little too hot for him. He had to decide whether he would land on German ground or whether he would fly back to the English lines. Of course he tried the latter, after having endeavored in vain to escape me by loopings and such like tricks. At that time his first bullets were flying around me, for hitherto neither of us had been able to do any shooting.

When he had come down to about three hundred feet, he tried to escape by flying in a zig-zag course during which, as is well known, it is difficult for an observer to shoot. That was my most favourable moment. I followed him at an altitude of from 250 feet to 150 feet, firing all the time. The Englishman could not help falling. But the jamming of my gun nearly robbed me of my success.

My opponent fell, shot through the head, 150 feet behind our line. His machine gun was dug out of the ground, and it ornaments the entrance of my dwelling.

MY RECORD DAY

The weather was glorious. We were ready for starting. I had as a visitor a gentleman who had never seen a fight in the air or anything resembling it, and he had just assured me that it would tremendously interest him to witness an aerial battle.

We climbed into our machines and laughed heartily at our visitor's eagerness. Friend Schäfer thought that we might give him some fun. We placed him before a telescope, and off we went.

The day began well. We had scarcely flown to an altitude of six thousand feet when an English squadron of five machines was seen coming our way. We attacked them by a rush as if we were cavalry, and the hostile squadron lay destroyed on the ground. None of our men was even wounded. Of our enemies three had plunged to the ground, and two had come down in flames.

The good fellow down below was not a little surprised. He had imagined that the affair would look quite different, that it would be far more dramatic. He thought the whole encounter had looked quite harmless until suddenly some machines came falling down looking like rockets. I have gradually become accustomed to seeing machines falling down, but I must say it impressed me very deeply when I saw the first Englishman fall, and I have often seen the event again in my dreams.

As the day had begun so propitiously, we sat down and had a decent breakfast. All of us were as hungry as wolves. In the meantime our machines were again made ready for starting. Fresh cartridges were got, and then we went off again.

In the evening we could send off the proud report: "Six German machines have destroyed thirteen hostile aeroplanes."

Boelcke's Squadron had only once been able to make a similar report. At that time we had shot down eight machines. Today one of us had brought low four of his opponents. The hero was a Lieutenant Wolff, a delicate-looking little fellow in whom nobody could have suspected a redoubtable hero. My brother had destroyed two, Schäfer two, Festner two and I three.

We went to bed in the evening tremendously proud but also terribly tired. On the following day, we read with noisy approval about our deeds of the previous day in the official communiqué. On the next day, we downed eight hostile machines.

A very amusing thing occurred. One of the Englishmen whom we had shot down and whom we had made a prisoner was talking with us. Of course he inquired after the red aeroplane. It is not unknown even among the troops in the trenches and is called by them "le diable rouge." In the squadron to which he belonged, there was a rumour that the red machine was occupied by a girl, by a kind of Jeanne d'Arc. He was intensely surprised when I assured him that the supposed girl was standing in front of him. He did not intend to make a joke. He was actually convinced that only a girl could sit in the extravagantly painted machine.

The most beautiful being in all creation is the genuine Danish hound, my little lapdog, my Moritz. I bought him in Ostend from a brave Belgian for five marks. His mother was a beautiful animal, and one of his fathers also was pure-bred. I am convinced of that. I could select one of the litter, and I chose the prettiest. Zeumer took another puppy and called it Max.

Max came to a sudden end. He was run over by a motor car. Moritz flourished exceedingly. He slept with me in my bed and received a most excellent education. He never left me while I was in Ostend and obtained my entire affection. Month by month Moritz grew, and gradually my tender little lapdog became a colossal, big beast.

Once I even took him with me. He was my first observer. He behaved very sensibly. He seemed much interested in everything and looked at the world from above. Only my mechanics were dissatisfied when they had to clean the machine. Afterwards Moritz was very merry.

Moritz is more than a year old, and he is still as childlike as if he were still in his teens. He is very fond of playing billiards. In doing this he has destroyed many billiard balls and particularly many a billiard cloth. He has a great passion for the chase. My mechanics are highly satisfied with his sporting inclinations, for he has caught for them many a nice hare. I do not much approve of his hunting proclivities. Consequently he gets a whacking if I catch him at it.

He has a silly peculiarity. He likes to accompany the flying machines at the start. Frequently the normal death of a flying man's dog is death from the propeller. One day he rushed in front of a flying machine which had been started. The aeroplane caught him up and a beautiful propeller was smashed to bits. Moritz howled terribly and a measure which I had hitherto omitted was taken. I had always refused to have his ears cut. One of his ears was cut off by the propeller. A long ear and a short ear do not go well together.

Moritz has taken a very sensible view of the world war and of our enemies. When in the summer of 1916 he saw for the first time Russian natives—the train had stopped and Moritz was being taken for a walk—he chased the Russian crowd with loud barking. He has no great opinion of Frenchmen, although he is, after all, a Belgian. Once, when I had settled in new quarters, I ordered the people to clean the house. When I came back in the evening, nothing had been done. I got angry and asked the Frenchman to come and see me. When he opened the door, Moritz greeted him rather brusquely. Immediately I understood why no cleaning had been done.

During the full moon nights of the month of April, our English friends were particularly industrious. This was during the Battle of Arras. Probably they had found out that we had comfortably installed ourselves on a beautiful large flying ground at Douai.

One night when we were in the officers' mess, the telephone started ringing, and we were told, "The English are coming." There was a great hullabaloo. We had bomb-proof shelters. They had been got ready by our excellent Simon. Simon is our architect, surveyor, and builder.

We dived down into shelter, and we heard actually at first a very gentle humming and then the noise of engines. The searchlights had apparently got notice at the same time as we, for they started getting ready.

The nearest enemy was still too far away to be attacked. We were colossally merry. The only thing we feared was that the English would not succeed in finding our aerodrome. To find some fixed spot at night is by no means easy. It was particularly difficult to find us because our aerodrome was not situated on an important highway or near water or a railway, by which one can be guided during one's flight at night. The Englishmen were apparently flying at a great altitude. At first they circled around our entire establishment. We began to think that they had given up and were looking for another objective. Suddenly we noticed that the nearest one had switched off his engine. So he was coming lower. Wolff said, "Now the matter is becoming serious."

We had two carbines and began shooting at the Englishman. We could not see him. Still the noise of our shooting was a sedative to our nerves.

Suddenly he was taken up by the searchlights. There was shouting all over the flying ground. Our friend was sitting in a prehistoric packing case. We could clearly recognize the type. He was half a mile away from us and was flying straight towards us.

He went lower and lower. At last he had come down to an altitude of about three hundred feet. Then he started his engine again and came straight towards the spot where we were standing.

Wolff thought that he took an interest in the other side of our establishment, and before long the first bomb fell, and it was followed by a number of other missiles.

Our friend amused us with very pretty fireworks. They could have frightened only a coward. Broadly speaking, I find that bomb throwing at night has only a morale effect. Those who are easily frightened are strongly affected when bombs fall at night. The others don't care.

We were much amused at the Englishman's performance and thought the English would come quite often on a visit. The flying piano dropped its bombs at last from an altitude of 150 feet. That was rather impertinent, for in a moonlit night I think I can hit a wild pig at 150 feet with a rifle. Why then should I not succeed in hitting the Englishman? It would have been a novelty to down an English airman from the ground.

From above I had already had the honour of downing a number of Englishmen, but I had never tried to tackle an aviator from below.

When the Englishman had gone, we went back to mess and discussed among ourselves how we should receive the English should they pay us another visit on the following night. In the course of the next day, our orderlies and other fellows were made to work with great energy. They had to ram into the ground piles which were to be used as a foundation for machine guns during the coming night.

We went to the butts and tried the English machine guns which we had taken from the enemy, arranged the sights for night shooting, and were very curious as to what was going to happen. I will not betray the number of our machine guns. Anyhow, they were to be sufficient for the purpose. Every one of my officers was armed with one.

We were again sitting at mess. Of course we were discussing the problem of night fliers. Suddenly an orderly rushed in shouting, "They are there! They are there!" and disappeared in the next bomb-proof in his scanty attire. We all rushed to our machine guns. Some of the men who were known to be good shots had also been given a machine gun. All the rest were provided with carbines. The whole squadron was armed to the teeth to give a warm reception to our kindly visitors.

The first Englishman arrived, exactly as on the previous evening, at a very great altitude. He went then down to 150 feet and to our greatest joy began making for the place where our barracks were. He got into the glare of the searchlight.

When he was only three hundred yards away, someone fired the first shot, and all the rest of us joined in. A rush of cavalry or of storming troops could not have been met more efficiently than the attack of that single impertinent individual flying at 150 feet.

Quick firing from many guns received him. Of course he could not hear the noise of the machine guns. The roar of his motor prevented that. However, he must have seen the flashes of our guns. Therefore I thought it tremendously plucky that our man did not swerve but continued going straight ahead in accordance with his plan.

At the moment he was perpendicularly above us, we jumped quickly into our bomb-proof. It would have been too silly for flying men to die by a rotten bomb.

As soon as he had passed over our heads, we rushed out again and fired after him with our machine guns and rifles.

Friend Schäfer asserted that he had hit the man. Schäfer is quite a good shot. Still, in this case I did not believe him. Besides, every one of us had as good a chance at making a hit as he had.

We had achieved something, for the enemy had dropped his bombs rather aimlessly, owing to our shooting. One of them, it is true, had exploded only a few yards from the "petit rouge" but had not hurt him.

During the night the fun recommenced several times. I was already in bed, fast asleep, when I heard in a dream antiaircraft firing. I woke up and discovered that the dream was reality. One of the Englishmen flew at so low an altitude over my habitation that in my fright I pulled the blanket over my head. The next moment I heard an incredible bang just outside my window. The panes had fallen a victim to the bomb. I rushed out of my room in my shirt in order to fire a few shots after him. They were firing from everywhere. Unfortunately, I had overslept my opportunity.

The next morning we were extremely surprised and delighted to discover that we had shot down from the ground no fewer than three Englishmen. They had landed not far from our aerodrome and had been made prisoners.

As a rule we had hit the engines and had forced the airmen to come down on our side of the front. After all, Schäfer was possibly right in his assertion. At any rate, we were very well satisfied with our success. The English were distinctly less satisfied, for they preferred avoiding our base. It was a pity that they gave us a wide berth, for they gave us lots of fun. Let us hope that they come back to us next month.

SCHÄFER LANDS BETWEEN THE LINES

We went on a shooting expedition on the twentieth of April. We came home very late and lost Schäfer on the way.

Of course everyone hoped that he would come to hand before dark. It struck nine, it struck ten, but no Schäfer was visible. His benzine could not last so long. Consequently, he had landed somewhere, for no one was willing to admit that he had been shot down. No one dared to mention the possibility. Still, everyone was afraid for him.

The ubiquitous telephone was set in motion in order to find out whether a flying man had come down anywhere. Nobody could give us information. No division and no brigade had seen anything of him. We felt very uncomfortable. At last we went to bed. All of us were perfectly convinced that he would turn up in the end.

At two o'clock, after midnight, I was suddenly awakened. The telephone orderly, beaming with pleasure, reported to me, "Schäfer is in the Village of Y. and would like to be fetched home."

The next morning when we were sitting at breakfast, the door opened, and my dear pilot stood before me. His clothes were as filthy as those of an infantryman who has fought at Arras for a fortnight. He was greeted with a general "Hurrah!" Schäfer was tremendously happy and elated and tremendously excited about his adventure. When he had finished his breakfast, he told us the following tale:

I was flying along the front, intending to return home. Suddenly I noticed far below me something that looked like an infantry flier. I attacked him, shot him down, and meant to fly back. However, the English in the trenches did not mean me to get away and started peppering me like anything. My salvation lay in the rapidity of my machine, for those rascals, of course, would forget that they had to aim far in front of me if they wished to hit me.

I was at an altitude of perhaps six hundred feet. Suddenly, I heard a smash, and my engine stopped running. There was nothing to do but to land. I asked myself whether I should be able to get away from the English position. It seemed very questionable. The English noticed my predicament and started shooting like mad.

As my engine was no longer running, I could hear every single shot. The position became awkward. I came down and landed. Before my machine had come to a standstill, they squirted upon me heaps of bullets from machine guns in the hedge of the village of Monchy near Arras. My machine became splashed with bullets.

I jumped out of it and down into the first shell hole. Squatting there, I reflected and tried to realize exactly where I was. Gradually it became clear to me that I had landed outside the English lines but cursedly near them. Happily it was rather late in the evening, and that was my salvation.

Before long the first shell came along. Of course they were gas shells, and I had no mask with me. My eyes started watering like anything. Before darkness set in, the English ascertained the distance of the spot where I had landed with machine guns. Part of them aimed at my machine and part at my shell crater. The bullets constantly hit its rim.

In order to quiet my nerves, I lit a cigarette. Then I took off my heavy fur coat and prepared everything for a leap and a run. Every minute seemed to me an hour.

Gradually it became dark but only very gradually. Around me I heard partridges giving a concert. As an experienced shot, I recognized from their voices that they felt quite happy and contented, that there was no danger of my being surprised in my hiding place.

At last it became quite dark. Suddenly and quite close to me, a couple of partridges flew up. A second couple followed. It was obvious that danger was approaching. No doubt a patrol was on the way to wish me a happy evening.

I had no time to lose. Now or never. First I crept very cautiously on my chest from shell hole to shell hole. After creeping industriously for about an hour and a half, I noticed I was nearing humans. Were they English, or were they Germans? They came nearer, and I could almost have fallen round their necks, when I discovered our own musketeers. They were a German patrol who were nosing about in No Man's Land.

One of the men conducted me to the commander of his company. I was told that in the evening I had landed about fifty yards in front of the enemy lines and that our infantry had given me up for lost. I had a good supper, and then I started on my way home. Behind me there was far more shooting than in front of me. Every path, every trench, every bush, every hollow was under enemy fire. The English attacked on the next morning, and consequently, they had to begin their artillery preparation the evening before. So I had chosen an unfavorable day for my enterprise. I reached the first telephone only at two o'clock in the morning when I phoned to the squadron.

We were all very happy to have our Schäfer again with us. He went to bed. Any other man would have taken a rest from flying for twenty-four hours. But on the afternoon of this very day, Friend Schäfer attacked a low-flying B.E. above Monchy.

THE ANTI-RICHTHOFEN SQUADRON

The English had hit upon a splendid joke. They intended to catch me or to bring me down. For that purpose they had actually organized a special squadron which flew about in that part which we frequented as a rule.

We discovered its particular aim by the fact that its aggressive activity was principally directed against our red machines.

I would say that all the machines of the squadron had been painted red because our English friends had by and by perceived that I was sitting in a blood-red bandbox. Suddenly there were quite a lot of red machines, and the English opened their eyes wide when one fine day they saw a dozen red barges steaming along instead of a single one. Our new trick did not prevent them from making an attempt at attacking us. I preferred their new tactics. It is better that one's customers come to one's shop than to have to look for them abroad.

We flew to the front, hoping to find our enemy. After about twenty minutes, the first arrived and attacked us. That had not happened to us for a long time. The English had abandoned their celebrated offensive tactics to some extent. They had found them somewhat too expensive.

Our aggressors were three Spad one-seater machines. Their occupants thought themselves very superior to us because of the excellence of their apparatus. Wolff, my brother, and I were flying together. We were three against three. That was as it ought to be.

Immediately at the beginning of the encounter, the aggressive became a defensive. Our superiority became clear. I tackled my opponent and could see how my brother and Wolff handled each his own enemy. The usual waltzing began. We were circling around one another. A favourable wind came to our aid. It drove us, fighting, away from the front in the direction of Germany.

My man was the first who fell down. I suppose I had smashed up his engine. At any rate, he made up his mind to land. I no longer gave pardon to him. Therefore, I attacked him a second time, and the consequence was that his whole machine went to pieces. His planes dropped off like pieces of paper, and the body of the machine fell like a stone, burning fiercely. It dropped into a morass. It was impossible to dig it out, and I have never discovered the name of my opponent. He had disappeared. Only the end of the tail was visible and marked the place where he had dug his own grave.

Simultaneously with me, Wolff and my brother had attacked their opponents and had forced them to land not far from my victim.

We were very happy and flew home and hoped that the Anti-Richthofen Squadron would often return to the fray.

We Are Visited by My Father

My father had announced that he would visit his two sons on the twenty-ninth of April. My father is commander of a little town in the vicinity of Lille. Therefore he does not live very far away from us. I have occasionally seen him on my flights.

He intended to arrive by train at nine o'clock. At half past nine, he came to our aerodrome. We just happened to have returned from an expedition. My brother was the first to climb out of his machine, and he greeted the old gentleman with the words, "Good day, Father. I have just shot down an Englishman." Immediately after, I also climbed out of my machine and greeted him, "Good day, Father. I have just shot down an Englishman." The old gentleman felt very happy, and he was delighted. That was obvious. He is not one of those fathers who are afraid for their sons. I think he would like best to get into a machine himself and help us shoot. We breakfasted with him, and then we went flying again.

In the meantime, an aerial fight took place above our aerodrome. My father looked on and was greatly interested. We did not take a hand in the fight, for we were standing on the ground and looked on ourselves.

An English squadron had broken through and was being attacked above our aerodrome by some of our own reconnoitering aeroplanes. Suddenly one of the machines started turning over and over. Then it recovered itself and came gliding down normally. We saw, with regret this time, that it was a German machine.

The Englishman flew on. The German aeroplane had apparently been damaged. It was quite correctly handled. It came down and tried to land on our flying ground. The room was rather narrow for the large machine. Besides, the ground was unfamiliar to the pilot. Hence, the landing was not quite smooth. We ran towards the aeroplane and discovered with regret that one of the occupants of the machine, the machine gunner, had been killed. The spectacle was new to my father. It made him serious.

The day promised to be a favorable one for us. The weather was wonderfully clear. The antiaircraft guns were constantly audible. Obviously, there was much aircraft about.

Towards midday we flew once more. This time, I was again lucky and shot down my second Englishman of the day. The governor recovered his good spirits.

After the midday dinner, I slept a little. I was again quite fresh. Wolff had fought the enemy in the meantime with his group of machines and had himself bagged an enemy. Schäfer also had eaten one. In the afternoon my brother and I accompanied by Schäfer, Festner, and Allmenröder flew twice more.

The first afternoon flight was a failure. The second was all the better. Soon after we had come to the front, a hostile squadron met us. Unfortunately they occupied a higher altitude, so we could not do anything. We tried to climb to their level but did not succeed. We had to let them go.

We flew along the front. My brother was next to me, in front of the others. Suddenly I noticed two hostile artillery fliers approaching our front in the most impertinent and provocative manner. I waved to my brother, and he understood my meaning. We flew side by side, increasing our speed. Each of us felt certain that he was superior to the enemy. It was a great thing that we could absolutely rely on one another, and that was the principal thing. One has to know one's flying partner.

My brother was the first to approach his enemy. He attacked the first, and I took care of the second. At the last moment, I quickly looked round in order to feel sure that there was no third aeroplane about. We were alone and could see eye to eye. Soon I had got on the favorable side of my opponent. A short spell of quick firing, and the enemy machine went to pieces. I never had a more rapid success.

While I was still looking where my enemy's fragments were falling, I noticed my brother. He was scarcely five hundred yards away from me and was still fighting his opponent.

I had time to study the struggle and must say that I myself could not have done any better than he did. He had rushed his man, and both were turning around one another. Suddenly, the enemy machine reared. That is a certain indication of a hit. Probably the pilot was shot in the head.

The machine fell, and the planes of the enemy apparatus went to pieces. They fell quite close to my victim. I flew towards my brother, and we congratulated one another by waving. We were highly satisfied with our performance and flew off. It is a splendid thing when one can fly together with one's brother and do so well.

In the meantime, the other fellows of the squadron had drawn near and were watching the spectacle of the fight of the two brothers. Of course they could not help us, for only one man can shoot down an opponent. If one airman has tackled his enemy, the others cannot assist. They can only look on and protect his back. Otherwise, he might be attacked in the rear.

We flew on and went to a higher altitude, for there was apparently a meeting somewhere in the air for the members of the Anti-Richthofen Club. They could recognize us from far away. In the powerful sunlight, the beautiful red color of our machines could be seen at a long distance.

We closed our ranks, for we knew that our English friends pursued the same business as we. Unfortunately, they were again too high. So we had to wait for their attack. The celebrated triplanes and Spads were perfectly new machines. However, the quality of the box matters little. Success depends upon the man who sits in it. The English airmen played a cautious game but would not bite. We offered to fight them, either on one side of the front or on the other. But they said, "No, thank you." What is the good of bringing out a squadron against us and then turning tail?

At last, one of the men plucked up courage and dropped down upon our rear machine. Naturally battle was accepted, although our position was unfavorable. If you wish to do business, you must, after all, adapt yourself to the desires of your customers. Therefore we all turned round. The Englishman noticed what was going on and got away. The battle had begun.

Another Englishman tried a similar trick on me, and I greeted him at once with quick fire from my two machine guns. He tried to escape me by dropping down. That was fatal to him. When he got beneath me, I remained on top of him. Everything in the air that is beneath me, especially if it is a one-seater, a chaser, is lost, for it cannot shoot to the rear.

My opponent had a very good and very fast machine. However, he did not succeed in reaching the English lines. I began to fire at him when we were above Lens. I started shooting when I was much too far away. That was merely a trick of mine. I did not mean so much to hit him as to frighten him, and I succeeded in catching him. He began flying curves, and this enabled me to draw near. I tried the same manoeuver a second and a third time. Every time my foolish friend started making his curves, I gradually edged quite close to him.

I approached him almost to touching distance. I aimed very carefully. I waited a moment, and when I was at most at a distance of fifty yards from him, I started with both the machine guns at the same time. I heard a slight hissing noise, a certain sign that the benzine tanks had been hit. Then I saw a bright flame, and my lord disappeared below.

This was the fourth victim of the day. My brother had bagged two. Apparently, we had invited our father to a treat. His joy was wonderful.

I had invited several gentlemen for the evening. Among these was my dear Wedel, who happened to be in the neighborhood. We had a great treat. The two brothers had bagged six Englishmen in a single day. That is a whole flying squadron.

I believe the English cease to feel any sympathy for us.

I Fly Home

I had shot down fifty aeroplanes. That was a good number, but I would have preferred fifty-two. So I went up one day and had another two, although it was against orders.

As a matter of fact, I had been allowed to bag only forty-one. Anyone will be able to guess why the number was fixed at forty-one. Just for that reason, I wanted to avoid that figure. I am not out for breaking records. Besides, generally speaking, we of the Flying Corps do not think of records at all. We merely think of our duty. Boelcke might have shot down a hundred aeroplanes but for his accident, and many others of our dear dead comrades might have vastly increased their bag but for their sudden deaths. Still, it is some fun to have downed half a hundred aeroplanes. After all, I had succeeded in obtaining permission to bring down fifty machines before going on leave.

I hope that I may live to celebrate a second lot of fifty.

In the evening of that particular day, the telephone bell was ringing. Headquarters wished to speak to me. It seemed to me the height of fun to be connected with the holy of holies.

Over the wire they gave me the cheerful news that His Majesty had expressed the wish to make my personal acquaintance and had fixed the date for me. I had to make an appearance on the second of May. The notification reached me on the thirtieth of April at nine o'clock in the evening. I should not have been able to fulfil the wish of our All-Highest War-Lord by taking the train. I therefore thought I would travel by air, especially as that mode of locomotion is far pleasanter. I started the next morning, not in my single-seater "le petit rouge," but in a big, fat double-seater.

I took a seat at the rear, not at the sticks. The man who had to do the flying was Lieut. Krefft, one of the officers of my squadron. He was just going on furlough to recover his strength, so that it suited him admirably to act as my pilot. He reached home more quickly traveling by air, and he preferred the trip by aeroplane.

I started on the journey rather hastily. The only luggage which I took with me was my toothbrush. Therefore, I had to dress for the journey in the clothes in which I was to appear at headquarters. Now, a soldier does not carry with him many beautiful uniforms when he goes to war, and the scarcity of nice clothes is particularly great in the case of such a poor front hog as myself.

My brother undertook the command of the aeroplane squadron in my absence. I took leave with a few words, for I hoped soon to recommence my work among those dear fellows.

The flight went via Namur, Liège, Aix la Chapelle, and Cologne. It was lovely for once to sail through the air without any thoughts of war. The weather was wonderful. We had rarely had such a perfect time. Probably the men at the front would be extremely busy.

Soon our own captive balloons were lost to sight. The thunder of the Battle of Arras was only heard in the distance. Beneath us all was peace. We saw steamers on the rivers and fast trains on the railways. We easily overtook everything below. The wind was in our favor. The earth seemed as flat as a threshing floor. The beautiful mountains of the Meuse were not recognizable as mountains. One could not even trace them by their shadows, for the sun was right above us. We only knew that they were there, and with a little imagination, we could hide ourselves in the cool glades of that delightful country.

It had become late. Clouds were gathering below and hid from us the earth. We flew on, taking our direction by means of the sun and the compass. The vicinity of Holland was disagreeable to us. We decided to go lower in order to find out where we were. We went beneath the cloud and discovered that we were above Namur.

We then went on to Aix la Chapelle. We left that town to our left, and about midday we reached Cologne. We both were in high spirits. We had before us a long leave of absence. The weather was beautiful. We had succeeded in all our undertakings. We had reached Cologne. We could be certain to get to headquarters in time, whatever might happen.

Our coming had been announced in Cologne by telegram. People were looking out for us. On the previous day, the newspapers had reported my fifty-second aerial victory. One can imagine what kind of a reception they had prepared for us.

Having been flying for three hours, I had a slight headache. Therefore, I thought I would take forty winks before going to headquarters. From Cologne we flew along the Rhine for some distance. I knew the country well. I had often journeyed that way by steamer, by motor car, and by railway, and now I was traveling by aeroplane. It is difficult to say which of these is the most pleasant form of locomotion. Of course, one can see the details of the landscape better from the steamer. However, the commanding view one gets from an aeroplane has also its attractions. The Rhine is a very beautiful river, from above as well as from any other viewpoint.

We flew rather low in order not to lose the sensation that we were traveling among mountains, for after all the most beautiful part of the Rhine are the tree-clad hills and castles. Of course we could not make out individual houses. It is a pity that one cannot fly slowly and quickly. If it had been possible, I would have flown quite slowly.

The beautiful views which we saw vanished only too quickly. Nevertheless, when one flies high in the air, one never has the sensation that one is proceeding at a fast pace. If you are sitting in a motor car or in a fast train, you have the impression of tremendous speed. On the other hand, you seem to be advancing slowly when you fly in an aeroplane at a considerable speed. You notice the celerity of your progress only when you have not looked out of your machine for four or five minutes and then try to find out where you are. Then the aspect of the country appears suddenly completely changed. The terrain which you passed over a little while ago looks quite different under a different angle, and you do not recognize the scenery you have passed. Herein lies the reason that an airman can easily lose his way if he forgets for a moment to examine the territory.

In the afternoon we arrived at headquarters and were cordially received by some comrades with whom I was acquainted and who worked at the holiest of holies. I absolutely pitied those poor ink-spillers. They get only half the fun in war.

First of all I went to the general commanding the Air Forces.

On the next morning came the great moment when I was to meet Hindenburg and Ludendorf. I had to wait for quite a while.

I should find it difficult to describe my encounter with these generals. I saw Hindenburg first and then Ludendorf.

It is a weird feeling to be in the room where the fate of the world is decided. I was quite glad when I was again outside the holiest of holies and when I had been commanded to lunch with His Majesty. The day was the day of my birth, and somebody had apparently told His Majesty. He congratulated me in the first place on my success and, in the second, on my twenty-fifth birthday. At the same time, he handed me a small birthday present.

Formerly I would never have believed it possible that on my twenty-fifth birthday I would be sitting at the right of General Field Marshal von Hindenburg and that I would be mentioned by him in a speech.

On the day following, I was to take midday dinner with Her Majesty. And so I went to Homburg. Her Majesty also gave me a birthday present, and I had the great pleasure to show her how to start an aeroplane. In the evening I was again invited by General Field Marshal von Hindenburg. The day following I flew to Freiburg to do some shooting. At Freiburg

I made use of the flying machine which was going to Berlin by air. In Nuremberg I replenished my tanks with benzine. A thunderstorm was coming on. I was in a great hurry to get to Berlin. Various more or less interesting things awaited me there. So I flew on, the thunderstorm notwithstanding. I enjoyed the clouds and the beastly weather. The rain fell in streams. Sometimes it hailed. Afterwards the propeller had the most extraordinary aspect. The hail stones had damaged it considerably. The blades looked like saws.

Unfortunately I enjoyed the bad weather so much that I quite forgot to look about me. When I remembered that one has to look out, it was too late. I had no longer any idea where I was. That was a nice position to be in! I had lost my way in my own country! My people at home would laugh when they knew it! However, there it was and couldn't be helped. I had no idea where I was. Owing to a powerful wind, I had been driven out of my course and off my map. Guided by sun and compass, I tried to get the direction of Berlin.

Towns, villages, hills, and forests were slipping away below me. I did not recognize a thing. I tried in vain to compare the picture beneath my map. Everything was different. I found it impossible to recognize the country. Later on I discovered the impossibility of finding my way, for I was flying about sixty miles outside my map.

After having flown for a couple of hours, my guide and I resolved to land somewhere in the open. That is always unpleasant. One cannot tell how the surface of the ground is in reality. If one of the wheels gets into a hole, one's box is converted into matchwood.

We tried to read the name written upon a station, but of course that was impossible; it was too small. So we had to land. We did it with a heavy heart, for nothing else could be done. We looked for a meadow which appeared suitable from above and tried our luck. Close inspection unfortunately showed that the meadow was not as pleasant as it seemed. The fact was obviously proved by the slightly bent frame of our machine. We had made ourselves gloriously ridiculous. We had first lost our way and then smashed the machine. So we had to continue our journey with the commonplace conveyance, by railway train. Slowly but surely, we reached Berlin. We had landed in the neighborhood of Leipzig. If we had not landed so stupidly, we would certainly have reached Berlin. But sometimes you make a mistake, whatever you do.

Some days later I arrived in Schweidnitz, my own town. Although I got there at seven o'clock in the morning, there was a large crowd at the station. I was very cordially received. In the afternoon various demonstrations took place to honour me, among others, one of the local Boy Scouts.

It became clear to me that the people at home took a vivid interest in their fighting soldiers after all.

My Brother

I had not yet passed eight days of my leave when I received the telegram: "Lothar is wounded but not mortally." That was all. Inquiries showed that he had been very rash. He flew against the enemy, together with Allmenröder. Beneath him and a good distance on the other side of the front, he saw in the air a lonely Englishman crawling about. He was one of those hostile infantry fliers who make themselves particularly disagreeable to our troops. We molest them a great deal. Whether they really achieve anything in crawling along the ground is very problematical.

My brother was at an altitude of about six thousand feet, while the Englishman was at about three thousand feet. He quietly approached the Englishman, prepared to plunge, and in a few seconds was upon him. The Englishman thought he would avoid a duel, and he disappeared likewise by a plunge. My brother, without hesitation, plunged after. He didn't care at all whether he was on one side of the front or the other. He was animated by a single thought: "I must down that fellow." That is, of course, the correct way of managing things. Now and then I myself have acted that way. However, if my brother does not have at least one success on every flight, he gets tired of the whole thing.

Only a little above the ground, my brother obtained a favorable position towards the English flier and could shoot into his shop windows. The Englishman fell. There was nothing more to be done.

After such a struggle, especially at a low altitude, in the course of which one has so often been twisting and turning and circling to the right and to the left, the average mortal has no longer the slightest notion of his position. On that day it happened that the air was somewhat misty.

The weather was particularly unfavorable. My brother quickly took his bearings and discovered only then that he was a long distance behind the front. He was behind the ridge of Vimy. The top of that hill is about three hundred feet higher than the country around. My brother, so the observers on the ground reported, had disappeared behind the Vimy height.

It is not a particularly pleasant feeling to fly home over enemy country. One is shot at and cannot shoot back. It is true, however, that a hit is rare. My brother approached the line. At a low altitude, one can hear every shot that is fired, and firing sounds then very much like the noise made by chestnuts which are being roasted. Suddenly, he felt that he had been hit. That was queer to him.

My brother is one of those men who cannot see their own blood. If somebody else was bleeding, it would not impress him very greatly, but the sight of his own blood upsets him. He felt his blood running down his right leg in a warm stream. At the same time, he noticed a pain in his hip. Below, the shooting continued. It followed that he was still over hostile ground.

At last the firing gradually ceased. He had crossed the front. Now he must be nimble, for his strength was rapidly ebbing away. He saw a wood and next to the wood a meadow. Straight for the meadow he flew, and mechanically, almost unconsciously, he switched off the engine. At the same moment, he lost consciousness.

My brother was in a single-seater. No one could help him. It is a miracle that he came to the ground, for no flying machine lands or starts automatically. There is a rumor that they have at Cologne an old Taube which will start by itself as soon as the pilot takes his seat, which makes the regulation curve and which lands again after exactly five minutes. Many men pretend to have seen that miraculous machine. I have not seen it. But still I am convinced that the tale is true. Now, my brother was not in such a miraculous automatic machine. Nevertheless he had not hurt himself in landing. He recovered consciousness only in hospital and was sent to Douai.

It is a curious feeling to see one's brother fighting with an Englishman. Once I saw that Lothar, who was lagging behind the squadron, was being attacked by an English aviator. It would have been easy for him to avoid battle. He need only plunge. But he would not do that. That would not even occur to him. He does not know how to run away. Happily I had observed what was going on and was looking for my chance.

I noticed that the Englishman went for my brother and shot at him. My brother tried to reach the Englishman's altitude, disregarding the shots. Suddenly his machine turned a somersault and plunged perpendicularly, turning round and round. It was not an intended plunge but a regular fall. That is not a nice thing to look at, especially if the falling airman is one's own brother. Gradually I had to accustom myself to that sight, for it was one of my brother's tricks. As soon as he felt sure that the Englishman was his superior, he acted as if he had been shot.

The Englishman rushed after him. My brother recovered his balance and in a moment had got above his enemy. The hostile aeroplane could not equally quickly get ready for what was to come. My brother caught it at a favorable angle, and a few seconds after, it went down in flames. When a machine is burning, all is lost, for it falls to the ground burning.

Once I was on the ground next to a benzine tank. It contained one hundred litres of benzine which exploded and burnt. The heat was so great that I could not bear to be within ten yards of it. One can therefore imagine what it means if a tank containing a large quantity of this devilish liquid explodes a few inches in front of one while the blast from the propeller blows the flame into one's face. I believe a man must lose consciousness at the very first moment.

Sometimes miracles do happen. For instance, I once saw an English aeroplane falling down in flames. The flames burst out only at an altitude of 1,500 feet. The whole machine was burning. When we had flown home, we were told that one of the occupants of the machine had jumped from an altitude of 150 feet. It was the observer. One hundred and fifty feet is the height of a good-sized steeple. Supposing somebody should jump from its top to the ground, what would be his condition? Most men would break their bones in jumping from a first-floor window. At any rate, this good fellow jumped from a burning machine at an altitude of 150 feet, from a machine which had been burning for over a minute, and nothing happened to him except a simple fracture of the leg. Soon after his adventure, he made a statement from which it appears that his nerve had not suffered.

Another time, I shot down an Englishman. The pilot had been fatally wounded in the head. The machine fell perpendicularly to earth from an altitude of nine thousand feet. Some time later I came gliding down and saw on the ground nothing but a heap of twisted debris. To my surprise I was told that the observer had only damaged his skull and that his condition was not dangerous. Some people have luck indeed.

Once upon a time, Boelcke shot down a Nieuport machine. I was present. The aeroplane fell like a stone. When we inspected it, we found that it had been driven up to the middle into the loamy soil. The occupant had been shot in the abdomen and had lost consciousness and had wrenched his arm out of its socket on striking the ground. He did not die of his fall.

On the other hand, it has happened that a good friend of mine in landing had a slight accident. One of the wheels of his machine got into a rabbit hole. The aeroplane was traveling at no speed and quite slowly went on its head. It seemed to reflect whether it should fall to the one side or to the other, turned over, and the poor fellow's back was broken.

My brother Lothar is lieutenant in the 4th Dragoons. Before the war he was at the War Academy. He was made an officer at the outbreak and began the war as a cavalry man exactly as I did. I know nothing about his actions, for he never speaks of himself. However, I have been told the following story:

In the winter of 1914, Lothar's regiment was on the Warthe. The Russians were on the other side of the river. Nobody knew whether they intended to stay there or to go back. The water was frozen partly along the shore. So it was difficult to ride through the river. There were, of course, no bridges, for the Russians had destroyed them. So my brother swam across, ascertained the position of the Russians, and swam back again. He did that during a severe Russian winter when the thermometer was very low. After a few minutes, his clothes were frozen solid. Yet he asserted that he had felt quite warm notwithstanding. He kept on his horse all day long until he got to his quarters in the evening, yet he did not catch a chill.

In winter 1915, he followed my urgent advice and went into the flying service. He also became an observer and became a pilot only a year later. Acting as an observer is certainly not a bad training, particularly for a chasing airman. In March 1917, he passed his third examination and came at once to my squadron.

When he arrived he was a very young and innocent pilot who never thought of looping and such like tricks. He was quite satisfied if he succeeded in starting his machine and in landing successfully. A fortnight later I took him with me against the enemy for the first time. I asked him to fly close behind me in order that he might see exactly how the fighting was done.

After the third flight with him, I suddenly noticed he parted company with me. He rushed at an Englishman and killed him. My heart leapt with joy when I saw it. The event proved once more that there is no art in shooting down an aeroplane. The thing is done by the personality or by the fighting determination of the airman. I am not a Pégoud, and I do not wish to be a Pégoud. I am only a soldier who does his duty.

Four weeks later my brother had shot down a total of twenty Englishmen. His record as a flier is probably unique. It has probably not happened in any other case that a pilot, a fortnight after his third examination, has shot down his first enemy and that he has shot down twenty during the first four weeks of his fighting life.

My brother's twenty-second opponent was the celebrated Captain Ball. He was by far the best English flier. Major Hawker, who in his time was as renowned as Captain Ball, I had pressed to my bosom some months previously. It was a particular pleasure to me that it fell to my brother to settle England's second flying champion.

Captain Ball flew a triplane and encountered my brother flying by himself at the front. Each tried to catch the other. Neither gave his opponent a chance. Every encounter was a short one. They were constantly dashing at one another. Neither succeeded in getting behind the other. Suddenly both resolved to fire a few well-aimed shots during the few moments of the encounter. Both rushed at one another and fired. Both had before them their engine. The probability of a hit was very small, for their speed was twice as great as normally. It was improbable that either should succeed. My brother, who was a little lower, had pulled his machine around too hard, and the result was that it overturned. For a moment his aeroplane became unsteerable. But presently he recovered control and found out that his opponent had smashed both his benzine tanks. Therefore, he had to stop the engine and land quickly. Otherwise, his machine might burst into flames.

His next idea was: "What has become of my opponent?" At the moment when his machine turned its somersault, he had seen that the enemy's machine was rearing up in the air and had also turned a somersault. He therefore could not be very far. His whole thought was: "Is he above me or beneath me?" He was not above, but he saw the triplane falling down in a series of somersaults. It fell, fell, fell until it came to the ground, where it was smashed to pieces. This happened on German territory. Both opponents had hit one another with their machine guns. My brother's machine had had both benzine tanks smashed, and at the same moment, Captain Ball had been shot through the head. He carried with him some photographs and cuttings from the newspapers of his town where he had been greatly feted. In Boelcke's time Captain Ball destroyed thirty-six German machines. He, too, had found his master. Was it by chance that a prominent man such as he also should die an ordinary soldier's death?

Captain Ball was certainly the commander of the Anti-Richthofen Squadron. I believe that the Englishmen will now give up their attempt to catch me. I should regret it, for in that case, I should miss many opportunities to make myself beloved by them.

Had my brother not been wounded on the fifth of May, he would probably on my return from furlough, also have been given a leave of absence with fifty-two hostile machines to his credit.

My father discriminates between a sportsman and a butcher. The former shoots for fun. When I have shot down an Englishman, my hunting passion is satisfied for a quarter of an hour. Therefore I do not succeed in shooting two Englishmen in succession. If one of them comes down, I have the feeling of complete satisfaction. Only much, much later, I have overcome my instinct and have become a butcher.

My brother is differently constituted. I had an opportunity of observing him when he was shooting down his fourth and fifth opponents. We were attacking in a squadron. I started the dance. I had settled my opponent very quickly. When I looked around, I noticed my brother rushing after an English machine which was bursting into flames and exploded. Next to it was another Englishman. My brother, though following number one, immediately directed his machine gun against number two, although his first opponent was still in the air and had not yet fallen. His second victim also fell after a short struggle.

When we met at home, he asked me proudly, "How many have you shot down?" I said quite modestly, "One." He turned his back upon me and said, "I did two." Thereupon I sent him forward to make inquiries. He was to find out the names of his victims, etc. He returned late in the afternoon having been able to find only a single Englishman.

He had looked carelessly, as is usual amongst such butchers. Only on the following day, I received a report as to the place where the second had come down.

We all had seen his fall.

I Shoot a Bison

When visiting headquarters I met the Prince von Pless. He permitted me to shoot a bison on his estate. The bison has died out. On the whole earth, there are only two spots where bisons may be found. These are the Pless estate and in the Bialowicz estate of the ex-czar. The Bialowicz forest has, of course, suffered terribly through the war. Many a magnificent bison which ought to have been shot either by the czar or by some other monarch has been eaten by German musketeers.

Through the kindness of the prince, I was permitted to shoot so rare an animal. In a few decades, none will be left.

I arrived at Pless on the afternoon of the twenty-sixth of May and had to start immediately from the station if I wished to kill a bull the same evening. We drove along the celebrated road, through the giant preserves of the prince, which has been frequented by many crowned heads. After about an hour, we got out and had to walk half an hour to come to the shooting place. The drivers had already been placed in position. The signal was given to them, and they began the drive.

I stood at an elevated spot which had been occupied, according to the head forester, by His Majesty, who from thence had shot many a bison. We waited some considerable time. Suddenly I saw among the timber a gigantic black monster, rolling along. It came straight in my direction. I noticed it before the head forester had. I got ready for firing and must say that I felt somewhat feverish.

It was a mighty bull. When he was at a distance of two hundred yards, there was still some hope for him. I thought it was too far for a shot. Of course I could have hit the monster because it was impossible to miss such a huge beast. However, it would have been unpleasant to search for him. Besides it would have been ridiculous had I missed him, so I thought I would wait until he came nearer.

Probably he noticed the drivers, for he suddenly turned and came rushing towards me at a sharp angle and at a speed which seemed to me incredible. It was a bad position for a shot, and in a moment he disappeared behind a group of stout trees.

I heard him snorting and stamping. I lost sight of him. I have no idea whether he smelt me or not. At any rate, he had disappeared. I caught another glimpse of him at a long distance, and he was gone.

I do not know whether it was the unaccustomed aspect of the animal or whether something else affected me. At any rate, at the moment when the bull came near, I had the same feeling, the same feverishness which seizes me when I am sitting in my aeroplane and notice an Englishman at so great a distance that I have to fly perhaps five minutes in order to get near him. The only difference is that the Englishman defends himself. Possibly, different feelings would have moved me had I been standing on level ground and not on an elevated position.

Before long, a second bison came near. He was also a huge fellow. He made it easier for me to fire my shot. At a distance of eighty yards, I fired at him, but I had missed my opportunity to shoot him in the shoulder. A month before, Hindenburg had told me when talking of bison, "You must take a lot of cartridges with you. I have spent on such a fellow half a dozen for he does not die easily. His heart lies so deep that one misses it as a rule." That was really so. Although I knew exactly where the bison's heart was, I had missed it. I fired a second shot and a third. Hit for the third time, the bull stopped perhaps fifty yards from me.

Five minutes later the beast was dead. The shooting was finished. All three bullets had hit him close above the heart.

We drove now, past the beautiful hunting box of the prince, through the forest, in which the guests of Prince Pless shoot every year deer and other animals. Then we looked at the interior of the house in Promnitz. It is situated on a peninsula. It commands beautiful views, and for three miles around, there is no human being. One has no longer the feeling that one is in a preserve of the ordinary kind when one visits the estate of Prince Pless, for the preserve extends to a million acres. It contains glorious stags which have never been seen by man. No forester knows them. Occasionally they are shot. One can tramp about for weeks without seeing a bison. During certain times of the year, it is impossible to find one. They like quietude, and they can hide themselves in the gigantic forests and tangled woods. We saw many beautiful deer.

After about two hours, we arrived at Pless, just before it became dark.

Had I not become a professional chaser, I should have turned an infantry flier. After all, it must be a very satisfactory feeling to be able to aid those troops whose work is hardest. The infantry flier can do a great deal to assist the man on foot. For that reason his is a very grateful task.

In the course of the Battle of Arras, I observed many of these splendid fellows. They flew in any weather and at any time at a low altitude over the enemy and tried to act as connecting links with our hard-pressed troops. I can understand that one can fight with enthusiasm when one is given such a task. I dare say many an airman has shouted, "Hurrah!" when after an assault he saw the hostile masses stream back or when our smart infantry leaped from the trenches and fought the aggressors eye to eye. Many a time, after a chasing expedition, I have fired my remaining cartridges into the enemy trenches. Although I may have done little practical good, such firing affects the enemy's morale.

I have also been an artillery flier. In my time it was a novelty to regulate the firing of one's own artillery by wireless telegraphy. To do this well, an airman requires special talent. I could not do the work for long. I prefer fighting. Very likely, artillery officers make the best artillery fliers. At least, they have the necessary knowledge of the arm which they serve.

I have done a lot of reconnoitering by aeroplane, particularly in Russia during the war of movement. Then I acted once more as a cavalryman. The only difference was that I rode a Pegasus made of steel. My days spent with friend Holck among the Russians were among the finest in my life.

In the Western theatre, the eye of the reconnaissance flier sees things which are very different from those to which the cavalrymen get accustomed. Villages and towns, railways and roads seem lifeless and dead. Yet there is a colossal traffic going on all the time, but it is hidden from the flying men with great skill. Only a wonderfully trained, practised, and observant eye can see anything definite when one is traveling at a great height and at a terrific speed. I have excellent eyes, but it seems doubtful to me whether there is anyone who can see anything definite when he looks down upon a road from an altitude of fifteen thousand feet. As the eye is an imperfect object for observation, one replaces it by the photographic apparatus. Everything that seems important to one must be photographed. Besides, one must photograph those things which one is told to photograph. If one comes home and if the plates have gone wrong, the whole flight has been for nothing.

It often happens to flying men who do reconnoitering that they get involved in a fight. However, their task is more important than fighting. Frequently a photographic plate is more valuable than the shooting down of a squadron. Hence the flying photographer should, as a rule, not take a hand in fighting.

Nowadays it is a difficult task to reconnoitre efficiently in the West.

THE GERMAN FLYING MACHINES

In the course of the war, the German flying machines have experienced great changes. That is probably generally known. There is a colossal difference between a giant plane and a chaser plane.

The chaser plane is small, fast, quick at turning. It carries nothing apart from the pilot except machine guns and cartridges.

The giant plane is a colossus. Its only duty is to carry as much weight as possible, and it is able to do this owing to the huge surface of its planes. It is worthwhile to look at the gigantic English plane which landed smoothly on the German side of the front. The giant plane can carry an unbelievable weight. It will easily fly away, dragging from three to five tons. Its benzine tanks look as large as railroad cars. In going about in such a colossus, one has no longer the sensation that one is flying. One is driving. In going about in a giant plane, the direction depends no longer on one's instinct but on the technical instruments which one carries.

A giant plane has a huge number of horsepower. I do not know exactly how many, but they are many thousand. The greater the horsepower is, the better. It seems not impossible that the day may come when a whole division will be transported in such a thing. In its body one can go for a walk. In one of its corners, there is an indescribable something. It contains an apparatus for wireless telephony, by means of which one can converse with the people down below. In another corner are hanging the most attractive liver sausages which one can imagine. They are the famous bombs which cause such a fright to the good people down below. At every corner is a gun. The whole thing is a flying fortress, and the planes with their stays and supports look like arcades. I have never been able to feel enthusiasm for these giant barges. I find them horrible, unsportsmanlike, boring, and clumsy. I rather like a machine of the type of "le petit rouge."

If one is in a small chaser plane, it is quite immaterial whether one flies on one's back, whether one flies up or down, stands on one's head, etc. One can play any tricks one likes, for in such a machine one can fly like a bird. The only difference is that one does not fly with wings, as does the bird albatross. The thing is, after all, merely a flying engine. I think things will come to this, that we shall be able to buy a flying suit for half a crown. One gets into it. On the one end, there is a little engine and a little propeller. You stick your arms into planes and your legs into the tail. Then you will do a few leaps in order to start, and away you will go up into the air like a bird.

My dear reader, I hear you laughing at my story. But we do not know yet whether our children will laugh at it. Everyone would have laughed fifty years ago if somebody had spoken about flying above Berlin. I remember the sensation which was caused when, in 1910, Zeppelin came for the first time to Berlin. Now no Berlin street man looks up into the air when an airship is coming along.

Besides giant planes and little chaser planes, there are innumerable other types of flying machines, and they are of all sizes. Inventiveness has not yet come to an end. Who can tell what machine we shall employ a year hence in order to perforate the atmosphere?

CHAPTER TWELVE

Learning to Kill People and Break Their Stuff

Peter Aleshire

THE IPs KEEP PILING ON THE BRICKS—LISTENING FOR THE SOUND OF cracking.

As soon as the B-coursers learn the basics of flying to the range, lining up on a target, flying in under radar, popping up, rolling over, and diving in toward the target at just the right angle—they up the ante. In the final missions of the air-to-ground training, the IPs throw in some simulated MiG fighters, waiting to pounce soon after the F-16s deliver their bombs.

The F-16's evolved flexibility makes it one of the most useful jets in Air Force history. The development of smart bombs has made the F-16 a lethally effective bomber—especially in close air support. Once, it took fighter-bombers and B-52s dozens of missions dropping hundreds of bombs to destroy a specific target—like a bridge. Now, four F-16s can destroy almost any target for which they have coordinates. Of course, versions of the F-16's GPS bombs can also be dropped wholesale from B-52s and strike fixed targets with the same transforming accuracy. But B-52s and other dedicated bombers remain vulnerable to fighters and so require heavy escorts of F-16s or F-15s. By contrast, not only can the Viper precisely deliver bombs, it can outfight virtually any other jet— with the exception, over long ranges, of the F-15. Moreover, F-16s have also largely taken on the Wild Weasel role, so they remain the primary SAM-killers—likewise able to fight through enemy fighters while loaded with bombs.

All of that has complicated the already-complex job of the F-16 pilots. They must learn most of the tactics and weapons used by the dogfighting F-15 pilots, plus the complicated bomb-delivery tasks of the bomber pilots—all without a navigator, a weapons officer, or a backseat pair of eyes. As a result, although the F-16 remains one of the easiest planes in the world to fly, it's one of the toughest to employ.

As the B-coursers have discovered with each new layer of bricks.

In this case, Igor and Jack learn how complicated and unpredictable the task of dropping bombs gets when you've got MiGs—even F-16s acting like MiGs—laying an ambush on the escape route back to base.

The plan is simple enough. Fly to the range. Descend to 500 feet for a breathtaking hurtle along the sun-blasted desert ridges below enemy radar to within 100 miles of the target. It takes about ten minutes to cover 100 miles in an F-16, tooling along without afterburners. Near the target they will climb to 20,000 feet and then dive toward the target in an inverted arc, to release the bombs at a precise heading and angle. It's not as gut-wrenching as the low-angle attacks they've been practicing, but it more closely resembles a real-world mission—since smart bombs and SAM-killing Wild Weasels have mostly eliminated risky, treetop approaches.

Then all they have to do is get home without getting shot down.

Igor and Jack do all the mission planning: programming the navigational steer points, precisely plotting the path the jets will follow on the map, drawing the diagram of the bomb run, complete with the precise speeds and angles. The plan builds in deconfliction to minimize the chance of a midair collision. When they started, it would have taken them six hours to develop the mission plan. This time it takes just ninety minutes. The IPs can do it in half that.

They'll be bombing three bermed fortifications suitable for basing SAMs. The plan calls for two jets to hit the center target, with the other two jets splitting to hit the revetments to each side. They're treating the target like a SAM site, with a central van containing the targeting radar and the missiles themselves splayed off to the side. The plan choreographs the arrival of the jets so they don't fly across one another's path on their approach—when the pilot's attention will be focused on the target.

The takeoff proceeds flawlessly, each two-ship lifting off in formation. Once, every takeoff required intense concentration and anticipation. Once, working out the details of ground operations—taxiing, accelerating down the runway, lifting off in formation, turning to the precise headings necessary to avoid other jets and the subdivisions sprawling out beneath them—seemed a major accomplishment. Now, it's all routine, like the stretch from the garage to the freeway on the morning commute.

Approaching the target, they follow the steer points programmed into the ship's computer on cartridges prepared during the mission-planning phase.

The cloudless sky arching over the canopy is brilliant, blue, and featureless. The horizon stretches out beneath them, brown and rumpled, the edge between tawny earth and brilliant sky clearly etched. Flying an F-16 remains exhilarating—when the pilots have a moment to pay attention between checking the radars and the steer points and their position in formation.

Igor flies with his habitual, methodical care—attending to the mantra of "Near rocks, far rocks." The pilots have learned to shift their attention constantly, a habit intended to make sure that no critical task slips out of their "situational awareness." So Igor moves his eyes deliberately to the closest mountain ridges, making sure he's on the preprogrammed flight path and has plenty of elevation to clear the "close rocks." Then he shifts his attention to the higher, more distant mountains—the "far rocks"—to quickly calculate whether he needs to change altitude or direction. Now he shifts his attention inside the cockpit, to check the radar that would warn him of approaching planes. His eyes flick to the speed, altitude, and the time and distance to the next steer point. But he only lets his attention remain inside the cockpit for a few seconds before shifting again to the "near rocks," then over to Opie, flying lead. Now he turns and looks back over his shoulder, the wingman habit that could save all their lives in combat. Then his attention shifts again to inside the cockpit. It's all a matter of intensively trained routine—the distillation and reiteration of lifesaving habits of vigilance and double-checking. At the beginning of the training, the B-coursers could only really pay attention to a few things on each mission. Often when flying in formation, they spent all their time just maintaining the proper position off the wing of the lead fighter. The lead could fly into the side of a mountain and the punk would follow him in, never taking his eyes off the wing of the doomed jet. Now, the flight formation is just one item in the ceaseless cross-check.

Soon, they approach the target, marked by the splitting of a dirt road skirting the edge of a wash between two low, saguaro-spiked, sun-bronzed mountain ranges. Igor recognizes the topography immediately from the aerial photos he studied before the mission. Rex's humiliation in strafing the wrong target gave them all a walking-past-your-grave chill. Ever since, they've all been studying their targeting photos with extra intensity. They're all proud, self-critical overachievers—with a horror of failure and ridicule. Even the unflappable Stihl felt like he wanted to crawl into a hole and hide after nearly busting his recent bomb run. They each dread the thought of anyone ever talking about them with that kind of pitying condescension most of them employ already when talking about Rex. All of which makes Rex's dogged, uncomplaining persistence the more remarkable.

Igor lines up the small smudge of the SAM site on the canopy rail of his cockpit, using those visual clues to guide his approach. He double-checks the target, which lies at the end of a three-pronged side road. In studying the photographs, Igor had already cautioned himself not to mistakenly target a different series of mounds on a four-pronged fork off the road that led him in toward the SAM site. As he approaches, the target begins to disappear under the nose of the jet, so he shifts to the right and rolls halfway over so he can keep the target in sight. He manipulates the control stick intuitively now.

The jet seems an extension of himself, thanks to the computer-mediated controls. Originally, the engineers made the stick itself solid, unmoving, since the computer could translate the pressure on the stick from the pilot's hands as easily as the stick's actual movement. But the pilots hated that. They wanted to move the stick, to gain that sense of control. Now F-16 pilots often wrestle the stick, sometimes straining their muscles in the violent maneuvering of combat, although the computer pays attention to only the first few increments of that pressure. But an experienced F-16 pilot flies the jet with a light touch, never looking down. Sometimes, it almost seems as if the jet is reading his mind—straining like a racehorse at the slightest shift of the reins. Moreover, the enormous thrust of the Viper creates its own gravity and orientation. So as he rolls into his turn, Igor instinctively puts just enough arc into his turn to press his body into the seat at about 1 g, even though he's three-quarters upside down. This manipulation of g-forces often makes it feel like the F-16 isn't really turning or climbing or diving or rolling at all. Rather, it seems like the world is shifting—twirling—out there beyond the bubble arch of the cockpit. The horizon shifts to vertical, then becomes the floor. The earth tilts and becomes the sky. And all the while, the force of the jet's path makes it seem like he's sitting comfortably in level flight.

Igor comes out of the rolling turn so that now he is flying at a carefully calculated angle to the target, keeping it in sight for the final 10 miles of the approach.

Suddenly, Opie's calm but penetrating voice sounds in his earphones.

"We have a lock and a SAM launch at your five o'clock," he says.

Of course, it's not really a SAM lock. But the rules of the mission include maneuvering to evade a SAM strike. So Igor veers abruptly into a violent, classified maneuver designed to break the radar lock of a SAM missile. Usually, the antiaircraft missiles follow a radar signal from the ground, so if the ground station loses the radar lock, the SAM will go off course or explode prematurely. Essentially, the evasion involves abrupt, gut-wrenching maneuvers to turn the jet edge-on to the radar signal from the ground, breaking the lock. The maneuver, which depends on the agility of the F-16, proved effective repeatedly in Bosnia and Iraq. Opie studies the sequence of Igor and Jack's violent evasive maneuvers until he's satisfied, then declares that the missiles have missed.

"You're still alive," he adds helpfully.

They reassemble. Early in the course, simply corralling four jets in so vast a sweep of sky and precisely matching their headings and speed would have been a major focus of a whole flight. Now it's done in an offhand way, in the midst of more important tasks.

When it's time for the bombing run, Opie rolls in first, followed by Igor and the other two jets in sequence. The jets execute a "Pappy Peel," named after World War II ace Pappy Boyington: a line of jets plummet-ing toward the target in single file.

The first pass goes off smoothly. Each jet must dive at a 45-degree angle at 430 knots and release its bomb at precisely the moment the computer calls the shot. Every jet hits the right dive angle, releases right on time, and then banks away from the target—ready for more evasive maneuvers if Opie calls another SAM launch.

Igor imagines himself hurtling down at the target on an imaginary wire strung tight at a 45-degree angle to the ground. He knows he can drift to 48 or 50 degrees, but flattening to 35 degrees will make it harder to hit the target, and going steeper than 55 degrees will take him into his own blast pattern—either way, he will bust the ride. During the mission planning, Igor spent twenty minutes calculating the dive angle and speed for his assigned weapons and altitude. "Then you go out there and make those numbers work," he says. "You measure to a millimeter, draw with a crayon, and hack with an ax," he jokes.

On the first pass, he's 50 feet too high but right on a 45-degree angle when he drops the bomb. He looks at the airspeed indicator and notes that he's just 5 miles per hour too fast, so he pickles and drops the 24-pound concrete-filled steel bomb. But he screws up. He looked at the airspeed indicator, which gives his absolute speed relative to the ground; he should have looked at the Mach airspeed indicator, which gives his speed relative to the speed of sound. The speed of sound varies signifi-cantly with altitude—as it propagates through the different densities of air. The restrictions on the release of the bombs are based on Mach speed, which more accurately indicates the pressure of the air on the jet and the bombs slung to the underside. In fact, if Igor had checked the Mach speed indicator, he would have seen that he was diving so fast that he would have been in danger of ripping real 500-pound bombs off the pylons on the underside of the wings. He flirted with the limit that would have automatically busted the ride—but "by the luck of God and the grace given to fighter pilots," he didn't exceed it.

As he goes around for the next pass, he recognizes his mistake. Shaken, he prays the tape will show he didn't quite screw the pooch—then steadies himself and fixes his concentration on the Mach speed indicator. Of course, that's the whole point of training. Hopefully, the peerless young hotshot is completely humiliated and busted because he's looking at the wrong airspeed indicator. That burns the distinction between the two gauges into his brain. As a result, he'll never make that mistake again—when it counts and the bomb slung under his wing really could kill him if he went in too fast.

Every other pass is textbook—within 10 miles per hour of the right speed, within 3 degrees of the right angle, within 100 feet of the right altitude for the drop. He's got it nailed.

Every bomb hit inside his targeted revetment—even the first one.

Several days earlier, Igor and Stihl had made a jaunt down to the firing range, waiting for a lull between runs. They went out onto the range to look at a cluster of rusting, armored half-tracks they'd bombed the day before. Stihl located the truck he'd hit with his 24-pound steel bomb—which had plunged down through the hood, punching a hole the size of a person's head.

Very cool.

"When you drop a bomb with a fragment pattern of 3,000 feet," says Igor, "and you drop it within 50 yards of your target, you're going to kill it. Last pass, no kidding, hit dead center of where it was supposed to hit. That feels pretty good."

After finishing their runs, Opie calls for a range check. The range sprawls for hundreds of miles along the Mexican–U.S. border. The Border Patrol crackdown on the major crossing points like San Diego, Nogales, and El Paso have driven the smuggler networks into the vast, unpatrollable stretches of the desert—especially in the millions of unpopulated acres devoted to the gunnery range. During the great western immigrations of the 1800s, this stretch of desert was dubbed the "Devil's Highway" for its killing heat and the lack of water. It was littered with the bones of reckless and unprepared California gold seekers. Now the F-16 and A-10 pilots who practice on the range regularly report groups of people and bodies sprawled, shriveled, and twisted in the sand. That's a pain. Usually ends up shutting down a chunk of airspace for hours, as the Border Patrol heads out into the desert to round up the illegals or recover the bodies—nameless people risking death to pick lettuce and wash dishes.

No one has cleared the range for a couple of hours, so Opie and Igor swoop down low and scrutinize the territory in an outward spiral—looking for any furtive motion among the rocks and saguaros and thirsty green Palo Verde. It's a kick, whipping along at 800 feet, eyes fixed on the ground—flying the jet by instinct in tight, terrain-hugging patterns—the proximity to the ground giving them the sense of speed normally elusive in the featureless sky.

Opie pronounces himself satisfied. Igor did blow the first run, but he recognized the mistake himself. "If a guy has no idea what was going on, then when you say, 'How was that attack?' You don't hear anything. 'What was your dive angle?' You don't hear anything. That means he was pretty far behind the jet. No SA [situational awareness] on how his pass went."

The whole training has been leading up to this point. Most F-16 pilots want to become aces—go tip to tip with a MiG. But they'll spend most of their careers training intensively for combat most will never see. If they finally go into combat, they'll mostly drop bombs. Partly, that's because the F-15s dominate the dogfighting mission. But mostly it's because no other air force in the world stands a chance against the U.S. in a dogfighting war. Even in fights with substantial air forces in the years since Vietnam, the U.S. fighters established complete air supremacy within days. As a result, the F-15s mostly end up boring holes in the sky, while the F-16s blow things up.

The sequence of missions builds a mental picture in the minds of the B-coursers, stacking one brick atop the next as they acquire skills. "First, you just learn to get to and from the range," says Igor. "Then you're building this mental picture. You're on the first pass to put the bombs on the target and kill it. You're thinking, 'Holy cow,' because the real picture is so much smaller than the aerials. But mostly you're trying to keep the navigational system up to speed and fly formation and put the target in the steer point. By the third [air-to-ground] ride, you can kind of breathe a little bit. By the fifth and sixth rides, you have a grasp of the big picture—and you can do three different things at the same time without even really knowing you're doing them—like updating the navigational system, staying in formation, listening to the radio. You have an idea where you are, where you need to be, what side to be on—like in chess, where you have to think ahead of where you're going."

"Then we add more stuff," says Opie.

Let's see, can he fight his way in and deal with some air-to-air threats, getting jumped on the way out of the target? Every time they get comfortable, we task them with something else. So maybe I'll call, "Break right, bandit at six o'clock," and see how they react. The key is, they've got to stay ahead of the airplane. I know they're having a rough day if they're drifting out of formation. They're not saying anything on the radio. They're freaking falling behind the aircraft.

Gradually, flying becomes automatic. "It's like when you're driving down the highway on a four-lane road," says Igor.

I drive down the road, and I know who's in front, how fast I'm closing, who's behind, who's in either lane on either side. You have a 360-degree picture—so you can react and avoid getting into an accident. And if you mounted a radar detector, you'd be checking for cops. And looking at all the underpasses for speed traps. Meanwhile, you're talking and listening to the radio. Same thing when you're flying. Whenever you're doing a turn, you're checking to make sure it's a level turn—so you're not running into the ground or changing altitude. You automatically check, thinking, "If I turn that direction, can I hit anything? Am I going to hit anything going this direction—yeah—but I have twenty seconds, so I can look behind me." So you look back and then check left and right—it's just a fluid environment. You're doing what you need to do.

"When we first started in T-38s in basic," adds Igor, "we were flying at 1,000 feet—that was really impressive. Then we dropped down to 500 feet at 360 knots. That was really impressive. Then you get here and do it at 420 knots at 500 feet—that was no different. Once you're going fast, a little faster is not a big deal," says Igor.

"I had a blast today," he says of the flight.

It was a ton of fun, it's a great feeling, being ahead of the jet. You've got everything waxed. You're in perfect position—and here's Interstate 10, so you do a little wing flash for the civilians. Or you're going to split a mountain—that's sweet. You just put that mountain right between your jets. You get so you can do something most people would say is insanely dangerous and enjoy it. It's way crazy cool. Your mind is operating so fast you can count fence posts at 5,000 feet and 500 knots. You fly over I-10, and you can just in a flash see the blue car with a semi behind it—and twelve or fourteen cactus on top of that mountain—and a bird went by just above to the left while I was doing my radar fix. Your cross-check is so reactive and automated that you don't miss anything.

The danger adds to the thrill. That includes the possibility that someone out there wants to kill you.

On the way out through "Bad Guy Land," a cluster of blips suddenly appears on the radar screen, a flight of jets at 22.5 miles, angling across the path of the returning flight of Vipers.

"Nacho three," says Opie, calling Crash's attention to the radar image. Crash is the flight lead of the second two-ship element, with Jack as his wingman, trailing 4 miles to the rear. Each of the four ships in the flight has a code—Nacho one through four. "Target group Bull's-Eye, 260. 55. 15,000," Opie adds, giving the group's altitude and a steer point as reference. The "Bull's-Eye" refers to a reference point, in this case the Gila Bend airport, and the "55" is the distance in miles from that point. The code allows pilots to describe over the radio the position of anything relative to a known reference point rather than their own positions; any pilot who knows the Bull's-Eye point will understand. In combat, Bull's-Eye is kept secret and shifted during the engagement, so that enemy pilots can't figure out the position of the U.S. jets by listening in on their communications. So now Igor knows that Opie's talking about the contacts on his radar flying at 15,000 feet 55 miles from the Bull's-Eye on a 260-degree heading.

"Three's targeted," says Crash, as soon as his tracking radar locks the still-invisible jets.

"Nacho two, sort, 260, 56, 15,000, west," says Opie, telling Igor to track a specific aircraft in the group on his radar. The radar now shows four "bogeys" in two groups. Igor will track the group to the west and stay with them if they split. If they spot the approaching four-ship, they will probably try to outflank Igor's flight.

Jack, flying on Crash's wing, now starts scanning the sky anxiously for enemy fighters, especially anyone creeping up from behind. He's trailing the formation, covering the vulnerable six-o'clock position for Opie, Igor, and Crash, which leaves his own rear area dangerously exposed.

"Targeting" Crash to that group makes Crash and his wingman responsible for killing them if they prove hostile. By sorting Igor to the western two-ship in the group, Opie has made sure Igor will stay with that group if they split. Until such a split takes place and the bogeys remain a single group, Crash will control who takes a shot.

Now the eight jets converge. The four bogeys remain on a steady heading, now moving away from Opie's four-ship. But the Vipers have a 100-knot speed advantage and quickly close the distance. Igor's fingers move constantly on the control stick, shifting radar views and getting his air-to-air missiles ready as he continues the habitual cross-checking—near rocks, far rocks, check your six.

Opie lets them converge. He has lots of options now. Having made Crash responsible for taking the shot, Opie can maneuver for position or close in for a visual identification. Since Opie has sorted Igor to keep track of the western group, the flight should react smoothly to a split by the enemy jets. So far the enemy jets give no sign they know they're being stalked, although Opie's flight has closed to within 15 miles.

Suddenly Igor's computer sounds a warning tone, indicating that he's just been swept by the enemy's radar—followed by Betty's soft but insistent warning.

"Three's targeted," comes Crash's voice. "Group. Bull's-Eye, 262, 40, 15,000. Declare," he adds, asking Opie to declare the unidentified jets hostile so Crash can kill them.

"Badger declares group Bull's-Eye 265, 40, 15,000 hostile," says Opie, filling in for "Badger"—the AWACS plane that would sort out the bewilderment of aircraft during a real engagement. The comprehensive coverage by AWACS controllers at the edge of the battlefield has played a crucial role in every major air engagement since Vietnam, dramatically increasing the advantage American pilots already enjoy.

"Nacho three, Fox three," says Crash, indicating he has launched a simulated air-to-air missile.

"Nacho four, Fox three," adds Jack, having been sorted to the western set as well by his flight lead.

Crash and Jack each launch two missiles—with perfect parameters. The four unidentified jets fly straight and level to their deaths. Of course, they were just four Vipers on their way to the range—with no idea they'd just been incorporated into Igor and Jack's training.

Still, it's a kick—killing the bad guys. Of course, next time, the bad guys will shoot back. The easy days of turkey shooting have ended. The large force deployment looms now, the culmination of the training.

This time, the best IPs will be doing their level best to kill the punks—and anyone else who gets in their way.

SOURCES

Aleshire, Peter. "Learning to Kill People and Break Their Stuff." In *Eye of the Viper: The Making of an F-16 Pilot*. Guilford, CT: Lyons Press, 2005.

Brown, Don. "Fallen Angel: The Final Seconds of Extortion 17." In *Call Sign Extortion 17: The Shoot-Down of SEAL Team Six*. Guilford, CT: Lyons Press, 2015.

Deighton, Len. "*Kanalkampf*: The Battles over the Channel." In *The Battle of Britain*. London: HarperCollins, 1980.

Dorr, Robert F. "Thunderjets over Korea." In *Air Combat: An Oral History of Fighter Pilots*. New York: Bill Fawcett, 2006. Used by permission of Berkley, an imprint of Penguin Publishing Group, a division of Penguin Random House.

Lundstrom, John. "The Skies over Midway." In *The First Team: Pacific Naval Air Combat from Pearl Harbor to Midway*. Annapolis, MD: Naval Institute Press, 2005.

Michel, Marshall L., III. "The Fiercest Battles." In *Clashes: Air Combat over North Vietnam, 1965–1972*. Annapolis, MD: Naval Institute Press, 1997.

Scott, Group Captain A. J. L. "Sixty Squadron, R.A.F." In *Sixty Squadron, R.A.F.: A History of the Squadron from Its Formation*. London: William Heinemann, 1920.

Smith, Col. Robert Barr, and Laurence J. Yadon. "Home Town Hero." In *Greatest Air Aces Stories Ever Told: The Men of the American, British, and Commonwealth Air Forces Who Fought for the Sky in Two World Wars*. Guilford, CT: Lyons Press, 2017.

Stout, Jay A. "Hornets Get into the Fight." In *Hammer from Above: Marine Air Combat over Iraq*. New York: Presidio Press, an imprint of Random House, a division of Penguin Random House, 2005.

Toland, John. "Tallyho! Bandits over Clark." In *But Not in Shame: The Six Months after Pearl Harbor*. New York: Ballantine Books, a division of Penguin Random House, 1963.

von Richthofen, Captain Baron Manfred. "The Red Baron Remembers." In *The Red Battle Flyer*. New York: Robert M. McBride, 1918.

Whitcomb, Darrel. "The Night They Saved Vega 31." *Air Force Magazine*. December 2006.